PENGUI...

A GIRL,
a smock
AND
a simple
PLAN

Chris Daffey was born in Melbourne in 1972. He worked as a lawyer for a number of years before going part-time to pursue other interests. This is his first book.

CHRIS DAFFEY

A Girl, a Smock and a simple Plan

PENGUIN BOOKS

To contact the author, go to chrisdaffey@bigpond.com

Penguin Books

Published by the Penguin Group
Penguin Books Australia Ltd
250 Camberwell Road, Camberwell, Victoria 3124, Australia
Penguin Books Ltd
80 Strand, London WC2R 0RL, England
Penguin Putnam Inc.
375 Hudson Street, New York, New York 10014, USA
Penguin Books, a division of Pearson Canada
10 Alcorn Avenue, Toronto, Ontario, Canada M4V 3B2
Penguin Books (NZ) Ltd
Cnr Rosedale and Airborne Roads, Albany, Auckland, New Zealand
Penguin Books (South Africa) (Pty) Ltd
24 Sturdee Avenue, Rosebank, Johannesburg 2196, South Africa
Penguin Books India (P) Ltd
11, Community Centre, Panchsheel Park, New Delhi 110 017, India

First published by Penguin Books Australia Ltd 2003

1 3 5 7 9 10 8 6 4 2

Copyright © Chris Daffey 2003

The moral right of the author has been asserted

All rights reserved. Without limiting the rights under copyright reserved above, no part of this publication may be reproduced, stored in or introduced into a retrieval system, or transmitted, in any form or by any means (electronic, mechanical, photocopying, recording or otherwise), without the prior written permission of both the copyright owner and the above publisher of this book.

Design by John Canty, Penguin Design Studio
Cover image © photolibrary.com
Typeset in 11/16 Minion by Post Pre-press Group, Brisbane, Queensland
Printed and bound in Australia by McPherson's Printing Group,
Maryborough, Victoria

National Library of Australia
Cataloguing-in-Publication data:

Daffey, Chris.
A girl, a smock and a simple plan.

ISBN 0 14 028961 5.

1. Australia – Biography. I. Title

920.71

www.penguin.com.au

For Pop

With thanks to my family, Lisa, Ben, Tony, Ray and Margaret, Hermione, Dick Thomas, Clare Forster, the wonderfully patient Anne Rogan and the students and staff of Templestowe Heights Primary School.

contents

Introduction — xi

1. Lucas Tordby sings the Blues — 1
2. The sweet smell of Dewberries — 17
3. A girl, a smock and a simple plan — 35
4. Tea and biscuits with Richie Benaud — 47
5. Tips from an old Druid — 62
6. The Golden Boy — 73
7. The SRC — 100
8. Sex, lies and videotape — 128

9	Stuart Lund's brain	145
10	Green, green, you're my team!	164
11	The mean streets of Lower Templestowe	186
12	Crime and punishment	210
13	Mr Dribbles goes bananas	229
14	It's all about hair	249
15	The race-tuned, VH SS Group Three Holden	275
16	The Ball	294

Introduction

The following book is based on a true story. By this I mean that much of it is true and much of it is not. The true parts relate to myself, my family, the primary school I attended many years ago, and the girl who I spent much of grade six trying to impress. I have attempted to keep the untrue bits to a minimum, but some changes were unavoidable. Names have been altered, details have been fiddled with, and Peter Pendergast didn't actually *die* during the First Eleven cricket team try-outs (he was just badly injured).

If you are going to read this book, you should know that it is a love story – or, more accurately, a *like* story. It is about the lengths a person will go to to gain the attention of another; about the ridiculous things we all do when confronted with the first major trauma of our lives – a crush.

So sit back, relax and cast your mind back to an age where things were simple. A time when bad was bad, good was grouse, and red-headed children were hunted for sport.

Welcome to my childhood.

1

Lucas Tordby sings the Blues

As far as seething melting pots of economic and racial tension go, Lower Templestowe was pretty soft. It was the type of suburb where the 'haves' and 'have nots' were distinguished by the presence or absence of sports pinstripes on their SL Commodores. It was the kind of neighbourhood where price competition between Uncle Gino's Pizza World and Kim Sung's Imperial Palace was the closest thing you could find to ethnic conflict. By and large, it was a safe place to grow up. But even in a suburb where 'crime sprees' were defined as the theft of hose fittings from more than two houses, a child couldn't be guaranteed a fear-free existence.

Terror came in many forms when you were a kid. There was fear of bullies and bigger kids; fear of teachers; fear of parents; fear of neighbours' dogs; fear of chicken pox; fear of the yellow stuff you had to bathe in once you got chicken pox; fear of injections; fear of doctors; fear of dentists; fear of anyone who used the words 'this isn't going to hurt a bit'; and, most harrowing of all, the fear of being unpopular.

It was this final fear that held a certain Lucas Tordby in its grip on a blustery Friday morning in the middle of February. Lucas was Templestowe Heights Primary School's least favourite person. He had earned this title not because of anything he had ever done, but because of a whole range of things that he simply couldn't help: big eyes; orange hair; a tendency to squeal when you poked him; and a soft, doughy, feminine appearance, such that if you cut him open you'd expect him to leak puppies.

Physical attributes aside, Lucas was a fairly normal kid in all other respects. A bit of a loner perhaps, but that was more thrust upon him than a conscious choice. If there was one thing in life that Lucas Tordby hated, it was the public spotlight. For this, and other reasons, he stood trembling with fear.

All of grade six had assembled there that day, on a spacious, carpeted expanse, universally known as the 'multi-purpose room'. The title of that room probably overstated the case a little bit. As far as I could tell, it had very few purposes. It wasn't quite big enough for proper concerts or productions. It didn't have portable floors or an amazing retractable roof so that you could stage moto-cross rallies or ice spectaculars or anything. It was basically just a big room that wasn't a classroom and didn't easily lend itself to another name. In recent times, it had played host to a gym class, a couple of science exhibitions and a series of gut-wrenchingly terrible 'discos'. (If you ever want to see something embarrassing, try a room full of eleven-year-olds getting down to Huey Lewis and the News at two o'clock in the afternoon.) The discos had been the first in a number of new initiatives from the irrepressible Mrs Newport. Performing arts classes was the latest.

'Sorry about all this, children!' she suddenly burst out, waving her hands around and unleashing one of her customary 200-watt smiles. 'I know you must be getting a little impatient by now,' (beam, tilt of head, sympathetic upturning of palms) 'but we're having a little trouble getting the sound going. I've sent Mr Weathershaw off to fetch a new tape machine – though we're not really sure what the problem is yet.'

'But don't worry!' she exploded with redoubled zeal. 'We'll have it fixed up in a jiffy and then we'll get the show on the road!'

She emphasised this point by thrusting the end of a power cord into the air, as if that were somehow relevant (prompting me to speculate that if a lack of power really was the problem, all she'd have to do was plug it into her mouth). After a moment or so of messing about with the cord, she continued.

'I know you're all very excited about today's act,' she glowed, glancing over her shoulder and shooting an encouraging smile at Lucas, 'but you're just going to have to sit tight until Mr Weathershaw returns. In the meantime, how about we have a bit of a singalong? Who's up for a couple of verses of *Dr Knickerbocker?*'

Ninety-five individual facial expressions suddenly screamed 'hell no!'.

'Or maybe you could just chat amongst yourselves for a while?'

The expressions morphed into something approximating approval.

'Okay then, but don't go getting carried away, children – keep it hushed!' And with her finger pressed to her lips in an exaggerated shushing motion, Mrs Newport slowly turned her back on the crowd and recommenced her tinkering with the speakers. But not before giving us one last long, lingering beam.

In many ways, Mrs Newport was a fairly standard primary school teacher. She was kind, she was mindlessly enthusiastic, she used words like 'silly-billy' and 'poppet' a lot, and she wasn't afraid to pair skivvies with floral skirts. In other ways, she was not so standard. The main thing that set Mrs Newport apart from the rest of her Templestowe Heights colleagues was that she was young – young and 'progressive'. If Mrs Newport had a mission in life, it was to systematically tear down the old primary school system and replace it with a warmer, fuzzier one. She wanted kids to be able to 'express themselves' and to 'harness their creative energies' – concepts that sounded fine in theory, but were often catastrophic in practice. For my part, I was wary of her program for reform. Innovation had its casualties and Lucas Tordby was about to become one of them.

Of all the ideas Mrs Newport came up with, performing arts classes was definitely the worst. The basic premise was simple. At some stage during the year, each kid in grade six had to take part in a play, read a poem, sing a song or perform some other act in front of their peers. Not just the kids who *wanted* to do it, mind you – every kid – no matter how inept or unpopular they were and no matter how many notes they had from their parents saying they got 'stage fright' or 'asthma' or whatever. *Everyone.*

The reasoning behind this must have been that if you didn't make stuff like that compulsory, no-one would ever do it. By forcing kids up onto the stage, Mrs Newport must have hoped to encourage an appreciation of the arts, or perhaps unearth some previously undiscovered talent. Well, if that were the aim, Friday morning arts classes had been an abject and dismal failure. Amongst the sea of mediocrity they had produced so far, the only standout performances had been:

- Billy Gibson's 'World of Nature' (in which Billy dramatically produced a bug from his pocket and then stamped on it); and
- Anton Georgio's 'Amazing Anton' (in which Anton donned a hat and cap, muttered a few magic words, and then demonstrated how many marbles he could ram into his nose).

In the ongoing search for a future Mel Gibson or Peter Allen, genuine talent was looking thin on the ground.

This was why we'd all gathered in the multi-purpose room

that day – to watch an act that promised nothing in terms of skill and everything in terms of humiliation. I was sitting up the front near the stage (or, more accurately, near the end of the room which had been designated as the stage). On either side of me were my two best friends – Martin Timms on the right and Simon Jackson on the left. It was Martin who first broke the silence.

'I betcha Tordby's packin' darkies,' he half said and half whispered.

'For sure,' I muttered back, glancing over at Lucas (who, on cue, adopted a suitably horrified expression).

'You've gotta feel sorry for him really – the poor little bugger. I mean, if I was like him, Daff – you know – all fat and stuff – I wouldn't want to stand up in front of everyone and perform some act, just so people could hang it on me.'

'No, of course not. Neither would I.'

'I mean, kids like Lucas shouldn't have to do things like that. They should just be left alone – cut off from everyone else. Maybe even sent to a special school or something.'

I stopped for a moment to digest what Martin was saying. Although it might not sound like it, I was sure his heart was in the right place on this issue. He just hated to see needless suffering.

'What, you mean like a special school for fat kids?'

'Noooo, not just the fat kids. I mean *all* the losers. Ship 'em off somewhere where they can play in peace and hang out with their own kind and stuff. Like in the movies.'

'The movies? What movies?'

Martin paused at this point, unable to come up with a movie in which overweight primary school children were herded into special schools for their own protection.

'Well, you know what I mean, Daff.'

'Um . . . yeah.'

No, not really.

I should, at this stage, point out that people at school called me 'Daff' – as in 'Daffey'. They also sometimes called me 'Duck' – as in 'Daffy Duck' – the lack of an 'e' in the cartoon character's name not being enough to save me from years of torment. Not that 'Duck' was always used as an insult. It just depended on how it was said and who was saying it.

After Martin made his point about special schools, our conversation petered out a little. Although I had no idea what he was on about, I didn't directly challenge his argument. Martin was, after all, the leader of our little gang of three.

Martin got to be leader not because he was smarter or more worldly than Simon or me (though he may have been those things too), but because of the natural authority that came with owning a Gray-Nicolls double-scoop and having a higher batting average than us. Martin's prowess as a sportsman made him a well-respected member of the school community, but he had never managed to work his way into the cool crowd. He was good-looking, in a friendly sort of way, athletic and pretty likeable, but he couldn't quite crack it for a ticket to the big time. Why this was the case was hard to tell, but it may have had something to do with his manner. Whereas most sporty kids at school had a kind of cocky charm to them, our friend tended to be more serious – almost adult-like at times – and people never really warmed to that.

Just as Martin was born to be the leader of our group, Simon was destined to bring up the rear. It's hard to think of a way to describe Simon's personality without sounding overly harsh. Suffice to say this: he was thin, he was freckly, he had every episode of *Dr Who* on tape, and he had an uncanny knack of getting under people's skin. Why then were we friends with him? I blame mothers. Mothers had this weird rule that if they knew another mother who also had a kid at school your age, you were obliged to become their friend (or at least give friendship a red hot go). This wouldn't have been so bad if it wasn't for the *quality* of kids you had to adopt. It was never:

'This is Helena, a statuesque blonde from Finland who's new in town. Help her out a bit.'

It was always:

'This is Marvin, a serial dipstick and compulsive bed-wetter. Take him under your wing, show him the ropes, make it clear to everyone at school that he's YOUR FRIEND!'

Our relationship with Simon was a bit like that. His mother went to school with Martin's mother a hundred years ago and because of that, Martin and I were destined to pay through the nose. Not that Simon was *that* bad. He was just bad.

While Martin and I had been discussing Lucas's plight,

Simon had been happily thumping away at a Game 'n Watch. It was called Oil Panic. Oil Panic was a bit like Donkey Kong. It was a twin-screen game like Donkey Kong, but it came in a white case, whereas Donkey Kong came in an orange one. The plot of the game, if you can call it that, also differed from its more successful counterpart. Where Donkey Kong involved scrambling up ladders and avoiding barrels thrown by gorillas (which sounds sort of fun), Oil Panic involved running around the Mario Bros restaurant and catching stray drops of oil with a pan. As a result, Donkey Kong sold about a billion copies, while Oil Panic sold about fifty.

Having spent the entire morning engrossed in the game, Simon suddenly let out a cry of despair and dropped it to the floor.

'Damn it! I don't believe it. I had it, I actually had it. I mean, I was this close!' he exclaimed, turning towards us and holding up a pair of pinched fingers.

'No-one cares, Simon,' Martin replied bluntly, sick to death of his friend's daily Nintendo sagas.

'What do you mean, *no-one cares*? I almost clocked the thing! Do you understand – *clocked it*! I bet you don't know anyone else around here who's almost clocked Oil Panic!'

'That's because no-one has it, Sime. Oil Panic sucks.'

Simon responded to this insult by opening and closing his mouth rapidly without making any sound, as if Martin had just said something awful about his mother. 'That's not true – that's not true at all! It's a great game. Better than any of the crap *you've* got. Better than your stupid, boring Donkey Kong, which *everyone* has!'

'Okay, Sime. Whatever! It's not *our* fault you asked for Donkey Kong for Christmas and your parents got you Oil Panic. Don't blame it on us!'

He was right, of course. Poor old Simon. Few things sting an eleven-year-old quite as much as telling everyone you were getting a certain thing for Christmas, and then copping something else. At first, Simon had been ashamed of his new game. But over time, his grief had turned into anger and then an unbearable compensatory pride.

'Well, you're not having a go of it then, Martin,' he declared, after stewing on it for a moment.

'Suits me.'

'And neither are you, *Daff.*'

'Hey, I didn't say anything!'

But Simon had made up his mind. He sat there, clutching the game to his chest, determined to pay us back by sulking, by refusing to let us near his game, and by not saying another word to us. Not now, and not ever. This lasted about thirty seconds.

'So what's happening with the act? Have I missed something?'

Martin looked away and snorted with contempt.

'They reckon the tape recorder's busted,' I volunteered, 'so they've gone off to get another one.'

'Oh. Well, I hope they hurry up. This Tordby thing's going to be a pisser!'

That said, Simon happily returned to his Game 'n Watch, buoyed by the knowledge that someone was about to suffer and it wasn't going to be him.

As it happened, we didn't have to wait long for the tape recorder to turn up, and when it did, Mrs Newport heralded its arrival like the coming of a new messiah.

'Children, children,' she exclaimed, raising both hands into the air in the way people do when they're announcing something momentous. 'The problem has been fixed! We are right to go!'

The crowd bobbed up and down and murmured approvingly. The delays were over. Bring on the sacrificial lamb.

After a brief and unnecessarily positive introduction from Mrs Newport, Lucas rose from his chair and shuffled clumsily across the stage. He looked ill. His face had that expression people get when they've been waiting ages for something horrible to happen and then suddenly it's upon them. Like when you're in a hospital waiting room about to have an operation. You're sitting there saying to yourself:

'Don't worry, it's going to be okay. Don't worry, it's going
to be okay. Don't worry, it's going to be okay . . .'
and then BANG, the doctor walks in holding a needle the size of a small sword and you think to yourself,

'No, actually, it's not going to be okay. I am going to *DIE*!'
There may not have been any needles or surgeons around, but Lucas had the look of a man who was about to lose his spleen.

When he reached the microphone he took it in his left hand and then looked away to the right, as if preparing himself for a big opening line. This was definitely a bad sign. I put my hand over my face to shield myself from the impending horror, and resisted the temptation to laugh at him before he'd given me reason to. I didn't have to wait long. As the first few bars of Sheena Easton's *Morning Train* rang out through the multi-purpose room, Lucas Tordby turned slowly towards the crowd, swayed his hips awkwardly and prepared to greet infamy.

It's hard to imagine what Lucas could have been thinking when he opted to bite the bullet and perform a musical number. It was a ballsy call by anyone's standards and an amazing decision for someone who couldn't sing. Lucas had the type of voice the FBI blasts through loudspeakers to end a siege. From the moment he opened his mouth, it bounced disconcertingly between the gravelly bass of Joe Cocker and the high-pitched squeal of Alvin and the Chipmunks. If the kids watching him had cared at all about the courage needed to stand up on stage and do that, Lucas would have received a standing ovation. As it was, he was lucky to get through the first few lines unharmed. As bad as Lucas's voice was, however, it paled in comparison with his choice of song. No matter how well he sang it, there was no escaping the fact Sheena Easton was a woman, her 'baby' was a man and Lucas Tordby had no business being right there 'waitin' for him'.

The crowd's response to all of this was predictable and

severe. We'd been expecting a shocker from Lucas, but no-one could have hoped for something as shit as this. While he flounced about the stage howling and wailing, the audience peppered him with a stream of laughter and abuse. Not that any of it was audible. Since there were teachers around, any giggles had to be stifled behind hands and any insults had to be mouthed at their target.

The reactions of Martin, Simon and myself were better than this, but not by much. The simple fact is that it's hard to remain respectful of someone when everyone around you is pissing themselves. But as Lucas's act went from bad, to worse, to something worse than worse, I started to think about what it must have been like to actually *be* Lucas. Did Lucas know that Lucas sucked? Was there a time when things were different? Had he always known his life was going to turn out this way?

You see, the way I looked at it, the hardest part about primary school for Lucas must have been his lack of preparation for it. When he first strolled through the gates on his way to Mrs McCauley's Prep Grade M, he would have had no idea whatsoever that he'd be handed a business card that said 'Lucas Tordby – Dropkick.' In fact, like almost all of us, he would have had quite the opposite idea. Years of being smothered by parental affection and encouragement leaves your average pre-schooler thinking he is the smartest, best-looking, most advanced 'little bundle of joy' in the world ever. Parents rarely opt for honesty in assessing their children. No mother ever turns to her six-year-old daughter and says, 'Marcy, you're as dumb as you are hideous, but I love you anyway.' It's just praise, praise and more praise until every little trooper turning up for their first day of school thinks they're God's gift to humanity. If only parents fessed up to the lies they've told before they packed their kids off to school. If only fathers grabbed their sons by the shoulders before they sailed out the door and said:

> 'You know all that stuff your mother and I told you about you being cute and clever and adorable? Well, it's a bunch of cobblers. You're actually a bit of a bonehead, Son, and you might cop a little stick out there because of it.'

Maybe then we would have had at least some idea of what we were in for. But no, there was none of that. It was all 'have a great day', 'enjoy yourself' and 'you'll make lots of fantastic new friends'. It was like storming the beaches of Normandy with no real conception of how the enemy was going to attack you. You arrived on the shores of a dangerous foreign place with a bunch of guys you hardly knew, and before you knew it someone was calling you a fat-arse and laughing at your *Hey Hey It's Saturday* albums and you'd been blown to bits before you stepped out of the boat.

In my case, the first few minutes of that battle were telling. Within moments of stepping through Templestowe Heights Primary's front gate, I knew more about myself than I'd learnt in the five years preceding. On the plus side, I discovered that I had a socially acceptable hair colour, was of average height and weight, and was at least quick-witted enough to fend off your average moron. On the downside, I had a noticeable overbite and a surname akin to a target on my arse. In the fight for my self-esteem, it quickly became apparent that while I wasn't exactly cannon fodder, Private Christopher Daffey was no Navy Seal either.

As I sat there that day watching Lucas grind what little there was of his reputation into dust, I was grateful that I'd at least been given a fighting chance; that God, or whoever was in charge of handing out DNA up there, had set the odds of me having a happy childhood at even money, rather than a squillion to one. Had things been just a little different – had I been born with a lazy eye, facial moles or a pair of ears that could collect television signals – life at primary school would have been infinitely more difficult. Had fate been just a touch harsher, then maybe I'd be the one up on stage belting out the words 'My baby takes the mornin' train' to a room full of people who hated me.

Lucas's act was a stark reminder of just how hard primary school could be on a kid. When the curtain finally fell and he trudged off the stage to riotous, insincere applause, a small knot of panic began to form inside me. In just a few short months, it would be me up on stage. This date loomed ahead of me like an appointment with oblivion. If anything was going to spoil my well-laid plans for my grade six year, it would be a humiliating cock-up in front of the entire known world. One false step, one ill-conceived impression or appalling mime, and everything I was working towards would be smashed to pieces. And she'd be there to see it all. She, who meant more to me than life, death, even *Star Wars*.

I was afraid, and I had reason to be.

2

The sweet smell of Dewberries

SLEEP PROVED DIFFICULT in the nights following the Tordby debacle. Each time I drifted off, my mind would fill with disturbing images involving Lucas, myself and a series of unspeakably bad cabaret acts. It was one of those dreams that made perfect sense in some respects, but was completely bewildering in others. The act bit made sense: I was afraid of screwing my act up; I was afraid of screwing my act up as badly as Lucas; I was afraid of ending up *like* Lucas – a failure, a stuff-up, a goofy pathetic loser. All of this was perfectly understandable. It was the little things that kept me guessing. Like how come we were dancing at my nan's place? Why was Lucas bald? And what was with all those miniature schnauzers? The answers to these questions were beyond me and speculation proved pointless. It wasn't until the following Wednesday that I was able to put it all behind me and get through the night without trauma.

Wednesday was geography day; or at least it was for Mr Weathershaw's Grade 6W. My form teacher's classroom was located at the northern end of one of two tan-bricked buildings that ran up the centre of the school. On this particular morning, he was running late, and students were left to themselves to file in and make their way to their seats.

After saying a quick hello to Martin and Simon (who sat on either side of me), I settled down and began searching through my desk. It was one of those classic primary school two-seaters – the kind with wooden flip-top lids, inkwells on the side, and tiny stickers somewhere underneath that read:

'Bulk-bought by the Education Department in 1904 – *never to be retired.*'

Along with an atlas, some exercise books and a heap of other junk was a carefully wrapped brown-paper package tucked away in the corner. Glancing around to make sure no-one was looking, I reached inside and patted it nervously. 'Today is going to be the day, my friend,' I whispered to the parcel.

Each day since the start of the year, I'd gone through this ritual: open the desk, pat the parcel, promise it big things for the day ahead. And each day I'd chickened out when the time came. But today was going to be different. Today, I was determined to march right up to her at lunch, hand her the package, and tell her . . . And tell her . . . Well, I'd figure out what to say once I got there. A direct confrontation was definitely risky, but I had nothing to lose. Other than my pride, of course. And maybe my dignity. And self-respect would probably go too, come to think of it. In fact, the more I looked at it, the worse it seemed. Just as what little courage I had threatened to evaporate, a tall, spindly man strode into the room and bid the class good morning. Mr Weathershaw had arrived.

Mr Weathershaw was a strange old relic from the fifties. He had gnarled, leathery skin, a stern manner and a pair of massive sideburns which people called 'sideboards' or 'mutton chops' or some other weird term that reminded me of Governor Bligh and the rum rebellion. Along with being the hairiest man I'd ever seen, he was also the worst dressed. If what he wore to school was any indication, Mr Weathershaw owned exactly two jumpers and two pairs of pants. This gave him a staggering four combinations to mix and match. In the jumper department, he could opt for his flagship garment (a red woollen number with an Advance Australia triangle sewn into the corner), or his 'special occasions pullover' (a brown, loose-fitting top that looked like it was designed to clothe monks). As for pants, he had a choice between blue cords and gray pinstripes. Some kids maintained that he actually had two pairs of gray pinstripes. This theory gained a lot of momentum over the years, but was finally put to rest when Bruce Sanguinetti tagged a pair with a piece of gum. The more times the gum fronted up, the less likely it seemed he had two.

Mr Weathershaw's teaching methods were at least as outdated as his wardrobe. In contrast to our female grade six teacher, Mrs Newport, and her 'you can never do enough brainstorming' approach to education, Mr Weathershaw put his faith in the time-honoured 'four Rs' method of instruction: reading, writing, arithmetic, and ramming the name of every capital city in the entire fucking world down kids' throats. I have never understood the importance he placed upon learning one tiny piece of information about every nation on earth. After all, it wasn't as if this knowledge really increased our understanding of the world around us.

'Okay, Chris, the test begins now. What is the capital of Chad?'
'That's an easy one, Mr Weathershaw – N'djamena.'
'Great. Well done. Next question – *where* is Chad?'
'Ahhhhh, dunno.'
'Who is the leader of Chad?'
'Dunno that either.'
'What are Chad's most important primary industries?'
'Pass.'
'What are people from Chad called?'
'Ummmm . . . Chads? Chadders? Chaddies? Stuffed if I know.'

It was a strange way of educating, but our teacher swore by it.

After taking a moment or two to compose himself, Mr Weathershaw went to work.

'Yes, hmm, sorry I'm late, children,' he began in a thin,

nasally and perpetually rushed tone. 'Couldn't be helped, couldn't be helped. Now, I hope everyone's brought their atlases in today, because we've got a lot to get through,' he continued, waving around his own tattered textbook (which still referred to Australia as 'New Holland'). 'Without opening your books, I wonder if anyone could tell me the capital of, hmmm, let's see . . . *Ceylon*?'

This request was greeted by puzzled silence.

'Come along now, children. Ceylon. The jewel upon India's brow! The tear drop of the sub-continent! Famous for its tea, cricketers and elephants!'

'Don't you mean Sri Lanka?' came Sally Higgs's voice from the back of the class.

'Sri Lanka?' our teacher repeated, twisting his mouth around these alien words. 'Yes, of course. That's right. Well done, Sally! Ten house points to you. Now, for twenty house points, tell me the capital!'

Sally furrowed her brow and then shrugged.

'Anyone else? Can anyone else tell me the capital of Sri Lanka?'

Silence.

'Hmmmmm,' said Mr Weathershaw. 'I see what's going on. Too early in the morning for you, is it? Stayed up 'til all hours last night watching the goggle box, did you? Yes, I see. I get it.'

Most of the class averted their eyes at this point and there were a few isolated giggles at the phrase 'goggle box'.

'Come along now, someone must know the answer. Don't make me pick a volunteer. You know how you hate that!'

We certainly did. There was nothing worse than being plucked out from amongst your classmates and used as a kind of demonstration model for stupidity. ('Yes, you – Mark, up the back – please tell the class how dumb you are.')

As Mr Weathershaw scoured the room for an appropriate victim, everyone did their utmost to deflect attention away from themselves. From where our teacher was sitting, it must have looked hilarious. Squirming before him was a sea of frightened children, all trying desperately to come up with body language that said 'now is not the appropriate time to ask me a question'.

I opted for what could be called the 'child in distress' routine. This involved staring out the window with a panicked expression on my face, as if I'd just remembered something horrible – something so traumatic that no decent human being would dare interrupt my grief. Martin went for a more conventional approach. He simply nudged his pen off the desk, bent over to pick it up, and stayed down there for as long as it took. As impressive as our performances were, neither came close to matching Simon's ridiculous display. Each time our teacher's gaze drifted near him, he let out a stifled gasp, clamped a hand over the top of his face, and began writhing in agony – as if there was suddenly something drastically wrong with his eyes.

'Yes, okay, class,' Mr Weathershaw sighed. 'Here's what I'm

going to do. I'm going to ask you a series of questions over the next hour and I expect people to answer them. At the end of that hour, I'll pick out the worst two performers in class. These two children will have the honour of accompanying me during lunchtime – *on yard duty*!'

The class snapped to attention. In terms of enjoyable school-time activities, yard duty ranked right up there with bush craft and papier-mâché barn animals. It consisted of trailing after your teacher at lunchtime, picking up rubbish and emptying garbage bins. It was soul-destroying stuff and the mere mention of it was enough to prompt a dramatic increase in the class participation rate. Children who only moments earlier were rendered speechless by mysterious ailments were suddenly clamouring to get their hands in the air and answer a question. Of course, it didn't change the fact that none of us knew the capital of Sri Lanka (or any of the countries he mentioned). But we did know the names of some cities, and they were going to have to do.

When the sixty minutes were up, it was a real struggle to pick the two worst (though not half the struggle it would've been to pick the two best). In the end, it came down to chance, and it was Simon and me who drew the short straws. This was because Simon kept insisting that Bogotá was the capital of everything, and I was unlucky enough to agree with him on one occasion.

✳✳✳✳✳

Yard duty commenced down by the portable classrooms at the southern end of the school. While Mr Weathershaw limbered up and ran through some pre-duty exercises, Simon and I kicked around clods of tanbark and quietly fumed.

Naturally, we were pretty disappointed with our selection. The hour we had off for lunch was an invaluable respite from the rigours of a five-hour working day. Now that it had been transformed into collecting refuse with our form teacher, Wednesday was shaping up to be wall-to-wall Weathershaw. From 9 a.m. to 10.30 a.m. we had him for geography. From 10.45 a.m. to 1.15 p.m. we had him for mathematics. And from 2.15 p.m. to 3.30 p.m. he conducted a class that was loosely termed 'social studies', but could be more accurately described as 'Mr Weathershaw tours Europe, circa 1958'. It was the grand-daddy of all slide shows and our teacher's favourite way of rounding out the middle of the week.

Over-exposure to my teacher wasn't the only thing worrying me. With lunchtime dead and buried, I'd lost my chance to give her the present. Again! If I wanted to stick to my morning resolution, I'd have to wait until after school. This was a much more daunting prospect. Compared with a casual lunchtime rendezvous, tailing a girl as she left the building seemed a little less like spontaneous interest, and a little more like calculated stalking. I'd have to chance it anyway, of course. The Plan said 'by Wednesday' and so Wednesday it had to be.

We got underway as soon as our teacher finished stretching. It was exhausting work. While Simon and I stumbled after him, Mr Weathershaw blazed a trail ahead of us and acted as a type of rapidly moving 'scout' in the never-ending search for refuse. It was a role at which he was frighteningly proficient. As he shoved his way through the activity around him, he used one eye to scan for litter and the other to police the playground. He was so quick at what he did that the kids he told off probably wouldn't have even seen him. The only evidence he was there at all was a faint whiff of Shelltox Ministrips and an endless series of barked commands:

'Play fair, Cathy!', 'Put it back in your pants, Devon!', 'You over there, with the spud gun – don't think I don't know what's going on!'

The man may have been in his late fifties, but the old bastard sure was agile.

In what seemed like no time at all, the three of us managed to clean a path all the way from the school's back fence, past the basketball courts and up into the New Adventure Playground (a collection of play equipment constructed almost entirely out of pine logs). Once we reached the playground, it became clear that our task was about to get harder. It was the last week of summer and the area was packed with kids making the most of the sunshine and warm northerly winds. As we approached the crowds, Mr Weathershaw raised his right hand as if to steady us and then muttered some words of caution.

'Christopher, Simon, stay close, we could be in for a little rough-housing!'

I shot a quick look at my friend to make sure that sounded as stupid to him as it did to me. Simon responded by putting a finger to his temple and twisting his hand back and forth – universal code for 'Mr Weathershaw is mental'.

The New Adventure Playground was primarily the domain of younger kids. As the three of us pushed on towards the centre of it, I noticed how the hoarse cries of older students kicking balls had been replaced by the shrill squeals of nine-year-olds kicking each other. Wherever I looked, there were masses of them: running around, chasing their friends, and crawling all over the play equipment. From what I could tell, virtually every kid from grade three down was out there that day. And those who weren't were probably doing exactly the same thing on the other side of the school, at the *Old* Adventure Playground.

The Old Adventure Playground was much like the new one except that a lot of the stuff in it was made with rocks – huge, brown, porous rocks set in concrete and fashioned into walls and steps and things. Why one playground was called the 'Old' and the other 'New' was anyone's guess. Nobody could recall a time when both did not exist and kids did not have the choice of two surprisingly similar adventures at lunchtime. But, in theory at least, there must have been such a time – a Dark Age where playtime was bleak and optionless – where the Old Adventure Playground was *The* Adventure Playground and steel-rendered monkey bars were the stuff of science fiction. Thankfully I did not live in such an era.

Having picked up papers all the way from the border of the playground to the Log Fort (a semi-submerged hideaway set into a hill), the yard duty crew rested for a moment and Simon burst into conversation.

'Hey, Daff, did I tell you about that new frisbee I got?' he asked excitedly.

'Nope. What's it like?'

'Well, remember the other one I had – the Official Championship one?'

'Yeah.'

'Well, this one's a Championship *Pro*!'

'Wow,' I replied, genuinely impressed. 'What's the difference?'

'The difference?' Simon asked incredulously. 'The difference is that this is the *Pro* one – as in the one *the professionals use*! It's got these cool grooves around the edge, and a picture of a trophy in the middle, and if you turn out all of the lights, it glows in the dark!'

'Gosh,' I said absently, turning my mind to the Utopian world of the professional frisbee thrower. (One of the many career options that you really think exists when you're a kid.)

'You can come over to my place after school and have a throw of it if you like. But you've got to promise not to chuck it on the roof.'

'Sure. Okay. That'd be ace,' I replied, before remembering the parcel and my mission after class. 'Um, actually, I can't.'

'Why not?'

'I've got stuff to do.'

'What do you mean? What stuff? Come on, Daff, you're holding out on me. Is it a secret? Do you have a secret???'

'No, really, Sime. It's nothing. I've just got things to do.'

Simon narrowed his eyes and stared at me warily. 'I bet you've told *Martin* about it, haven't you?'

'What? I don't know what you're talking about, Sime. It's nothing.'

'Yeah you have. And you're not going to tell *me*. Fine then. You're *banned* from using my frisbee!' Then he scooped up some rubbish, turned his head and strode away.

Conversations with Simon often ended like this. He'd start out normal, work his way round to offering you something, and then fly off the handle due to some perceived injustice. He was particularly sensitive to issues involving Martin. He was, it has to be said, a little jealous of his friend. This was because Martin was everything Simon was not. He was popular, he was good at sport, he could recite cricket statistics until you just wanted to kill him, and he had a well-liked and super-macho father (who coached the school footy team and had recently purchased a Holden dream car). For this reason, Simon constantly suspected that Martin was being favoured ahead of him. And most of the time, he was right.

I *had* told Martin about my plans for the afternoon. I'd also told him every single detail about my secret crush. I'd done this because Martin was reliable and worthy of my trust. Simon, on the other hand, was a blabbermouth! If you told him something, he'd tap his nose, wink his eye, point his finger, and do everything else that unreliable morons do to convince you that your secret is safe. Then, as soon as you were out of earshot, he'd blurt it out to the next passer-by. If I wanted the whole school to know I was in love, I'd tell Simon. Until then, he was out of the loop.

✳✳✳✳✳

Of all the places to wait for someone after class, I chose the breezeway. The breezeway was a short, open-ended corridor that ran across the end of the school and housed the girls' and boys' toilets. The breezeway smelt. No, it stunk. It was the type of smell that was unique to schools and could never be duplicated in the adult world: a subtle blend of stale urine, drying globs of wet tissues (which had been hurled against the ceiling for countless generations) and those little yellow soaps the cleaners tossed around to mask the smell of everything else.

The reason for choosing the breezeway was simple. The girl I was besotted with was in Mrs Newport's class. This meant that she exited the building at the southern end of the school and had to walk all the way to the northern end, past the breezeway, to get to her mum's car. It was in that hundred or so metres (between the breezeway and the Volvo station wagon) that I would make my move. The exact plan was as follows:

1. Race out of class and get to the breezeway as soon as possible (check).
2. Stand around for a few minutes, twiddling my thumbs and looking like an idiot (check).
3. Wait until she walks past (in progress).
4. Emerge casually from the breezeway and strike up a conversation (yet to be accomplished and too terrifying to contemplate).

The five or so minutes I spent waiting for her to arrive were some of the longest of my life. I tried as best I could to fill in the time constructively, but had to settle for staring down at the parcel in my hand and constantly dry-retching. I'd wrapped it well, if I do say so myself. So well, that you couldn't even tell it was perfume. Of course, I wasn't sure she even *wore* perfume, but that didn't matter. Television had taught me that there were only three things you could give to impress a girl – perfume, flowers, or a puppy. Since the latter items wouldn't have stood up well to three and a half weeks in my desk, I was glad I'd gone with perfume.

Acquiring the perfume had been easier than I could have hoped. My dad owned a chemist shop, so it was simply a matter of swiping a bottle when he wasn't looking. I chose this particular brand of perfume because of its impressive English-sounding name – 'Yardley' – and because it had one of those weird flowery descriptions that girls must love, like 'cinnamon musk' or 'moistened dewberries' or something stupid like that. Besides, it was the only one in Dad's shop that wasn't locked away in a glass display cabinet. In hindsight, this little fact should have rung some alarm bells.

Every girl in school must have walked past the breezeway that day, before *my* girl finally did. When I saw her, I almost fell over. Strolling nonchalantly along the path between the building and the Old Adventure Playground was Jenny Hartnett! The object of my fanatical affections. The centre of my primary school universe. Five and a bit feet of dazzling, dark-haired perfection!

So taken aback was I by Jenny's sudden appearance that I forgot all about my plans and watched her walk right on by. It wasn't until she was a good ten feet away that I finally sprang into action. Clambering down the stairs and clutching the parcel to my chest, I stumbled after her like a hippo chasing a swan. Although I moved quickly, my hesitation had cost me. Instead of emerging from the breezeway directly in line with her, I was a long way behind and had to play catch-up. I took a few clumsy strides in her direction and then threw my arm out to tap her on the back. *This* was the crucial moment!

As my hand sailed towards her and the rest of me hurried forward, my eyes opened wide with fear and expectation. It seemed to take forever to bridge the gap between us – that short, but immensely significant distance between fingertip and shoulder, between silence and conversation, between secret crush and going steady. It was a journey it was destined never to complete. Just as Jenny rounded the corner and my hand made its first fleeting contact with fabric, she collided with two girls coming the other way. It was the Gobbo twins. I was screwed.

'Sorry, Jenny!' the monsters chimed in unison, before swivelling around and fixing their gaze on my startled face. I tried to pull my hand back and make out as if I was stretching, or yawning, or something; but it was too late. They had me!

'Jenny,' (point, gesture, giggle) 'I think there's someone here to see you.'

I remember seeing these sculpture things once on television. They were called 'frozen moments'. The idea was that each sculpture was supposed to show a snapshot of a common, everyday thing in motion, like 'pouring coffee' or 'egg being broken'. When Jenny turned around and saw me standing there about an inch behind her, a very similar thing happened to me. For a moment or two, every single part of my body went completely rigid. I was left standing there, stockstill, with my mouth wide open and my hand still extended towards her. I'd become my very own frozen moment. And if someone had bothered to box, market and title me, I would have been known as 'man packing shit'.

'Hello,' Jenny ventured, smiling at me in a concerned kind of way.

'Hi,' I stammered back, grinning like an idiot and staring at a spot about a foot above her head.

'It's Chris, isn't it?'

I nodded.

'So, um, Chris, did you want to speak with me?'

Yes, I said without opening my mouth. *Yes, I did. I wanted to tell you that I'm completely in love with you and that it'd be really nice if you went out with me. Unfortunately, the two girls standing behind you are giggling and making faces and it's kind of putting me off. So instead, I'm going to say this:*

'Well, I was just . . . you know . . . in the neighbourhood . . . and I thought I'd . . . um . . . drop by.'

Shocker.

You see, what I was trying to do was say something *funny*. Something that pulled the iron out of the fire and turned the whole conversation around. Something witty. Something offhand and clever that proved I had a brain somewhere, even if it was temporarily out of order. It was a little joke at myself, you see – imitating the standard cornball line you hear on TV – using a casual, relaxed kind of tone, when I quite clearly wasn't. And it might have worked too, had I not been so consumed by terror that it came out like a mad guy saying something spooky, rather than a nervous guy trying to say something clever. I'd made a mistake, and now it was time to pay the penalty. After taking a few seconds to digest what I'd said, the Gobbos let loose.

'What do you mean you were *in the neighbourhood*?' (Donna)

'What neighbourhood? You mean school? That's not a *neighbourhood*.' (Trudy)

'And you weren't just *dropping by* either. You were following her!' (Donna)

It was a slaughterhouse.

I tried to think of things to say in my defence, but it was no use. Donna just kept pounding me with questions, and if Trudy smirked at me any harder, she was going to break her mouth. Needless to say, none of this was turning out as I'd hoped. When I'd pictured this event, Jenny had been alone for a start (it wasn't often that the Gobbo twins popped up in my fantasies). In addition, I'd been a much cooler customer; the type of customer who just sidled up to Jenny, said a couple of quick, throwaway lines (which were at once charming and hilarious), handed her the perfume and then strode away into the sunset – a suave, mysterious, present-giving enigma. Yes, it had been quite a dream. But this . . . this was horrible.

As the twins tore strips off me and Jenny looked on bemused, I felt the tension inside me rising. What could I do? What could I say? This was an ambush! Eventually, Jenny put a stop to it by raising a finger to hush them. Then she smiled at me warmly, put a reassuring hand on my shoulder and said, '*Were* you following me?'

I looked at Jenny, I looked at the Gobbos and then I just sort of ran off. In the circumstances, it was the most dignified exit I could think of.

3

A GiRL, a SMOCK AND a simple pLAN

THE FIRST GIRL I ever fell in love with wasn't Jenny Hartnett. Jenny Hartnett wasn't even the second girl I fell in love with. In fact, she probably didn't find her way into the first twenty. The thing that set Jenny apart from all the others was that she was the first girl I fell in love with who I'd actually met.

Before Jenny stepped into my life and screwed things up forever, I had a succession of wonderful girlfriends, all of whom spoke with an American accent, sat in the corner of my living room and screened between 4 and 6 p.m. daily. The first and most memorable was my beloved Jeannie of *I Dream of Jeannie* fame.

Before Jeannie and I started going out, I hardly noticed her really. She was just another member of a fine ensemble cast led superbly by the versatile Larry Hagman. Then, without warning, everything changed. One minute I was captivated by the comedic high jinks of Major Nelson and the long-suffering Doctor Bellows, and the next minute my whole life seemed to revolve around Jeannie's navel. It was terrifying. To make matters worse, I soon discovered that a similar transformation had occurred in all my favourite programs: the Six Million Dollar Man started looking like a cheap rip-off of the Bionic Woman (rather than the other way around); Maxwell Smart became half the agent 99 was; and Batman and Robin began to lose ground to the previously inane Batgirl and her startlingly conical breasts. At the tender age of ten, I'd clearly gone mad.

Jeannie remained the object of my affections for some months. In retrospect, it isn't hard to see why. Jeannie had a hell of a lot going for her as a girlfriend. She was gorgeous, she had a wardrobe full of lilac belly-dancing costumes, and if you ever got sick of her, you could trade her in for her evil twin sister (who I never once suspected was played by the same actress). Even more impressive than these qualities was the fact that Jeannie was magic. All she had to do was nod her head and blink her eyes and your room would be clean in an instant. For your average ten-year-old boy, it didn't get much better than that.

As good as she was, Jeannie's reign at the top didn't last forever. Slowly but surely she was overhauled by even more glamorous, larger-chested rivals. My selection criterion for new girlfriends was, with the benefit of hindsight, a pretty simple one, depending almost exclusively on a combination of breast size and a willingness to expose them in a G-rated timeslot. No-one scored better on this scale than Lynda Carter's ridiculously proportioned Wonder Woman.

For the star of a television series aimed squarely at children, Lynda Carter had a remarkably adult appeal. Even for boys too young to understand what sex was or how women fitted into the picture, there was something inherently desirable about a six-foot brunette who wore star-spangled bikinis and chased after men with lassos. From the moment she leapt onto our family's Rank Arena, I knew instinctively that half an hour alone with Wonder Woman would have to be a good thing. Exactly what would go on during that time, I had no idea. Perhaps, as some at school had suggested, she would rub her bottom against mine and then we'd have babies. Maybe, as others had surmised, it would have more to do with sticking my tongue in her mouth and that was how we'd make babies. Either way, babies seemed to be on the agenda and if that were the case, I was having none of it. At that stage of my life, the only sexual fantasy I had involving Wonder Woman consisted of:

- cornering her in a room;
- pumping her full of questions about the inconsistencies in her show (like, 'if you're so good at deflecting bullets with your enchanted bracelets, why doesn't someone just shoot you in the back?');
- and then yanking her top down and running like hell.

The jump from mindless crushes on television personalities to mindless crushes on girls my own age took a long while coming. Throughout most of my grade five year, TV starlets reigned supreme while my female peers suffered tremendously by comparison. Where Wonder Woman and Co were tall, curvaceous and spent their time casting spells and fighting crime, the girls I knew were short, scrawny and spent their time engrossed in skipping games and swapping pictures of kittens. It wasn't much of a contest and for a time I wasn't even aware there was one. Outside television, I was as untouchable as they came – immune from the mysterious forces that had already seen a number of my compatriots fall victim to 'going steady'. Girls simply held no interest for me and there was no power on earth strong enough to change that. That was, of course, until Jenny Hartnett.

*****

The circumstances that brought Jenny and I together could have been torn from the pages of an old-fashioned romantic novel. She was a damsel in distress, I was her knight in shining armour, and together we slew an evil fire-breathing dragon. Well, almost. In actual fact, I was probably more distressed than she was, a lack of protective clothing caused the problem in the first place, and the dragon wasn't so much slain as it was temporarily placated. But the basics were there, nonetheless.

It began in one of Mrs Kaufman's art classes towards the end of grade five. Jenny was in trouble because she'd forgotten to bring her smock. In the eyes of Mrs Kaufman (a tyrannical, hawk-like German woman), this was a crime which, in the scale of things, ranked somewhere between car theft and first-degree murder. Smocks were large, cloak-like garments designed to protect our clothing from paint spills and stray blobs of clay. As it happened, we were supposed to be making model planes that day and smocks probably weren't even necessary. After all, there was no real danger of Jenny tripping over and spilling balsawood on herself.

Had this argument been raised at the time, it wouldn't have carried much weight with Mrs Kaufman. Mrs Kaufman *hated* kids who forgot their smocks. Come to think of it, she wasn't a big fan of kids who remembered their smocks either. When she discovered that Jenny had left hers at home, she went absolutely berserk.

'Jenny – Jenny Hartnett! What would your parents say if I sent you home all covered in grease and grime?'

'But . . .' Jenny began in her defence.

'But nothing! No one else here has forgotten their smock. These children,' (waving her arm to indicate the rest of the class) '*always* remember their smocks. These children . . .'

And then she spotted me. I too was smockless and desperately trying to conceal that fact by pressing against Lucas Tordby and hoping somehow to merge into his. At the crucial moment, Lucas shifted himself sideways, I put my hand out to steady myself, and then tumbled forward in the manner of someone making a confession.

'Ah, Mister Daffey,' Mrs Kaufman sighed. 'You've forgotten your smock too. Well I'm glad you owned up, because I would have spotted you anyway!'

Under normal circumstances, one of Mrs Kaufman's smock-related rages would have seen out most of the class. On this occasion, however, the presence of multiple offenders seemed to take it out of her and she stopped after a couple of minutes. Jenny was naturally grateful. Had it been just her, she would have been crucified. As it was, she was mildly scolded and then forbidden from using oil-based paints. When our teacher's anger had subsided and the class recommenced, Jenny waved at me from across the room to get my attention. Then she did something that changed the course of my life. She looked at me, she smiled, and then she mouthed the words 'thank you'. And with that one sweet, simple gesture she dragged me kicking and screaming into the world of girls.

I hated the world of girls. From the moment I set foot in it I became anxious, distressed, unsettled and unsure. I preferred the world of mates. In that world, things were simple. Everything was okay so long as you were getting a few laughs in class, performing adequately on the sports field, and Australia was crapping all over England in the cricket. Women complicated everything. As soon as you threw girls into the equation, there were a million other factors to consider, like: What if no-one likes me? What if someone does like me, but then changes her mind? What if the only person that likes me is someone that I'd really prefer didn't? What if, what if . . . the questions were endless.

How you were supposed to find happiness under that sort of pressure, I didn't know. The only thing I did know was that Jenny's smile had had an effect on me that I didn't entirely understand. An effect that made everything up to that smile seem insignificant, and getting that smile again seem like the most important thing in the world.

The strangest part about it all was that I hardly knew the girl. If someone had asked me to write down every scrap of information I had on Jenny Hartnett, it would have come down to no more than this: she was attractive, she was successful, she had blue eyes and long, dark hair, and her reading level was 'black dot' (which meant she was pretty cluey). It wasn't much of a dossier, but somehow it was enough. Attraction, I was quickly learning, had nothing to do with reason – and when it struck, it was simply unstoppable.

The weeks that followed were fairly disappointing from a relationship point of view. To my dismay, I discovered that the Kaufman incident hadn't had quite the same life-altering impact on Jenny as it had on me. Despite my best attempts to get her attention (walking past her every thirty or so seconds, catching tennis balls spectacularly in front of her – that sort of stuff), I could have been excused for thinking that she didn't care at all. By the end of the month, I was at my wit's end. What had gone wrong? How could she have forgotten me?

What could I do to rekindle the flame that had burnt so briefly, and yet so brightly, between us? To my ten-year-old mind, the answer seemed obvious. I had to reconstruct the events that brought us together.

So began 'the great strike'. For a period stretching from the last month of grade five to the third term of grade six, I made leaving your smock at home my own personal crusade. Week in, week out, I sat there defiantly in my civvies, weathering the looks, the stares and every conceivable insult in the German language. And I did it all so I could send this simple message to my Jenny: 'Remember me? I'm the *smock guy*!'

Although it might not seem that clever now, I considered it a stroke of genius at the time. Not only would continually forgetting my smock help jog Jenny's memory, but it would also show her the type of man I was (or at least, the type of man I wanted her to *think* I was) – a rebel, an upstart, a teacher-defying tough guy who thumbed his nose at convention and played by his own rules.

Of course, there were other ways I could have been interpreted (a kid with an extraordinarily bad memory, for example), but I was confident that I was putting my best foot forward. Even when my ploy failed to deliver any tangible results, I never entirely lost faith in it. But as grade five wound its way to a close, it became clear that it wasn't enough. I needed something extra – some other ingenious ruse to help tip the odds in my favour. And then it came to me. What I needed was a *plan*. Not just any old plan though: a comprehensive, carefully constructed strategy designed to sweep Jenny off her feet and into my waiting arms. Over the two-month Christmas break, I went to work.

The first thing I realised about plan-making was that there was a lot more to it than just resolving to do one. Deciding what to actually put into the plan proved harder than I'd anticipated. Just how did a guy go about winning a girl's heart? I had no idea. When I hadn't come up with anything by January, I turned to television for the answer.

For countless hours, I sat in front of the box, taking down notes and studying the different methods used. Everything from:

- Sitcom Techniques: wait until she's walking down a corridor carrying an armful of books, and then smash into her and help pick them up;
to
- Day-time Soapie Solutions: abduct her, hold her hostage on an island, and continually feed her the line, 'I know it's hard to imagine now, my dear. But one day, you will *learn* to love me!'

Unfortunately, none of them seemed quite on the money (though the island thing had a certain appeal).

It wasn't until I'd clocked up almost a hundred hours that a hazy idea began to emerge. It wasn't so much what the characters *did*, but *who they were in the first place* that was important. No matter how many clever schemes or fiendish plots the bad guys hatched, women always flocked to the same sort of men: men who were rich, or charming, or good-looking, or all of the above. If that was what it took to get a girl, then I was in trouble.

For the first time I can remember, I was forced to have a good, hard look at myself. What was I good at? Where did my talents lie? If I couldn't trick Jenny into liking me, what else was there? I made a quick list.

Was I good at sport? No.

Was I good at art? No.

Could I sing or play an instrument? No (unless you counted the recorder – and no-one did).

Did I have the type of dashing good looks that made girls swoon and go weak at the knees? Welllllll . . . oh, come on, who do you think you're kidding? No.

Was I outstanding academically? Well, I did get an A+ for that project on John Batman . . .

You see this – *THIS* – was the problem. It wasn't so much that Jenny had forgotten me, but that even if she had remembered, she wouldn't have cared at all. Jenny was popular, smart, funny, gorgeous, interesting, talented. And I, by comparison, just wasn't good enough.

Finally, I had the answer I was looking for! If I wanted to get the girl, I had to pull my socks up, lift my game, straighten up and fly right, and all that other stuff. I had to become bigger, better, faster, smarter, more aesthetically pleasing. I had to go back to the drawing board and rebuild myself, brick by brick.

And so 'the plan' became *The Plan*. Brimming with enthusiasm, I took out a brand new four-coloured pen and listed all the areas of primary school life in which I could improve myself: sport, academia, the arts, student politics, everything. Then, on a fresh page, I set out a number of goals – goals which, if achieved, would propel me to the top of Templestowe Heights' social ladder and into Jenny's life.

1. Become member of important sporting team.
2. Get elected to student council.
3. Do a good act.
4. Perform well in inter-House competition.
5. Become known for my intelligence and speed with numbers.
6. If none of that works, talk to Jenny and get to know her.

In terms of timeframe, I gave myself the entire grade six year. After all, these things took time, didn't they? Just so long as by the end of that year, when the school gathered for its annual gala Ball, I'd be able to stride across the room and say, 'Hello, my love, care to dance?' Or words to that effect, anyway.

Although I was prepared to wait a whole year for success, I did allow myself one small concession. At the top of the list, I set out a goal that could only really be described as a 'short cut' – one last chance to win Jenny over quickly and easily, without having to overhaul my entire personality. I wrote this short cut down in green pen (to denote its special nature) and I gave myself until Wednesday the 23rd of February to achieve it.

And what a humiliating shemozzle it had turned out to be. Even a week after the incident at the breezeway, I still couldn't think about it without screwing up my face and shuddering violently. How the hell was I supposed to come back from *that*? It was hard to imagine. As I sat in my bedroom the following Thursday, I resolved to put it out of my mind and pretend it never happened. Instead, I turned my attention to the future – a future in which the slick, all-conquering winner I'd become would be scarcely recognisable from the blithering cretin Jenny had just seen. Then I took out a thick red texta and carefully ruled a line through the words 'Impress her with an inexpensive but tasteful gift'.

I'd made an arse of myself and now it was time to put in the hard yards. There'd be no more soft options, no more quick fixes. I had to knuckle down and get on with the job of making myself a better man.

I clicked my pen defiantly and looked down at my list.

Ah, Mr Bradbury . . .

4

Tea and biscuits with Richie Benaud

MATTHEW BRADBURY WAS from the old school of Phys. Ed. teachers. As such, he lived his life according to three simple maxims.

(a) Sport is good.
(b) It's never too cold to wear shorts.
(c) There's nothing on this earth you can't accomplish with a cleft chin, a pair of dark blue Stubbies and a can of Old Spice.

With his rugged physique, chiselled features and unhealthy obsession with blowing whistles, Matthew could be described as the perfect embodiment of the old school ethos. He was fit, he was impervious to all weather conditions and he ate more fibre in a week than most people consume in a lifetime.

In line with his no-nonsense outlook on life, Matthew had an equally straightforward approach to education. According to the Bradbury Big Book of Clever, there was no question too difficult, no dilemma too complex, that it couldn't be solved through a liberal application of common sense and a brisk jog around the block. So confident was Matt Bradbury in the power of his homespun logic that he frequently strayed outside the role of PE instructor and expressed opinions on a whole range of subjects, such as:

- Science and Technology ('Atoms are like tiny, tiny tennis balls, but smaller and more explosive');
- the Arts ('Has anyone in this class seen *Caddyshack*?'); and
- Sex Education ('Okay, boys, watch my hands move. You have one of these, they have one of those – BANG – there you have it. Any questions?').

Yep, it was a pretty black and white world out there for Matt Bradbury. And in that world there were only two types of cricketers – 'those who could play' and 'uncos'. On a scorching March afternoon, I fronted up to the school oval in the hope of distancing myself from the latter category.

*****

Like many primary school sportsgrounds, the school 'oval' was actually more of a rectangle than anything else. People just referred to it as an oval because it sounded stupid to say 'let's have a kick of the footy on the oblong'. To an eleven-year-old eye, the oval looked massive. Its loosely sown turf and countless sprinkler caps stretched nearly sixty metres from the St Marks' church fence to the sloping embankment separating the ground from the rest of the school. It was an awesome arena by primary school standards and the perfect venue for the epic struggle that was about to unfold. Thirty-six combatants strode onto the field that day, and only fifteen would walk off with a coveted place in the Templestowe Heights First Eleven. All my plans for my grade six year hinged on me being one of them.

Making the First Eleven was as impossible as it was desirable. To get in, you had to be good at cricket. I was shit at cricket. Well, shit's an exaggeration. I was stock-standard average – a talentless but gritty toiler who'd built a solid reputation in the backyard form of the game, but failed to make the jump to flat pitches and hard balls. With short boundaries, furry tennis balls and my sister bowling off spin, I was unstoppable. With long boundaries, polished Kookaburras and males my own age, I was bloody awful. I had more chance of sneezing bullion than I did of making the school cricket team, but I was determined to try anyway.

The rewards you received for making the First Eleven made even the most futile of attempts to get into it seem worthwhile. Membership of the side was like a gold pass to social acceptability. For those lucky enough to be selected in the squad each year, life was an endless parade of backslapping well-wishers, attractive girlfriends and fashionable parties (the kind with brand-name soft drinks and no games involving donkeys). The First Eleven was much less about sport than it was about status, and the list of certainties for this year's team read like a Who's Who of the playground elite. Amongst those almost guaranteed a spot were:

- Scott Brenner (a talented opening batsman and all-round nice guy who was expected to captain the side);
- Alex Milano (a flashy left-hander whose immaculate cover drive and ability to lay foot-long bogs were the stuff of legend);
- Marty Goldbloom (an insanely fast bowler);
- Mark 'show us your balls' Trimble (the best player in the school, but a woeful comedian and grade A arsehole); and
- last, but by no means least, Jeremy Ng (whose lightning reflexes and wizardry behind the stumps more than compensated for a loose grasp of English and an unpronounceable surname).

These were the kids who oozed the Right Stuff. These were the guys who held the playground in the palms of their hands. They were Templestowe Heights' finest, and if I'd ever had the opportunity, I'd have tied them all together, dropped them in an enormous tub of gelignite, and blown them all to bits. All of them. Even the nice ones.

✹✹✹✹✹

Mr Bradbury kicked off proceedings with a brief outline of the rules. It was standard trials format. Everyone was divided up into pairs and each pair got to bat and bowl for two overs. Once this had been explained to us in excruciating detail, Mr Bradbury clapped his hands together, blew his whistle a couple of times, and then signalled for the group to disperse. The trials had begun.

Having won the toss, my team filed off the ground and settled itself down on the embankment. Our opposition went in to field. Much to the relief of myself and the other cricketing minnows present that day, the division of the group into two teams had been attended to personally by Mr Bradbury (who'd posted up lists on the canteen noticeboard the day before). The alternative would have been to appoint two captains and let them pick the sides, player by player. That alternative was horrifying.

There are few times in life where your relative merit as a person is so brutally and publicly adjudged as when you stand before two captains waiting to be deemed worthy of their team. They look at you, they assess you, they weigh your strengths and weaknesses against those of your peers, and then slowly and methodically, they rank you:

'Mark, you're the best; Andy, you're second; Tim, Matt and Trent, you guys fit in the middle somewhere; Paulo, Max and that fat kid with his finger in his ear, you're all pretty shit...'

And so on and so forth, until thirty people are crowded around the two gangliest, least coordinated kids in the group, trying to decide which one is more tolerable than the other. After what seems like an eternity of last-minute deliberations, a decision is finally made. Slightly less awful Ross peels off to one side, leaving the truly, despicably awful Gavin to trudge off to a team that never expressed even the slightest preference in his favour. The verdict is in, the people have spoken.

'Gavin, you are quite simply the absolute worst. And there's no-one in the entire school we'd less like to have aboard than *you*.'

It was cruel, it was barbaric and it undoubtedly destroyed lives. But it produced fair teams, and that was what was important.

As luck would have it, I was on Scott Brenner's team. This was a good thing. The captain of the other side was Andrew McEvoy, and I didn't like him at all. Andrew was the Golden Boy of Templestowe Heights – good-looking, great at everything and the smarmiest prick in the entire world. If that wasn't bad enough, his star batsman (and best friend) was none other than Alex Trimble – and he was just *unbearable*. All up, it was a very fortuitous turn of events. Not only had I managed to evade the game's two top-seeded dickheads, I was also lucky enough to have Martin on my side.

Martin actually had a legitimate chance of making the side. He was a solid left-handed batsman, a handy medium pacer and was renowned for having a great 'cricket brain' (whatever the hell that meant). As we sat on the grass fiddling with our equipment, he attempted to impart some of his cricketing wisdom.

'Now don't forget what I showed you, Daff. Keep your eye on the ball, take each delivery on its merits, and for God's sake play straight!'

I nodded my head respectfully.

'Oh, and another thing,' he added, as I stuffed a worn plastic box down my pants. 'If you get hit in the goolies, don't let the opposition see your pain. Don't give 'em the satisfaction, Daffa. Don't give 'em the satisfaction.'

He was trying to be helpful, bless him. But all this talk of 'goolies' sent a shiver down my spine.

*****

While we sat waiting for play to commence, I scanned the lunchtime crowd for Jenny's face. From what I knew of her, she wasn't a massive sports fan, so I didn't expect to see her amongst the interested onlookers gathered by the side of the oval. Sure enough, the embankment was blissfully free of striking, olive-skinned brunettes. That is, unless you counted Theo Papadopoulos (which I didn't).

This was a massive relief. I'd been avoiding her religiously since the breezeway incident and the last thing I needed was her thumbing her nose at me from the stands. Her absence from the crowd meant I was under a little less pressure. Unless my failure to make the First Eleven was so spectacular that it became newsworthy, she'd never hear about it. On the other hand, if Lady Luck smiled upon me (and maybe slipped me a long brown envelope marked 'skills') and I made the team, she'd definitely hear about it. Mainly because I'd tell her. Yep, it was a win–win situation for Christopher Daffey, or at least a win–draw. And there was nothing like a risk-free, foregone conclusion to bring out my fighting spirit.

As expected, the opposition opened the bowling with Marty Goldbloom. My team responded by sending out a pair of perennial cricketing bunnies to face the music. The matching of hopelessly incompetent batsmen with murderous paceman and vice versa was standard practice in these matches. There was an automatic 'understanding' between captains that the batting side would arrange their batsmen in ascending order of competence, while the bowling side would do the opposite. It was a form of tacit collusion between the good players and was designed to eliminate the chance of one of them having a bad day and missing the team. You only had to glance at the ungainly duo clomping their way towards the pitch to realise how effective this system was.

Peter Pendergast looked like he'd last eaten a solid meal in 1974. He was five feet tall, built like a biro, and appeared to have barely enough energy to power his internal organs, let alone fend off a cricket ball. As appalling a sight as Pendergast was, though, you'd still happily hand him the strike in preference to the doofus walking out with him. Simon Jackson was a *woeful* sportsman. He wasn't fit, he wasn't fast, he wasn't strong, and he had no hand–eye coordination whatsoever. Combine these attributes with an unshakeable belief in his own abilities and you had a fairly fatal combination. Simon Jackson stunk, and everyone knew it but him.

Pendergast opted to face the first delivery of the day. It was a bold move. Rumour had it that Marty Goldbloom was expelled from his last school and almost jailed for killing a kid with a bean-ball. Apparently, one of the terms of his bond was that he had to restrict himself to medium pace or face imprisonment. Staring down the pitch at a convicted felon must have been a hard thing for Peter Pendergast. But if he was feeling the heat, he was showing no signs of it. As Marty began his long run from the canteen end, Peter calmly took guard and rolled his shoulders, like an in-form player with all the time in the world. If nothing more had happened, if all I'd seen that day was Peter's relaxed demeanour and casual stance, I would have been forced to conclude that he was a class batsman. This, presumably, was his plan. Think the goods, look the goods and maybe you'll *be* the goods. Peter was not the goods.

To say that Peter was beaten by the pace of Marty's first

delivery would be a gross distortion of the facts. As far as I could tell, he didn't even realise the ball had left Marty's hand until five minutes after it'd bounced off his face. To his credit, he maintained his defiant, professional stance until the very end. Even as the shiny red cherry exploded off the pitch and thundered towards his forehead, there was no movement at all in the Pendergast camp. He just stood there and continued looking like a batsman. When he still hadn't moved a muscle three minutes after impact, Mr Bradbury and most of the players rushed to his aid. There was a brief, ill-informed discussion about whether someone could be dead standing up (Mr Bradbury in favour, most of the kids against) and then Peter was carried from the field, stance intact. It was a strange dismissal, but it was the way he would have wanted to go.

Watching Peter's lifeless carcass make its way across the ground didn't do heaps for my confidence. Simon Jackson, on the other hand, seemed to revel in it. As Marty paced out his run and Mr Bradbury cautioned him about any further short stuff, Simon jogged cheerfully up and down and practised wild hook shots. Simon too, it seemed, was determined to go down looking like a cricketer, even if he couldn't play like one. The similarity between Simon's game plan and Peter's ended there. Whereas Peter had been content with mimicking a batsman at rest, Simon wanted to show the world he could play some shots. When Mr Bradbury directed Simon to face up to the next ball, rather than the new batsman, he was rapt. He'd waited eleven long years for a chance at glory, and in his hopelessly optimistic mind, this was it.

The first time Simon was bowled, he really did look shocked. He shouldn't have been, but he was. The ball wasn't even a good one by Marty's standards, but it was more than sufficient to knock over a batsman playing a square cut to a dead-straight yorker. Despite this setback, Simon was determined not to let Marty's accuracy deter him from playing his natural game. Over the next few balls, he played every shot in the book. He drove, he swept, he pulled, he hooked, and he never once got his bat near anything.

By the time Marty had finished his over, Simon's campaign was in disarray. He'd been caught once, bowled three times and stumped by the impossibly nimble Ng. At first, he tried to keep up the charade of a good batsman out of form. Each time the ball got past him, he'd spin around and stare at the shattered wicket in utter disbelief – as if it was the first time a delivery had slipped through his defences in years. Then he'd walk a few steps down the pitch, prod it with his bat and scratch his chin thoughtfully while contemplating nothing. But as time went by and more balls found their way into the woodwork, this ruse became progressively more implausible. On the third occasion that his stumps were broken, Simon merely sucked his lips together, raised his eyebrows slightly and mouthed something that looked like 'yep'.

✵✵✵✵✵

At the end of the first two overs, our team had three runs on the board at a cost of eight wickets and one life – and the opening bowlers had booked themselves a spot in the First Eleven. It was a great result for the status quo. As expected, the next few batsmen offered a little more resistance, and slowly but surely things began to level out. I was sent in just as the battle became evenly poised.

Naturally, I was nervous. Cricket balls are hard, unyielding things, and the prospect of having one lodged in my larynx did not sit well with me. Fortunately, I had a plan. Although Martin had stressed the importance of playing each ball on its merits, I'd made up my mind to do the exact opposite. You see, a player like Martin could *afford* to play a wait-and-see game. If the ball was good, he'd play it defensively. If it was bad, he'd rock back onto his back foot and club it to the fence. He was able to do this because he had a good eye and quick reflexes.

The same, however, could not be said for me. By the time *I* waited to see what a ball was doing, it was always doing something bad – like hitting me in the kidneys or crashing into the stumps. No, for me, batting had nothing to do with skill or quick reflexes. It was all about anticipation. The key was to guess what the bowler was going to do, and then play your shot accordingly. If you guessed right, you looked like a champion. If you guessed wrong, you looked like a complete berk. It was an all-or-nothing strategy, but I figured it was the only chance I had.

As I commenced my long journey out into the middle, my

mind began to race with the exciting possibilities a triumph might bring. I always did this. Whenever I got a sniff of success at anything, I'd extrapolate it in my mind until it was out of all sensible proportion. On this particular occasion, it began with the newspapers – wonderful, spinning newspapers with huge headlines, like the kind you see in films such as *The Bad News Bears* – 'Bears win first for season', 'Bears make it three in a row', 'Bears into playoffs', 'Bears win World Series', 'Where will it all end for those goddamned Bears?!?' Replace the word 'Bears' with 'Daffey' and ditch the baseball angle, and you've got a fair idea of the type of crap running through my mind.

'Daffey makes team!'

'Daffey shines in inter-school showdown!'

'Daffey freak selection in state squad!'

'Daffey who? Daffey how!'

'Daffey humbles England!'

'Daffey, best ever – Benaud.'

And so on and so forth, until I'm sitting next to the cream-suited one downing tea and biscuits and chatting about how I did it all for the love of the game.

It was a beautiful dream and I could've stayed in it forever. But as quickly as it came to me, it was abruptly torn away. All of a sudden the bowler was striding his way to the pitch, and reality was urgently jabbing me in the ribs.

My opponent was a kid called Steve Cohen. Steve was a good bowler, but he wasn't a great one. He was one of those players who look impressive enough in the run-up (all flailing arms, puffing cheeks and lengthy strides), but who fail to transfer any of that momentum into the ball itself. For a fast runner, he was an amazingly slow bowler. As he rolled his arm over and performed some rudimentary stretches, I fiddled with my gloves and tried to guess what he was going to do. What I came up with, was this:

- He knew I wasn't much of a batsman, so he'd use his first few balls to try and get me out.
- If that didn't work, he'd get pissed off and try and hit me in the head.
- And if even that failed, he'd be forced to pitch up his final ball in the hope of taking a wicket.

This was where I'd pounce.

Having worked out my plan of attack, it was just a matter of playing the appropriate shots: block, block, block, duck, duck, *DRIVE*!

And that's exactly what I did. I stonewalled Cohen's first three, got out of the way of the next two, and then prepared myself for one final, show-stopping slog. Everything depended on getting the right ball. If it was too full, he'd bowl me. If it was too short, he'd hit me. I needed something that was 'just so'. As Cohen thundered towards me, I shut my eyes, drew back my bat and prayed to God that it would be just short of a length. It was! I heard the ball crash into the pitch, felt it connect crisply with my bat, and then opened my eyes in time to see it sail over the St Marks church fence. It was the ultimate triumph of arse over skill.

'I told you it'd work!' Martin yelled, as I made my triumphant return to the embankment. 'You waited, you watched, and you kept your eye on the ball! Well done, Daff! Well done!'

I raised my bat appreciatively and thanked him for his advice. Why let the truth get in the way of a great innings?

It wasn't until I'd settled back down on the grass and removed my pads, that I realised the enormity of what had just happened. I was a chance. I was actually a chance. I'd faced six balls, none of them had humiliated me, and there was now a remote possibility of scraping into the squad. Of course, I still had to bowl, but maybe I'd get lucky there, too. Maybe I'd manage a couple of flukey inswingers or unplayable grubbers and then it'd all be over. Maybe, just maybe, I was actually, really, truly, destined to be a member of the First Eleven. And then Jenny would just *have* to like me.

Tips from an Old Druid

'Would you like some dessert?'

'No thanks.'

'How about some apple crumble?'

'Ahhh, no.'

'Ice-cream?'

'Nup.'

'What about some apple crumble *with* ice-cream?'

'No, really, I'm . . .'

'I just baked it?'

'I don't . . .'

'Just a little piece then?'

'For God's sake, *NO!!!* I don't want any ice-cream, I don't want any apple crumble, and I don't want any combinations of those things! I – DON'T – WANT – *ANYTHING!*'

(long pause)

'What about Ice Magic?'

I slammed the door shut in her face.

My mother, like all mothers, had no understanding of the words 'I am full'. She didn't have a great grasp of concepts like 'not for me, thanks' and 'I don't feel like any' either. For a long time, I'd assumed that this trait was peculiar to her. But lately I'd come to realise that all mums were like this – possessed of a strange desire to cram as much food down your throat as possible and *convinced* that changing the size, quantity or presentation of that food would alter your receptiveness to it.

On this occasion, I wasn't so much full as I was pissed off. I had, of course, missed out on the First Eleven and had chosen to express my disappointment by holing myself up in my bedroom and refusing to eat dessert. Once I was convinced Mum had gone away (and wasn't just lurking outside the door waiting to burst in and tell me there were some left-over pommes noisettes in the oven) I reached under my bed and pulled out my diary.

I wasn't a big keeper of diaries. Sure, I asked for one every year, and each year I'd *start off* okay. It was just that, after a while, I'd get bored of the whole thing. The first week of the year would be recorded in excruciating detail: what I was up to, what I got for Christmas, how I felt about what I got for Christmas, and so on. From there, things would go rapidly downhill. The second week would see a slimming down of entries, the third would barely rate a mention, and by the time February rocked round and the gloss of my new diary had worn thin, I'd have turfed it completely and thrown it behind a cupboard. To me, diaries were like goldfish: good for a week, okay for a month, and then ignored for the rest of the year.

Having said all that, diaries did have one important function in my life. I used them to record whinges. Each time something bad happened to me or I was worried about something, I'd dig around for an old diary and write it in there. The thinking behind it was that by recording my woes, I'd somehow ensure that there'd be a better time – a time in which I'd look back at what I'd written and scoff at my pathetic, trivial, eleven-year-old problems; a time when I'd throw my head back and have a good hard chuckle at the things I'd left behind:

> 'Ha! Can you believe I was concerned about *that*? Worried about some silly girl. Pissed off because I didn't make the First Eleven. It all seems so *insignificant* now that I'm worth a billion dollars and President of the World!'

Of course, this theory was a little reliant on the prospect of spectacular future success. But when I was eleven, I considered that a given.

On this particular evening, I had plenty to whinge about. After a few moments of careful deliberation, I put pen to paper and scribbled down the following entry:

'Failed to make the school cricket team. Batted well, but bowling was a disaster. Andrew McEvoy sent in his best batsman, Mark Trimble, and he smashed me all over the park. The bastards. I hope they both get rabies and die!'

Satisfied with my handiwork, I tossed the diary back under the bed and left Old Father Time to get on with the job of putting things right. Then I switched off the light and went to rejoin my family.

✱✱✱✱✱

'Pop!'
　No response.
　'Dad!'
　Still nothing.
　'ARTHUR!'
　'Ey?'
　'Turn it down!'
　'What?'
　'TURN IT *DOWN!*'
　My grandfather screwed up his face and fiddled with his hearing aid until it made a dreadful squealing sound.
　'Come again?'
　My mother, grandmother and younger sister Carolyn were almost out of patience. They'd been trying to speak to Pop for five minutes now, but had been unable to find a route into his

good ear. After a moment or two spent gathering composure, Mum made a final attempt at communication.

'Dad, TURN – THE – TELEVISION – DOWN!'

'Ey? Oh. Hang on a minute, Maur. They're announcing the numbers.'

That said, he turned away from her and refocussed his attention on the telly, which, as was customary when Pop was over, was jacked up to maximum volume.

My grandfather, or 'Pop' as my sister and I called him, had been taking out the same Tattslotto numbers each and every week since the game's inception. This probably doesn't sound that remarkable, but it was when you took into account Pop's general mistrust of all such things. Pop had certain 'doubts', shall we say, about the legitimacy of Tattslotto. In fact, he was convinced that the whole thing was a sham to raise funds for the Australian Liberal Party. The only possible reason we could think of for him entering all those times was to prove to us that he was right.

When it became clear that his numbers had failed to come up again, he turned the TV down and wheeled around in disgust.

'It's rigged you know!' he announced for the five millionth time. 'Bloody Liberals! You can't tell me that I can put in the same numbers all these years and still not win, without something being up. It's a disgrace, that's what it is!'

The rest of the family smirked and exchanged knowing glances.

'I don't think it's rigged,' my sister piped up. 'Why would people rig it?'

'Ey?'

'WHY WOULD PEOPLE RIG IT?'

'Ahhh, Carolyn, you've got a lot to learn about this world, m'girl. A lot to learn!'

'But how would they do it, Pop?' I interjected. 'All those little balls – it'd be impossible.'

'There are *ways*!' he nodded gravely, whirling his hand around to indicate some sort of sinister, all-powerful technology.

At this point, Mum and I started to giggle and Pop smiled at us to let us know he was half joking. (Not fully joking, mind you - *half* joking).

After the draw was over and Pop had deposited his ticket in the bin, my family settled into a silent equilibrium. Mum fussed about in the kitchen, Carolyn played Boggle, Nan stared into space, Pop sat down with one of his large-print books, and I fiddled with a Rubik's cube and dreamed about Jenny. The only person missing from this wild Saturday night scene was Dad, who happened to be out playing tennis. His absence aside, the scene was a fairly typical one for the Daffey family – a small, close-knit group that probably warrants further explanation.

Only four of us were actually Daffeys in the true sense of the word: Mum, Dad, Carolyn and me. Nan and Pop were Mum's parents and so, technically speaking, were Baileys. I counted them as part of my immediate family because they lived just around the corner and were as close to us as our parents. Nan and Pop were the sort of people you couldn't help but love. They were kind, they were generous, they had a pantry full of chocolate and creamy soda, and they were absolutely hilarious – sometimes intentionally, but more frequently not.

Leading the way in the unintentional department was Pop. Pop was a short, stout, practical man who distrusted everything in life outside the Australian Labor Party and the Carlton Football Club. When I was eleven, Pop was seventy-five. He'd retired almost a decade before, having worked for forty years in a government department called 'Central Drawing Office'. Pop's role at Central Drawing Office was actually a bit of a mystery. Despite a lifetime of crapping on about it, no-one had any real idea what he did there. He was a carpenter by trade and also something of a designer, so it was probably connected with that. All that was known from his stories, however, was that it involved stencils, microfiche and a foreman named 'Clarry'.

Despite his age, Pop was an incredibly active man. He cleaned, he gardened, he read, he fixed, he built, he studied and he still got around in his prized Sigma four-door sedan (though with an increasing level of danger to the general public). The same, however, could not be said for his wife. This was largely due to my grandmother's state of health. By the time she was seventy, Nan was the Guinness Book world record holder for having the largest number of strokes without being killed. She had her first in her early sixties and from then on racked up a couple each year. The combined effect of all of these life-threatening incidents was surprisingly small. Basically, the only differences between Nan and your average seventy-six year old woman were:

(a) that she spent a lot of time sitting in a chair;
(b) that she constantly moved her mouth up and down as if she were chewing something; and
(c) that the part of her brain responsible for 'tact' had been completely destroyed.

Aside from these things, Nan was fine and her mind was still as sharp as a razor. In particular, she had a freakish ability when it came to remembering names, dates and the average weighted price throughout history of a tub of Meadow Lea.

Together, Nan and Pop represented the very soul of the Daffey family. They were its most entertaining members, they were its most considerate members, and they took an inordinate amount of interest in all of our lives. Fifteen minutes into the book-reading, Boggle-playing equilibrium into which we had lapsed, Pop decided to express some of this interest.

'So, Chrissy, what's the matter with you this evening?' he asked, pushing his book away from himself to denote the change of tone.

'He missed out on the school cricket team,' Mum volunteered from the kitchen.

'*Mum!*'

'What was that, Maur?'

'HE MISSED OUT ON THE CRICKET TEAM!'

'Oh, well, that's marvellous then!' he beamed. 'So why would you be upset about that?'

'No, no, Pop. I *missed out* on the team – *I didn't get in.*'

'Ahhh, I see. Well, don't worry about it – there's always next year, you know. There's *always* next year.'

I was about to point out that next year was no good to me, but Pop didn't let me get a word in.

'You know, *I* played cricket when I was a young man. I wasn't much of a player though, but there was this guy on our team who could hit a thruppenny bit from twenty paces! What was his name again? We called him 'Twinkle Toes' or 'Jack Rabbit' or some damn thing. I played with him when I was at Central Drawing Office. He was in charge of the fiche – that was, before it became really small and we started calling it 'micro' fiche. What was his name? Winnie! Do you remember that guy I played cricket with? From the Drawing Office? Lived in Thornbury or something?'

For all intents and purposes, Nan hadn't even been in the room during this conversation. She'd just been sitting there, chowing down on an invisible meal and staring out into nothingness. But as soon as this question was directed at her, she awoke.

'Maurie Ruddock. His name was Maurie Ruddock. He lived in Northcote, not Thornbury – moved out in '42. Wife's name was Rose.'

Nan was amazing like that. I remember seeing the film *Rain Man* many years later and then belting home to spill a box of toothpicks in front of her. But alas, she was no good with maths or numbers – just names and dates.

While all this was going on, Mum had been rummaging around in a drawer for something. Just as Nan started spitting out Maurie's stats, she held up an object in triumph and walked over to hand it to Pop.

'Chris, Carolyn, take a look at this!'

Carolyn abandoned Boggle and, along with me, pressed close to Pop to see what he was holding. It was a photo – an old black and white photo of a cricket team. The caption at the top said 'The Druids Cricket Association – Premiers 1931–1932' and sitting on the far left was a young, athletic-looking man with a bat in his hand and a head full of hair. It was, unmistakably, Pop.

'Well, I'll be damned!' Pop said.

'Who the hell are the *Druids*?' I chipped in.

'I'd forgotten they even took a photo! There I am, right there. And there's Sid Leyland, and my brother Laurie, and here we go – Maurie Ruddock! What a player he was – an absolute champeen! Bit of a ratbag, mind you. Never let anyone borrow his pads.'

As I looked down at the photo and Pop ran through his old team-mates, I felt my earlier depression flooding back. The more I looked at the Druids Cricket Association Premiers, the more I wanted to be part of a team. Not *that* team, of course.

They were mostly dead for a start, and even when they were alive they looked a bit pasty. The Druids had that pre-colour, Bing Crosby look about them that meant that no matter how old you actually were, you always looked fifty: small bodies, big heads, enormous ears. No, I didn't want to be a Druid. But it would have been nice to be part of the Templestowe Heights First Eleven.

Once the team commentary was over and Mum and Carolyn had left us alone again, Pop noticed my distress and attempted to cheer me up.

'Things will turn out okay, you know,' he reassured me. 'One lesson you'll learn as you get older, Christopher, is that everyone has their talent. I was good at drawing, see, and your grandmother was good at sewing. You'll find something you're good at too – you just have to keep looking. And if you find you don't have any skills at all, you can *always* become a politician.'

I smiled at him gratefully and looked back down at the photo. The old guy was right. I may not have been able to impress Jenny with my cricketing skills, but I was sure to find *something* that would appeal to her. All I had to do was keep searching.

6

The Golden Boy

THE THREE WORST subjects I ever had to study at school, in descending order of awfulness, were these:

(a) bush craft (which I had in grade four and which consisted almost entirely of gluing gum nuts on pieces of paper);
(b) orienteering (for the same reasons everyone hates it); and
(c) Australian history (because not enough seemed to happen).

Bearing this list in mind, it was with some dread that I sat awaiting one of Mr Weathershaw's history classes, entitled 'Early Australians – Heroes, Explorers and Sheep-breeders'. Two weeks had passed since the First Eleven try-outs and not much had happened during that time. The only things worth noting were that Martin had made the team (and was feeling pretty pleased with himself), and that Simon had received a label gun for his birthday.

You really had to feel sorry for Simon. First there was Oil Panic and now this. He'd made it known to all and sundry that he was expecting, and likely to receive, a Prince tennis racquet for his birthday. It turned out the only two people not aware of this fact were his parents. Instead of an expensive new racquet, April 4 saw Simon unwrapping a second-hand clarinet and a device that made labels. He didn't even bother trying to talk up the clarinet, but he did what he could with the gun. It was one of those orange plastic ones that you hold like a pistol and that has a white disc on top where the labels come out. In addition to sticking his name on every single thing he owned, Simon also tried to play up the 'firearm' angle of his present. After all, it wasn't just a label *machine*, it was a label *gun*. But despite his best efforts to make the gift look cooler than it was, he was crucified. At the end of the day, kids were impressed by the type of gun that shot bullets – not the type of gun that shot names.

These events aside, the first weeks of April had been a fairly quiet time. I hadn't had any real chance to advance The Plan, so I instead concentrated on avoiding Jenny in the playground (in the hope that the passage of time might improve her memory of me). For what it's worth, this was going well. Unfortunately, no-one ever won over a girl by refusing to make visual contact with her. If I wanted Jenny to go with me, I had to do more than make a fool of myself and then disappear. This was where Stage Three came in: student politics!

In retrospect, I'd been mad to think that the First Eleven was the answer. I'd always been crap at cricket, and one lucky slog down the ground did not a Test Match batsman make. Even if I had bowled well; even if Andrew McEvoy hadn't decided to send in his star batsman, I probably wouldn't have made it. And even if I had, would Jenny have actually cared? I doubt it. She would, however, be absolutely thrilled when I carved myself into the greatest student politician since Tim Pierce campaigned for a twenty-two hour working week. I had, at least in my own mind, a natural flair for student politics. I was a listener, I was a consulter, and I had the one thing that every successful politician throughout history has had: a burning desire to hold office for my own selfish reasons.

My grandfather had been kidding when he suggested politics, but I was deadly serious. If what Mrs Newport had said on Monday morning was any indication, they would be calling for nominations later this afternoon. All I had to do was get through history and lunchtime and then strike.

✱✱✱✱✱

If there was any man on earth who could make a bad subject worse, it was Mr Weathershaw. This, after all, was the same man who came up with 'Dress as your favourite botanist' day. For this reason, I was pleasantly surprised to find he'd gone to some trouble to make 'Early Australians' a fun experience. Why he did this is not clear. Maybe it was because he was sick of kids not answering his questions. Maybe it was because he was afraid that Mrs Newport was making him look like a bit of a dinosaur. Who knows. Whatever the reason, something had possessed our teacher to go out and buy (with his own money) four copies of a *Sale of the Century*-type board game. He did it not for the questions, but for the buzzers.

In many ways, it was an inspired idea. His students were, at the best of times, reluctant to stick up their hands and answer a question. Why? Because there was nothing in it for us. Get it right and you were a nerd. Get it wrong and you were a moron. Either way, everything pointed to keeping your hands clasped firmly together and looking somewhere else. Buzzers changed all that. By their very nature, buzzers are objects that demand to be used. It's almost impossible to sit there with a buzzer in front of you and not give in to the overwhelming desire to thump the hell out of it. Yep, bringing buzzers to school was a master-stroke, and no-one was more enthused about it than Simon.

'This is going to be *GROUSE*!' he exclaimed, slamming his hand down on a rather flimsy looking buzzer. 'Bzzzt! (pause) *Bzzzt, bzzzt, bzzzt!*'

'Okay, Sime, I think we get the idea,' Martin smiled, raising his eyebrows and giving Simon one of his 'enough' looks.

Mr Weathershaw had asked the class to arrange itself into teams. Naturally, the three of us had chosen each other.

'Daff, before I forget,' Martin went on, 'I've been thinking about that act we have to do. Now I know it's not until the end of next term, but we probably should start planning. You saw what happened to Julie Greene.'

'Bzzzt!'

'Simon!'

'Sorry.'

I certainly had seen what happened to Julie Greene. The disastrous and ultimately bloody conclusion to her act had taught me two important lessons about the show business game: (1) always think your act through carefully and practise it like hell beforehand; and (2) never attempt to juggle porcelain figurines if you've got a poor aim and a big nose.

'Yeah, I think you're right, Mart,' I replied, after giggling to myself at the memory of it. 'How about we start this lunchtime?'

'Cool then, it's settled. We'll head down to the Log Fort and . . .'

'Bzzzt!'

'*SIMON!*'

'I can't help it!' Simon protested, clutching the buzzer to his chest and staring at us with wild eyes. 'Every time I try to put it down or think about something else, it *makes me buzz it*! I . . . I . . . can't stop!' he stammered, smiling wryly and moving his right hand into position over the buzzer.

'Don't do it, Sime!' Martin cautioned.

Without breaking eye contact, Simon slowly raised his hand up to chin level and opened his mouth wide to build the tension.

'Simon, I'm warning you!'

'*BZZZT, BZZZT, BZZZT, BZZZT!*'

'Okay, that's it!' Martin yelled, throwing himself at his friend and grappling for the buzzer.

We were, of course, supposed to be using this time constructively. Mr Weathershaw had asked us to spend the first ten minutes of class appointing a team captain and working out who would be in charge of pressing the buzzer. In a sense, we had already made those decisions. Martin got to be team captain (because Martin was always team captain) and I got to use the buzzer (because Simon was a dickhead).

After the buzzer had been wrestled away from him, Simon sat there sullenly, chewing on his fingernail and fiddling with his pencil case. Each item in that pencil case, I should point out, had a long purple sticker attached to it reading 'PROPERTY OF SIMON' – the pens, the pencils, the ruler, the jumbo-sized eraser shaped like Gene Simmons – everything. It was the sight of all those immaculately labelled objects that brought Simon back to life.

'Hey, who wants to borrow my label gun?' he queried, whipping the gun out of his desk and waving it in our faces. 'Daff?'

'No thanks, Sime,' I answered politely.

'Go on, have a go. It's really good for pens and things and makes this unreal clicking noise . . .'

'No, *really*, it's okay. I'll pass.'

'Oh. Okay then. Sure,' he whimpered back, disappointed that his gun had been rejected yet again.

'Martin?'

'Don't even think about it, Sime.'

Simon took this last rebuke poorly. Holding the gun close to him like an unwanted child, he turned his face away from us and looked down sadly at his label-heavy possessions. He was annoying like that, Simon. One minute he made you want to kill him, and the next he made you feel sorry for him. We'd all been there, after all. I remember once asking for a cricket bat for Christmas and instead copping a poxy board game called 'Korg: 20 000 BC'. The unexpected, shitful gift was something we all had to go through at one time or another. Simon just seemed to suffer more than most. After watching him for a while, I caved in.

'Sime, now that I think about it, I *would* like to borrow the gun for a sec.'

'Ah *ha!* I knew you wanted it, Daff!' he exploded with a smug 'I told you so' enthusiasm that had me immediately regretting my decision. 'Now hang on, Daff – don't touch it yet! I've got to show you how it works. It's *really* complicated. Now, you turn this wheel thing on top to choose the letter you want – say 'P' for 'property' – and then you . . .'

'Actually, Sime, I changed my mind.'

'What do you mean?'

'I don't want the gun anymore.'

'Are you *crazy*? You just asked to borrow it – it's . . .'

'*I DON'T WANT THE GUN!*'

And on the argument went, until the quiz got underway

and the halls rang with the sound of buzzers right through until lunch.

*****

Lunchtime was undoubtedly the best part of the school day. Although it only went for an hour, it somehow seemed to last much longer. You could eat, talk, run, fight, play, have a hit of bat tennis, conduct an entire cricket match, and still have twenty minutes left over to clog the drinking taps with sticks and to scratch 'Martin loves Yasmin Kronovsky' into the school fence. How this was possible I have no idea.

The first ten minutes of lunch were usually devoted to eating. What my friends and I ate during that period depended: (a) on what our parents packed for us; and (b) on our ability to barter our way out of trouble. Combine a fast mouth with a chocolate biscuit and you had 'feast'. Combine a slow wit with a packet of sultanas and you had 'famine'. In my case, I fell somewhere in between. In accordance with the strict instructions I'd given my mother, my lunchbox had contained exactly the same meal each day, every day, for the past six years:

- one peanut butter sandwich (cut in half, crusts removed);
- one drink bottle with 50/50 lemon-lime cordial (extra sweet);
- two Tim Tams wrapped in gladwrap (the jewel in my

lunchbox crown and worth their weight in gold on the free market); and
- one obligatory apple (for use in ball games and for throwing at cars).

Once we'd eaten all our food, it was time to get on with the serious job of playing. In terms of things we could do, our options were pretty much limitless. At our disposal was the combined creativity of countless generations of primary school students and the hundreds of different games they'd managed to invent. It would be impossible to list them all, but four of our favourites were these.

Tiggy

This game was also called 'tag' at some schools, but at Templestowe Heights we called it 'tiggy'. Tiggy began by selecting a person to be 'it'. This was usually done by a process of elimination. Everyone would form a big circle with their feet and one by one, kids would be released from that circle using a series of rhymes. No-one knew where the words for those rhymes had originally come from, but judging by the lyrics of some of them ('eanie meanie minie mo', for example) they can probably be traced all the way back to the Klu Klux Klan. Of all the rhymes used at our school, the most popular also happened to be the least offensive. In terms of speed and simplicity, nothing came close to matching the effortless grace of 'It – bit – dog – shit – you – are – not – it'.

Once a person had been chosen, he or she had to run after everyone else in the hope of 'tigging' someone. Once a person was tigged (which simply involved touching them with your hand) that person became 'it' and you were free to go. And that, in a nutshell, was the game.

Gang tiggy

Gang tiggy was like tiggy, but with more than one person 'it' at the same time. When someone was tigged, they teamed up with the tigger and joined the hunt for the remaining players.

Technically speaking, a game of gang tiggy only ended when all players had been caught. This wasn't always practical. Since there were often upwards of thirty kids in any one game and they had the entire school over which to disperse themselves, people were occasionally left behind. This was especially true of the heftier kids who relied on stealth rather than speed to evade capture. These kids knew they couldn't outrun their opponents, so instead, they chose to conceal themselves by burrowing under prickly bushes or burying themselves in tanbark. If they weren't found in the first ten or so minutes (and they usually weren't) people would get sick of looking and the game would be restarted without them. They would emerge eventually, of course. Many games later and well past the point people cared, chunky, leaf-spattered children would start popping up everywhere: confused, bewildered and entirely forgotten – like those Japanese soldiers who crawl out of the jungle thirty years later asking if 'the war' is over.

Brandy

Brandy was basically tiggy plus pain. The only difference between the games was that instead of tigging someone with your hand, you tigged them by 'branding' them with a ball. You'd think this would have added an extra element of skill to the game – that is, the ability to hit someone with a tennis ball from a reasonable distance. This, however, was not the case. In all the games of brandy I ever played, no-one ever bothered mucking around with a moving target. If you wanted to brand someone, you simply chased them around the school until they collapsed, and then threw the ball at them as hard as you could. In brandy, it wasn't so much about the thrill of the chase, as it was about the joy of the capture.

Kick the 'A'

Kick the 'A' involved defending a bunch of sticks shaped into an 'A.' One team had the job of guarding the sticks, while the other had the job of kicking them. Despite its simplicity, this game proved extremely popular at Templestowe Heights and was known by a number of names depending on the object being guarded: Kick the 'A' (the original); Kick the 'T' (if the sticks formed a 'T'); Kick the Can; Kick the Apple; Kick the Rock; and for a brief period during grade five, Kick George Redenbach.

The rest

As good as these four games were, they represented only the tip of the lunchtime entertainment iceberg. In addition to regular sports like cricket and football, the playground was constantly abuzz with an ever-evolving array of exciting activities, including such classics as card trading (which could be done either by swapping the cards or flicking them against walls), four square, downball, releaso, British bulldog, scarecrow, poison ball, marbles, attack piggyback, and the aptly named 'You play, you pay!'

The only category of games that my friends and I avoided was 'girls' games'. In part, this was because we weren't girls and so it wasn't appropriate to play them. By the time kids at our school hit grade six, the two sexes were engaged in a kind of 'voluntary segregation' and so the games we were involved in tended to be all-boy affairs. The second, more important reason, is that we never quite understood girls' games. For a start, they seemed to have no real point. Boys' games were easy to understand. They were either competitive or they were violent: you beat kids or you *beat* kids. Girls' games, on the other hand, were completely bewildering.

Take 'elastics' for example. What on earth was that all about? From the outside looking in, there seemed to be no more to it than watching a girl stick her legs through various combinations of elastic cord. What's entertaining about that? There were no big spills, hilarious accidents or broken bones; no girls raising their fists in triumph while others burst into tears. Nothing. Just a group of well-behaved women honing their skills and complimenting each other on their respective agility:

'Well done, Tilly – you really nailed that last combo! Keep up the good work!'

That's not a *game*. That's a joke! Where are the winners? Where are the losers? Where's the all-pervading stench of spiteful competition? Nowhere, that's where.

Elastics wasn't the only one, either. Who the hell came up with hopscotch? Hop, hop, hop, jump. Hop, hop, turn around, hop, jump, hop, hop. And the point was . . . ?

Girls even managed to butcher the fine art of card trading. As any boy knew, the only point to collecting a set of cards, was that there was *a set of cards to collect*. Without a finite number of cards in the series, where was the fun in collecting them? Why would you bother? This point seemed to be entirely lost on girls. Girls didn't collect *sets*, they just *collected*. Pink-edged cards depicting horses, kittens and other animals would be meticulously selected, grouped and then placed into albums. Why? So that one day you could announce to the world that you'd just got your fifteen-billionth snapshot of a Shetland pony? Well, congratulations! If anyone ever wanted to study the fundamental differences between men and woman, they should look no further than primary school lunch games.

Unfortunately for Simon, Martin and me, Tuesday the 11th of April was not a day on which we could draw such comparisons. There'd be no tiggy for us this lunchtime. No Kick the 'A' or poison ball. No four square, downball or footy card trading. We had an act to plan for; an act that could spell the end for all of us if we didn't come up with something good. This was no time for fun and games.

*****

Our brainstorming session was held at the Log Fort in the New Adventure Playground. The Fort had been our official headquarters since midway through grade five, when we had a brief flirtation with the idea that we were a 'gang'. Although we hadn't called ourselves the 'T-Birds' for a long time now, we still retained the clubhouse and occasionally spoke in reverential tones about our freewheeling 'wild days'.

The Fort itself wasn't much to look it. It was made out of pine logs and set into a muddy hill, giving it more of an underground bunker feel than a true fort. There was only one entrance, a kind of open doorway leading out to an unused section of the playground, one window and a plush-pile 'dirt and pine needles' floor covering. It was underneath this floor covering that the T-Birds had stockpiled our most valuable possessions. Locked away in a tin box buried carefully in the corner were a pocketknife, a packet of cigarettes and a collection of extremely soft-core 'pornography' (swimsuit ads, lingerie catalogues, that sort of thing). The safekeeping of this box had now become one of the Fort's principal functions, along with its more traditional role as a meeting place. When we arrived there that day, the first thing we did was dig it up, in part to check that it was still there, but mostly to remind ourselves what women looked like semi-naked. After satisfying ourselves on both of these fronts, we put the box to one side and Martin called the meeting to order.

'Now, before I ask if anyone else has any suggestions,' he began in his most polished tone, 'I'd like to read something which I wrote down last night.' He then fumbled around in his pocket for a few seconds and produced a crumpled piece of paper. 'You see, at first, I tried to think of all the different things we could do for our act. But I found that a bit hard. So instead, I thought it might be easier if we started off by eliminating the stuff we definitely *don't* want to do. So, I thought about all the acts we'd seen so far, and then I wrote this list.'

Martin hesitated at this point to gauge our receptiveness to his plan. Our blank stares proved encouragement enough.

'Okay, here we go then,' he said, clearing his throat and holding the list close to his face. 'The list of things we shouldn't do, number one. I don't want to be a part of anything that involves . . . (pause to decipher messy handwriting) . . . dressing up like girls.'

Simon let out an involuntary snort and I sniggered with approval. It was clearly a reference to last week's act – David Bentley's rather bewildering production of *HMAS Pinafore*. Emboldened by our reaction, Martin continued.

'Number two: acts that involve singing songs, especially if they're normally sung by a woman.'

Ah, now I understood what he was doing. He'd just picked

out all the worst acts we'd seen so far and listed them. Unhelpful, but amusing.

'Number three: acts that require you to dance' (Max Cameron's abominable 'Max Goes to Boogey-Town').

'Number four: actually, forget the numbers. I'll just read them. I don't want to do anything that involves: singing, dancing, juggling (Julie Greene and her porcelain cats), playing a musical instrument, poetry, or personal stories about friends, family or pets' (Tim Webber's touching, but ultimately flawed, 'The day we found out Snuffles had myxo').

Having exhausted his list, Martin lowered the page from his face and addressed us calmly. 'So, now that we've ruled those things out, what are we left with?'

This wasn't an easy question to answer. Now that all of these options had been removed, it was hard to come up with an act that we could still do.

'Ummm, not much,' I answered, after taking some time to think about it.

'Yep, you're right, Daff. There's *nothing*.'

'I've got an idea,' said Simon.

'What?'

'Well, I was watching one of my *Dr Who* videos last night – you know, the ones I tape off the TV – and . . .'

'Moving right along. Daff, any suggestions?'

'Hey, I wasn't finished!'

'Daff?'

'But I didn't even get to my idea about the act!'

'Let me guess, Sime. Does it have something to do with one of us being Dr Who?'

'Yeah, of course...'

'Well, that's it then.'

'But what about the battles? What about the Tardis?'

'*Fuck* the Tardis. Simon, if we do some dumb act based on *Dr Who*, we may as well just print T-shirts saying 'WE ARE DORKS'! It'd be instant death!'

'That's not true, you know. *I* watch *Dr Who*!'

Our leader met this with a smile and a raise of his eyebrows.

'Piss off, Martin. You wouldn't know anything! Remember that play Scott Thompson and his mates did – the space battle one set on the moon? It was crap and everything, but it was *safe*. They came on, they started shooting, everyone died, end of story. Impossible to stuff up. Impossible to get embarrassed. A dead-set winner!'

For the first time in a long while (perhaps ever), Simon actually succeeded in silencing Martin. Our leader sat there, scratching the top of his head and contemplating the horrifying possibility that Simon might actually have had a point.

'So what would your idea be then?' he proceeded cautiously.

'Well, we do the same thing, but with *Dr Who*.'

'Hmmmmmm,' he answered at some length, 'I don't know, Sime. I just don't know. Daff, what do you reckon? Any thoughts?'

I had no thoughts (or at least no thoughts worth sharing). The problem I faced in analysing the situation was that

I viewed everything in terms of what *Jenny* would like to see. Would Jenny like us to sing? Would Jenny like us to dance? Was Jenny the type of girl who would be impressed by a sci-fi show in which everyone got shot to shit in the first twenty seconds? I didn't think so. From what I knew about girls (and frankly, I didn't know a lot), I at least got the impression they preferred 'funny and clever' over 'violent and meaningless'. How I was going to raise this point without betraying my motives, I didn't know.

'I'm not sure, guys,' I began carefully, 'I mean, I see what Simon's saying about it being safe and everything. It's just that, I don't know – wouldn't you prefer an act that was a little more ... *impressive*? An act that's safe, but that also has a chance of being good? An act with a clever twist or a funny joke? An act that ... umm ... *people* ... will actually like?'

Yep, who could possibly see through that slick piece of subterfuge? Martin obviously. My friend bit down on his lip and shook his head knowingly, while Simon glanced around to see if he'd missed something.

'Daff, I know what you mean,' Martin began with equal caution. 'But you've gotta remember that just because *you* want the act ... umm ... in particular ... to be good and stuff, doesn't mean that your friends should have to ... umm ... risk it, so you can get a good ... umm ... result. If you get my meaning.'

Martin was as bad at this game as I was. I was about to formulate a suitably encrypted reply when something heavy slammed into the side of the Fort. The three of us stopped talking and stuck our heads out the window to see what was wrong. What we saw out there freaked us. It was Julian Crowler!

Julian was Templestowe Heights' resident bully. An enormous, grim-looking child, he specialised in beatings and extortion and was also the chief suspect in a series of highly publicised thefts. When we caught sight of Julian on this particular day, he was busy throttling some grade five kid against the wall of our Fort. The kid was actually two or three feet off the ground, with Julian's left hand wedged underneath his chin and Julian's right rummaging through his pockets.

Naturally, the three of us were concerned. We expressed this concern by shaking our heads, sighing meaningfully and then returning to our meeting. At first glance, this may seem a little heartless. But you have to remember how you viewed such things when you were at school. Bullying, far from being seen as a preventable menace, was looked upon as a type of 'natural phenomenon'. Seeing a bully in action was just like seeing a wildlife documentary. You're sitting there watching a cute little penguin frolic in the snow, and suddenly you hear the words,

'The polar bear is hungry.'

Then you watch in horror as an enormous bear appears out of nowhere and lopes toward the penguin. And then you start to barrack for the penguin – 'Carn little fella, get outta there – go, go, *GO!*' But it's all to no avail. The bear catches your furry little friend, scoops it up with its hand and then bites it in half. And you're sickened and you're sad and you're sorry. And you curse the bear, mourn the penguin and lament the cruelty of life. But one thing you don't do is hop onto the next plane bound for the Arctic, packing a gun and a set of bear traps. It's just the way of things. Likewise with bullies. Some kids are small, weak and hopeless, and other kids hit them and take their stuff. Fact. Can't do anything about it. Can't change it. Why worry?

Once the pounding noises and cries of anguish died down (and Julian had stuck his head in the window and peered around threateningly) we recommenced our discussion. It didn't go well. Basically, each of us wanted entirely different things: Martin pushed for 'safety first' without the science fiction; I acknowledged the importance of safety, but demanded something extra; while Simon just sat in the corner chanting, 'One, two, gimme *Dr Who*!' Clearly, something had to give.

When compromise finally came, it was in a rather unlikely form. Simon, against all expectations, threw his lot in with me. The deal he managed to strike with Martin was this: if he could think of a clever twist or sure-fire gag to add into the *Dr Who* format, Martin would agree to it. The twist or gag had to be *foolproof*, however. Martin was quite specific about this. This way, the act would be 'safe' as well as impressive and the twist or joke would cancel out the dweebiness of the subject matter. The debate was settled and everyone was happy.

By the time we re-emerged from the Fort, there wasn't

much of lunchtime left. We were way too late to join in any of the games and so had to be content as spectators. After spending a few rather unsatisfying minutes watching a group of girls skipping and singing songs, we made a quick dash for the breezeway to get a drink.

Apart from the girls' and boys' toilets, the breezeway also housed most of the school's drinking taps. The taps were divided into two troughs. On the left-hand side were the boys' taps and on the right-hand side were the girls'. Why one set of taps was designated for males and the other for females was anyone's guess. It was just custom. No, actually, it was more than custom. It was *law*. To drink at the girls' taps was to somehow throw your manhood into question. Just as no-one liked being accused of 'running like a girl' or 'throwing a ball like a girl', it seemed we also lived in fear of being told we 'drank water like a girl' too. Ridiculous as this may have been, I never once thought to buck the system.

While Martin and Simon disappeared into the bathrooms, I selected myself a tap. You could never be too careful in selecting a faucet. Since every tap had twigs or other items jammed into the nozzle, water issued forth at alarmingly different pressures. You either had 'dribblers' (taps so clogged with debris that you had to wrap your mouth around them and then *suck* the water out) or you had 'shooters' (taps clogged just enough so that kids who leaned over them would have their heads blown off). The trick was to walk down the trough, pressing the handle of each tap in turn and thereby assessing the danger. I was halfway through doing this when I spotted him.

Andrew McEvoy, aka the Golden Boy – most popular kid at school, captain of the opposing team in the cricket try-outs, best friend and mentor to Mark 'show us your balls' Trimble – was one of the few exceptions to the rule I've just described. This was a guy who *did* drink out of the girls' drinking taps. Why? Because he could. He was *so* cool that he could deliberately fly in the face of convention and get away with it. This was something he did often. When I spotted him, he was leaning against the girls' trough with his oafish buddy Trimble. After pausing for a while to make sure people noticed him, he flicked back his hair, leaned down towards a tap and took a long, deep, symbolic drink. Andrew McEvoy, you see, was above the law.

Spotting the Golden Boy was bad enough, but things got markedly worse when the Golden Boy spotted me. As soon as his eyes met mine, a wry smile crossed his face and he muttered something to his friend. Trimble's reaction was much more pronounced. Just as Martin and Simon re-emerged from the toilets, he laughed out loud and bounded up to me like a puppy wanting to play with something.

'Remember me, Ducky!' he shouted, swinging an invisible cricket bat through the air to remind me of his triumph.

Oh, God, not this again, I thought to myself, as memories of his swashbuckling innings came flooding back.

'C'mon, Ducky, you *must* remember *me*!' he repeated smugly.

'Oh yeah, it's coming to me now,' I replied. 'Aren't you that guy I saw on *That's Incredible*? The one that got trapped in a cave for a month and had to eat his own bogs?'

This was pretty snappy stuff as far as primary school wit was concerned. Realising that he'd just been mocked, Trimble furrowed his brow and prepared to respond in kind. He was interrupted by the arrival of Martin, Simon and McEvoy himself.

'Hello, Martin,' McEvoy oozed, the words spilling out of his mouth with a casual, all-consuming arrogance that had to be seen to be believed.

'Andrew,' Martin nodded back (thereby fulfilling the obligations of cordiality that existed between First Eleven cricket team members).

'And how are *you* today, Chris?' the Golden Boy continued.

'Um – fine I guess. Yourself?'

'Good. Great. Glad you asked. Actually, it's funny that I bumped into you today, Chris, because we were just having a bit of a chat about you. Weren't we, Mark?'

'Yeah, that's right, we were talking about you, Ducky!' Trimble confirmed with enthusiasm (though it was clear he had no idea where McEvoy was going with this).

'See, we both think it's a real shame and all, how you missed out on selection. We believe, and I think we speak for most of the guys on the team, that there's a place in the First Eleven for someone with your . . . umm . . . *talents*.'

What are you supposed to do in a situation like this? You

know someone's about to take the piss out of you, but they haven't quite reached for the pail yet. Steel yourself, feign indifference, lay on the sarcasm – that's all you can do.

'Really? Thanks. It's nice to know someone cares.'

'We do care, Chris,' he smiled back, 'we care enough to try and make a place for you. See, some of the other schools have an extra member in their squads. What's the one at Templestowe Valley called again? Trixie, that's it! Trixie. Cute little thing. Runs onto the ground during drinks and does tricks and stuff. They even knitted a sparkly little jumper for it. What sort is it again, Mark?'

'I think she's a Silky Terrier, Andrew,' Trimble grinned, delighted to play a part in the routine.

'Yeah, that's right – a Silky Terrier. Well, what do you think, Chris? The team really does need a mascot, and I reckon you'd look a million dollars in a sparkly top!'

I stared at him darkly.

'Anyway, no need to answer now. Why don't you just think on it for a while? In the meantime,' (leaning close to me and patting the side of my face) 'keep up the good work, champ. Keep up the good work.'

Then he turned on his heel, nodded to Martin and strode away.

It's hard to adequately explain just how insulting this last gesture was. On paper, and without any context, it might not seem that bad. He tapped my face, he told me to keep up the good work, and he called me a 'champ'. Big deal. But you have to read between the lines on this one. What he was really saying, was this:

> 'I'm calling you a champ because you're a loser, and I'm patting you on the face *because I can*. You see, no matter what you say after this – no matter what you think or what you do – nothing will ever change this simple fact: I am a schoolyard legend and you are a middle-class nobody. I am everything and you are nothing.'

And that is why it stung. As I watched him swagger down the breezeway clicking his fingers and playing with his blond hair, I felt a sudden, irresistible urge for vengeance. Trimble, I could take. He was loud, he was insulting, he had an abysmal sense of humour and he wasn't afraid to share it around, but he was bearable – the type of kid who might not have been too bad if he'd chosen a different best friend. Andrew McEvoy, on the other hand, was pure, unadulterated evil.

✱✱✱✱✱

'Can you believe that guy?' Simon ranted later that afternoon. 'During that whole conversation he had with you, Daff, he didn't even look at me once. Not once! Do you know what I think? I think he's afraid of me!'

Martin and I smiled at each other and searched Simon's face for a hint of irony. As always, there was none.

Mr Weathershaw's English class seemed particularly dull that afternoon. For my part, I was completely distracted by thoughts of violent retribution against the Golden Boy. The entire hour between 1.15 and 2.15 consisted of one long, waking fantasy in which McEvoy was killed in a variety of different ways, each one funnier than the last.

My favourite one bore considerable resemblance to the plot of a film which came out many years later: *Speed*. In *Speed*, a bad guy stuck a bomb under a bus and Sandra Bullock had to drive it around non-stop or else it would explode. If the speed dropped below sixty, the bus blew. My fantasy was a lot like that, except that instead of putting the bomb under a bus, I strapped it onto McEvoy's back and told him to get running. The great part about it was that no matter how hard he tried, *no-one can run forever . . .*

Run, run, run, run . . . pant . . . run, run, run . . . stumble . . . run, run . . . puff, wheeze . . . run . . . stagger, puff, stumble . . .

'I've just gotta to stop, Daff – I'm knackered!'

BOOM!

If only I'd thought to turn it into a movie.

So wrapped up was I in the demise of Andrew McEvoy that I completely forgot about the entire purpose of the day. It wasn't until Mr Weathershaw cleared his throat and muttered something about voting that it hit me. The nominations! The Student Representative Council nominations that I'd been waiting weeks for him to announce! My chance to throw myself into the world of student politics, my opportunity to dazzle Jenny with my skills as an orator, with my knack for diplomacy, and with my God-given talent to read the will of the people. The SRC was a road that led straight to Jenny's heart and I planned to hoon down it full speed ahead.

When the nomination sheet was finally passed into my hands (after circulating around the front of the classroom for what seemed like an eternity) I saw that the other classes had already listed their nominees. Scrawled across the top of the page in a variety of different pen colours, were the following names: Stuart Lund (the school brains trust), Sandra Peterson, Julie Greene, Jenny Hartnett, Scott Brenner, Lucas Tordby (some bastard playing a prank), and *Andrew McEvoy*.

I put pen to paper and signed my name. Stage Three was away, and this time, it was personal.

The SRC

TRUTH BE TOLD, organisations didn't get much dumber than the Templestowe Heights' Student Representative Council. Technically speaking, the Council was supposed to give children a voice in the day-to-day running of the school. Delegates were elected from each of grades four, five and six, and every week or so, these delegates would meet with teachers to discuss ways of improving student life. Factually speaking, it was a bit of a wank.

The main problem was one of policies. Teachers at Templestowe Heights often got carried away with the notion that their students were some sort of 'untapped reservoir of wisdom', that if they just opened their minds and listened to the children, the problems of the world would pack up shop and fade away. Nothing could have been further from the truth. Myself and my friends had *zero* to offer by way of political nous and you only had to look at the drivel the SRC came up with to realise how true this was. Each week, they'd put their heads together and produce a series of standing policies, most of which were clichéd, simplistic or just plain stupid.

- The school day should be shorter.
- The May holidays should start in March.
- Everyone should have access to a pony.

That sort of thing. Then, after submitting their recommendations, the Councillors would be applauded, complimented on their intellect and duly ignored. Naturally, I was keen to get in.

The benefits of getting a seat on the SRC were two-fold: (1) I'd get a nifty little badge that said 'SRC'; and (2) I'd get to work alongside Jenny. Jenny was a permanent fixture on the SRC. She was a Councillor in grade four, she was a Councillor in grade five, and barring some strange, unforeseen disaster, she'd be a Councillor again in grade six. Somehow I'd found it in my heart to forgive her for these transgressions. I figured she must have been different from your average SRC member because ... because ... well, for no reason actually: just because she was Jenny. I liked her, she liked me (or at least she *would* like me if she got to know me) and so anything she did in her spare time was AOK. In fact, not only did I forgive her for being a student politician, I was determined to join her. Achieving this, however, was not going to be easy.

Although nominations for the SRC were requested at the

start of first term (they'd been a little late this year), the actual elections weren't held until halfway through term two. This was Mrs Newport's idea. If elections were held early in the year, her reasoning went, people wouldn't get a chance to familiarise themselves with the candidates. By holding them in July, not only would students be able to recognise the names they were voting for, they'd also get a good look at the much-celebrated democratic process: the speeches, the policies, the unrealistic promises, and, most importantly of all, the smear campaigns ('Shelley Stevens has lice', 'Billy Watson is a Tasmanian', and so on).

Surviving this process was difficult enough. Getting elected was damn near impossible. There were only three grade six spots up for grabs, with each sex being guaranteed at least one place. The frontrunners for those positions were:

- McEvoy, Scott Brenner and Stuart Lund, for the guys; and
- Jenny, Julie Greene and Sandra Peterson, for the girls.

Between them, the male candidates had these things going for them: popularity, charm and intelligence (in that order). The girls possessed similar qualities, but had one significant advantage – the fact that they were girls. You see, it was rare for a female voter to throw her weight behind a male candidate, but it was quite common for guys to vote for them. This was because girls thought boys were pathetic and immature, and, deep down, we must have agreed with them.

When you took all of this into account, my chances didn't look overly good. I lacked the notoriety of McEvoy, the appeal of Brenner, the gray matter of Lund and I went to the bathroom standing up. In the race for SRC glory, I wasn't just a dark horse, I was a black mule.

✱ ✱ ✱ ✱ ✱

In the week following the nominations, my campaign swung into action. Martin graciously accepted the position of campaign manager, while Simon ungraciously complained that it should have been him.

The first thing we did was divide the school up into different demographic groups. We didn't use that term, of course; we called them 'blocks'. The reason we did this was to get an idea of all the different types of butt we'd have to kiss when it came to making policies. Compulsory Friday afternoon boot-ball games, for example, might impress the sporting crowd, but would leave Lucas Tordby and his compatriots out in the cold. What we needed was a policy mix that had something for everyone. Pie nights and aths days for the elite; chess clubs and table tennis bats for the not so elite. The first step in all of this was working out what the blocks were. After a couple of lunchtimes spent thinking about it, we met at the Log Fort to finalise our list.

'I've got one!' Simon announced, before Martin had the chance to take out his pen. 'How about those kids who never say anything? The ones you don't even know the names of?'

'What kids?'

'You know, Daff. The ones who never *ever* speak. Like that really short kid. What's his name again? I think he's Algerian or something!'

'You mean Ruftus? I'm not sure if that's his name, but that's what they call him. The one who wore a tie on his first day at school?'

'Yeah, that's him!' Simon roared, rocking back with laughter and slapping his leg with his hand.

'Once on camp,' he managed between giggles, 'Ruftus got bitten by a snake and he didn't even yell out or anything! He just held out his arm and made a face!'

This last revelation sent us all into hysterics. Every school had its share of quiet kids, but it was hard to imagine anyone as uncommunicative as Ruftus.

'There's a few of them, actually,' Simon continued after the commotion had died down. 'There's that Stretton kid. There's that guy with the funny eyes. And there's that Florence girl who sits up the front of class and makes paper cranes.'

'That still only makes four,' I pointed out. 'That's not much of a block. Besides, what sort of policies would we make for them?'

'I don't know. Maybe we could just give them stuff? Or introduce them to each other? Set them up with some friends!'

'Or maybe we could just *ask* them what they wanted?' Martin added thoughtfully.

Talk to them? Now there was a novel idea.

'Anyway,' Martin added, 'I think we should concentrate on the main groups for the moment. We can worry about the smaller ones later.'

This was sensible thinking. Martin was good at that. That's why I'd made him my campaign manager. If you ever wanted someone to put a serious, orderly slant on a big stack of mindless rubbish, Martin was your man. After opening up his Spirax notepad and uncapping his pen, he went to work.

'I think the biggest group, and the one we're most likely to get votes from, is the *normal* kids – the people who don't really fit into any group. Like you, Daff.'

I took this as a big compliment. No-one could pigeonhole this puppy, I thought to myself happily as Martin ploughed on.

'Then there's the kids who are really into sport and stuff. Like the First Eleven members and the guys who make the footy team. And there's the popular crowd – though that's usually pretty similar to the sports crowd.' Martin paused at this point and looked kind of embarrassed. By direct implication, he'd had just told us how hip and well liked he was. He hadn't meant it that way, of course. Martin was no boaster.

'Then you've got your tough kids and your bullies,' he continued, 'the weirdoes and the strange kids, and the nerds and the psycho nerds.'

(A brief note for those unfamiliar with the term 'psycho nerds' – psycho nerds were nerds who'd learnt the value of appearing ferocious. If anyone touched them or tried to hurt them, they'd just go nuts. The reason they did this was simple. Winning a fight at primary school had nothing to do with how strong you were, but everything to do with *how far you might go*. You might be convinced you could out-box a kid, but if you also knew that as soon as your back was turned, he'd jump up and stab you in the neck with a pencil, you'd think twice before picking on him. Psycho nerds turned this principle into a way of life. If challenged, they'd spit, scream, bark, bellow, froth at the mouth, piff rocks, hurl chairs, break bottles, and do everything they possibly could to give the impression they were some sort of 'loose cannon'. And they did all this just so they could have the following words said about them:

'Don't go near Robbo. Robbo's *mad*.')

'And finally,' Martin concluded, 'you've got *girls*, who probably should be split up into a whole bunch of their own categories, but since none of them are going to vote for us, I say we don't bother.'

Simon and I concurred. There was no point legislating for women if they were just going to shaft you at the polls anyway. Read-a-thons and 'starve yourself for the third world' days could be left to Jenny and the other female candidates. Us boys had smaller fish to fry.

Having successfully nutted out the different blocks, it was time to sit around congratulating ourselves on successfully nutting out the different blocks. We did this for the rest of lunch. We never got around to discussing specific policies, but we did have time to divide up some tasks and consider our general strategy. Martin decided that each of us should take responsibility for one or more of the blocks. He called them our 'folios' (confusing a term he'd heard on *Yes, Minister* with a term he'd heard in one of Mrs Kaufman's art classes).

'Daff, your folio will include the normal kids, and, if you think it's necessary, the girls. My folio will cover the cool, sporty and tough kid crowds. And Simon . . .'

'Hang on, *no way!*' Simon protested.

'. . . I'm proud to appoint you . . . Minister for Losers.'

Simon was understandably furious about the content of his folio. His anger only increased when Martin pointed out: (1) that he was the best man for the job; (2) that he could relate to his subjects; and (3) that he 'spoke their language', quote unquote.

He was being *wasted*, Simon argued – buried in a dead-end folio with little or no chance to display his considerable talents. If he were in charge, he insisted, I'd win the election by a landslide and McEvoy and his cohorts would be taught a valuable political lesson. For a moment or two, he almost sounded convincing, puffed up, as he was, by the power of self-conviction. But then we remembered who we were talking to and told him to shut the hell up. All work was honourable, Martin explained, and if Simon wasn't prepared to toe the party line, he was out on his ear. Simon accepted this ruling like a cab driver accepts a credit card. His mouth said 'okay then', his face said 'okay then', but an almost undetectable twitch of his eyes said, 'What I'd really like to do is fling it out the window and then smack you in the mouth.'

Minister for Losers he was, however. And Minister for Losers he would stay.

The final piece of planning took place after the bell had signalled the end of lunchtime. As we were walking back across the basketball courts, Martin raised an interesting point. What was it exactly that we were counting on to attract votes? What qualities did I possess as a person that would make ticking the box next to 'Chris Daffey' an electoral must? It was a good question and a hard one to answer. After a brief discussion, we concluded that it was more a matter of the bad traits I didn't have, than the good ones I did. Martin summed it up pretty well:

'The thing you've got going for you, Daff, is that not too many people hate you. You're not so good in class that people think you're a nerd, and you're not so good at sport that people think you're up yourself. You're what my mum calls "well rounded".'

Flattering though this was supposed to be, there weren't too many campaign slogans leaping out of that lot. 'Vote Daffey because he's just crap enough not to cause offence.' Fantastic.

No, I needed something extra. Some hidden gift that would endear me to the student body. Some undiscovered talent that would tip the electoral scales in my favour. But what could it be? What possible trait could I unearth that would lift my social standing?

*****

Charity work! Putting in the hard yards for those who need it most. Doing good for others at a minimal cost to yourself. Yep, that was the ticket alright. There's nothing like a display of carefully orchestrated benevolence to get the masses on side, and I planned to milk it to the max. It wouldn't be a completely cynical exercise either. Although I'd never done any charity work before, I had sometimes *thought about it*, and I certainly wouldn't have objected to doing a bit if someone had organised it for me and given me a good reason. Besides, I knew in my heart that I had a charitable nature. I once gave fifty cents to a pretty ordinary busker *and*, if I ever donated to a telethon, I wouldn't be one of those tight-arses who say they'll double the money if it's read out on TV. No, I figured I was a good person (or at least as good as most of the people I knew), so if I scored some good press simply by revealing my true generous self, then so be it.

The idea for the work actually came from Simon. We were sitting in one of Weathershaw's maths classes when he happened to mention the Neighbourhood Smiles Programme.

'Yeah, it's not too bad actually. We go out to some old person's place and clean it up and fix the garden and stuff. There's usually about ten of us. It's organised by that Jenny

Hartnett girl and they read out our names at assembly and everything!'

Bingo! Simon comes through for me again. The Neighbourhood Smiles Programme sounded too good to be true, and within a week I was on the job.

The place we had to clean up was owned by one Harold B. Myer. Harold was the same age as my grandfather and had about as much hair. It was at this point, however, that the similarities ended. Where Pop embodied all the good stereotypes about old people (wisdom, kindness, tendency to hand out gifts), Harold had dibs on all the bad ones (dementia, belligerence, tendency to dwell amongst cat faeces). Harold's house was the type that serial killers own in movies: few lights, no clear floor space, and the occasional mysterious swarm of flies. Not only was the house filthy and decrepit, Harold's aesthetics weren't too good either. If it weren't for the fact that he occasionally screamed out:

'Tell 'em to get the hell off my hydrangeas!'
I would have presumed that he was dead.

My job was to clear out the front yard. For this purpose, I'd been given a plastic bag and a weeding fork. These implements may have been useful had I been plucking weeds from amongst Harold's mythical hydrangeas, but proved manifestly inadequate against thirty years of carefully cultivated thorns. As I began peeling the skin off my arms to save the bushes the trouble, I caught a glimpse of Jenny. She was busy directing operations inside the house. I could just make her out through the front window chatting with Mr Linny, the school music teacher, who'd come out to supervise us. As always, she looked stunning. She had her hair up in pigtails and reminded me a bit of Mary Ann from *Gilligan's Island* (except not quite as 'would you like a fudge brownie, I just baked 'em fresh' as Mary Ann). Every now and then she'd look up and peer through the window, so I made sure I kept myself busy. After all, there was plenty to do, and this was no time to look like a loafer.

After hacking away at a rosebush for a while, I was joined by a pale irritating kid called Terrance Wheldon. Terrance had been sent to help. Unlike me, he was armed with a variety of objects that might actually be of use. In his right hand he had a rake, in his left a shovel, and being kicked along at his feet was an enormous plastic bin. My work brief, Terrance explained, had been changed by HQ. I was no longer to concentrate on clearing and pruning (a rather flattering term for the random destruction I'd been inflicting with the fork) but on gathering up and removing rubbish. He then pointed to the sea of refuse that lay at the base of the front fence. Harold's house, you see, was only one hundred metres away from the local high school. Since his garden was already such a mess, students had taken the liberty of treating it like a tip. Running all the way along the bottom of the fence was a semi-solid mass of packets, papers and old forgotten lunches. It was a sobering sight.

By the time we'd binned half of it, Terrance's company was wearing a bit thin. I hardly knew the kid really. In fact, up until that day, I don't think I'd ever said more than a couple of words to Terrance 'Spenda' Wheldon. Sure, I knew who he was and saw him around all the time, I'd just never had anything to do with him. I probably didn't even know his name was Terrance. First names were an easy thing to forget at primary school. Unless a name was so awful it was an insult unto itself ('Herman', for example), kids often searched for an offensive alternative. For this reason, no-one actually called Terrance 'Terrance' – it was too much of a nothing name. It was always Spenda. The exception was, of course, teachers, who didn't really go in for nicknames. This was probably a good thing. Constant ridicule from your peers was taken as a given at school – ridicule from those teaching you would have been something else entirely. It certainly would have made for a pretty demoralising role call.

'Please raise your hand to indicate that you're present. Is Porko here? Yep, good. Stinker? Yep. One-brow, BO, and Bushpig? Great. Bucky? Where's Bucky? Ah, there you are, you ugly little prick.'

Nicknames both defined and shaped your personality and no-one epitomised this principle more than Spenda.

'Hey, Spenda,' I began, after coming across a particularly hideous piece of rubbish, 'I'll give you twenty cents if you put that sandwich in the bin instead of me.'

Spenda looked at me warily and then crouched down to examine the sandwich I was referring to. He was right to be suspicious. From the look of it, the sandwich was, or had been, a cheese and tomato at some point in its life. It was hard to say what had happened since then, but it was clear that the sandwich's best days were behind it. After a couple of moments' contemplation, Spenda rose to his feet and shook his head decisively.

'No way, Duff. No way ut all,' he announced flatly. 'Ya kun put that thung in the bun yasulf.'

Spenda, as you may have already guessed, was born in New Zealand. If that wasn't bad enough, he was then shipped across to England where he'd stayed until fairly recently. Apparently, his parents were some sort of special accountants, or consultants, or consultants to accountants, or some other thing that meant they had to move around a lot. Growing up in a bunch of different countries had done the same thing to Spenda's accent as occurs to famous Australians who live overseas. It starts off Australian with a quaint touch of foreign, progresses to foreign with a quaint touch of Australian, and eventually becomes a hideous mixture of both, so that they sound like an alien to everyone.

Weird though his voice was, it was adored by fellow students. My class even devised a game specifically aimed at hearing him speak, called 'Make Spenda say something'. We'd gather round him before the start of school and implore him to repeat clichéd, English-sounding lines from TV shows. When he refused, everyone would start chanting 'Spen-da, Spen-da, Spen-da, Spen-da' until he finally relented and screamed out *'COR BLIMEY, GUVNA!'* as loud as he could. Then everyone would cheer and go berserk and start pleading with him to do it again. At the time, it seemed like the funniest thing in the world.

'Uctually, Duff,' he continued, after staring at the sandwich for a while, 'why doesn't Muster Lunny take care of ut? We've been out here pucking up lutter for ages and he husn't lufted a funger!'

'Yeah, sure, maybe,' I replied. 'But I can't see him picking it up himself. Let's just pretend we never saw it.'

'Ahhh, okay, Duff. So long us ut's nut *me* who hus to put ut un the bun!'

Spenda paused at this point and sort of narrowed his eyes slightly, as if he was about to try something on.

'Ya know, Duff, buck un Unglund, thar was no such thung as buns.'

Oh God, here we go.

'Thar was no such thung as lutter either.'

'What are you talking about, Spenda?' I enquired wearily, knowing full well that Spenda was off on one of his legendary 'runs'.

'Wull, ya see, at my school un Unglund, we had people who would puck up the rubbush for us. As soon as you'd drop a wrupper or a piece of pupper, they'd run out from all over the place und grub thum before they hut the grund.'

'Really? You don't say. And where did *they* put the papers, Spenda?'

'They dudn't *put* thum unywhere!' Spenda announced, as if I was the dumbest guy in the state. 'They *utt* thum! We called thum the "luttle rubbush munchers". I even made frunds with one of thum. His name was Frunk.'

Spenda didn't get his nickname because he was generous with money. He didn't get his nickname because he was tight with money either. Spenda got his nickname because he was full of shit. It actually started out as 'S-bend', but was changed over time to the more easily pronounced 'Spenda'.

'Frunk und I whar really close we whar,' he plowed on. 'Ufter a while, we started up thus mussive gung that included virtually uveryone. We used to hung out toguther on the roof of the school and play games and ride bikes and thungs. That wus when they made me school cuptain.'

'Shut up, Spenda.'

Like many people who move from one place to another, Spenda had succumbed to the temptation to give his past a bit of a 'touch up'. Where the Spenda we'd come to know in Australia was annoying, unpopular and largely ignored by his fellow students, the Spenda that had existed in England was a different man entirely. If Spenda's account was to be believed, he had once enjoyed the status of a kind of 'god-like' figure – adored by his peers, worshipped by women, and appointed the captain of pretty much everything. You couldn't really blame the guy for stretching the truth a little. If I had moved to another country, I'm sure I would've done it as well. It probably wouldn't start off as an intentional thing. I'd just be in the middle of answering a simple question and then realise that I could lie and get away with it.

The thing was, though, Spenda didn't just confine his lies to stuff about himself. His extravagant and implausible boasts also extended to the country he used to live in. According to Spenda, everything in England was bigger, brighter and just plain better than it was in Australia. The girls were prettier, the Mars bars were tastier, and even the buses were twice as high as ours. I know now, of course, that the last of these things was actually true, but it all seemed like a heap of shit at the time.

Just as Spenda looked set to elaborate on his dreadful rubbish muncher story, he was interrupted by a visit from HQ. To my surprise and considerable horror, I was suddenly confronted with the smiling visage of Jenny.

'How's it going, guys?' she beamed, shoving her hands into her pockets and rocking back like one of the lads.

'Fun,' Spenda replied (meaning 'fine').

'Fun,' I replied too (meaning 'I'm too awkward to do anything but mindlessly parrot my friend here').

'That's, um, fantastic guys. I'm glad you're getting into it!' she smiled, looking from our faces to our filthy, bleeding hands and wondering just how 'into it' we could really be. 'I just came out to tell you that it's time to go back to school. Mr Linny says we have to finish what we're doing and pack up our things. Terry, you can collect up the tools. Chris, you can empty the bin and then carry it inside.'

Mmmm, I liked it when she took charge.

Terry (aka Spenda) moved off to retrieve his rake, leaving me to face Jenny alone.

'We meet again, huh?' she grinned cheerfully.

'Yeah, I guess so,' I answered (trying my best to give the impression that I didn't know what she was talking about).

'Well, it's nice to see you here. Do you do a lot of this sort of thing? Working with the elderly?'

'Um, yeah, of course. Tonnes of it.'

'*Really?*'

'Absolutely!' I confirmed, sensing a chance to get some runs on the board. 'I find working with old people very... umm... what's the word... *rewarding*. You know – helping them with things, cleaning up their stuff, making sure they live like normal people. I'm even considering doing a course in it!'

'Gosh, that's really lovely,' Jenny smiled. 'Who do you do it for? What are the programmes called? Maybe I can join up!'

Damn it. You've done it now, Daffey. You've done it now! I tried to think of some plausible charity names but my mind only offered me rubbish: 'Pensioners R Us', 'False teeth a-go-go', 'Don't get old, get even', and so on. Evasive action was necessary.

'Well, it's more of a casual thing really. My ummm... *grandfather*... needs a lot of help.' This, surely, was as low as I could go.

'Oh, I'm really sorry to hear that, Chris. What's the matter with him?' Jenny enquired, her voice bursting with pity and compassion.

'Ahh, you know, all sorts of things. Things that mean he can't do much for himself... or get around... or go shopping ... or anything. Things I really don't want to talk about.'

Nup, I could go lower.

'Oh,' she nodded sympathetically. 'Well, if you ever need a hand, just say so. Maybe we could get a group together and...'

'He doesn't like strangers!' I cut in a bit too quickly. 'Just family and friends – people he knows. Strangers scare him. Thanks for the offer, though,' I added hurriedly.

'That's okay. Any time. Well, I'd better keep going with the packing up. By the way, I see you've been nominated for the SRC this year. Good luck with it! It'd be great fun if you got in. Who knows, we might even end up on the Council together!'

And with those stupendously exciting words ringing in my ears, she smiled her sweet smile, turned her sweet head, and waltzed away in one of the ugliest pair of overalls I'd ever seen.

✶✶✶✶✶

For the next few days, I was in a golden mood. She'd said *fun* – it would be *fun* if I won the election, it would be *fun* if I was on the Council with her, it would be *fun* if I ran up to her in the playground, kissed her on the cheek and then asked her to go out with me (though this last point requires a fairly liberal interpretation of her words). Clearly, she was in love. Why else would she have said it? Why else would she have brought it up in the first place? Yep, there was no other explanation. My first decent conversation with the girl had been an outstanding success and now it was just a matter of time. Sure, I'd gone a bit overboard with the charity stuff – and I'd been forced to pretend that Pop was some sort of invalid – but those things aside, I'd handled myself brilliantly. I was no longer the 'breezeway blunderer', but the 'social conscience wonder boy' – the kid with a big heart and a can-do attitude. Everything was falling into place and I could hardly contain my enthusiasm.

My radiant mood lasted just long enough to realise my election campaign was in trouble. Despite a solid performance throughout late April/May, the Simon Gallup Poll (consisting of Simon, a clipboard and the sporadically asked question, 'So, you're voting for us, right?') had us lagging well behind our rivals. If the poll was accurate, the figures read like this:

McEvoy – 40 %

Brenner – 30 %

Me – 20 %

Lund – 10 % (after all, no-one likes an egghead).

Build into this equation the fact that Simon only asked ten people and that all of them were considered friends, and we were in some pretty serious shit.

The problem, as far as I could tell, had nothing to do with our policies. Like everyone else, we'd just rolled out the old chestnuts: more PE, less RE, hot food in the canteen all year round, and so on. We'd also tailored a few policies to please specific 'blocks'. The most popular of these had been our proposed ban on compulsory swimming lessons, which was aimed at the plump end of the spectrum and marketed with the words: 'No kid has to strip down to his Speedos if he doesn't want to'.

The problem wasn't lack of exposure either. I'd given a few talks to my class, Martin had put up posters everywhere, and Simon had handed out hundreds of flyers saying 'A vote for Daffey isn't a vote for *me*' (Martin's idea). My tireless work for the Neighbourhood Smiles Programme also got a regular mention at morning assembly. No, it wasn't a lack of publicity that was the problem. It was McEvoy.

In short, McEvoy was playing dirty pool. Every time we looked like making some headway, he'd unleash a withering burst of gutter tactics and cheap shots. Initially, he made much of the fact that I lived in Templestowe, rather than *Lower* Templestowe, and so wouldn't be on top of 'local issues'. When this failed to do much damage, he started telling people that my family was untrustworthy and that my mother stole from the canteen. Finally, when even these rumours had run out of steam, he resorted to the most common and most hated form of abuse at primary school: homophobic propaganda. To many, it soon became established fact that 'Chris Daffey liked boys' and that 'Simon was his bum chum'.

In public, we laughed the smears off. In private, we knew they were hurting us. It was still early days, of course (the elections weren't for eight weeks), but you couldn't help feeling that the writing was on the wall. Funnily enough, I didn't care as much as I thought I would. It was as if my conversation with

Jenny had coated me in a kind of all-purpose optimism which no calamity or setback could hope to dent. Sure, missing out on the SRC would be a bummer, but it couldn't alter destiny. Jenny and I were *meant* to be together – she'd virtually said so herself – so the election result was not absolutely crucial. Little did I know that McEvoy had one last nasty surprise left to spring on me – a surprise which would grab my good mood by the throat and throttle it to death. For one love-struck eleven-year-old, it was time to wake up and smell the coffee.

✶✶✶✶✶

The conversation started innocently enough. It was the last week before the May holidays and Martin, Simon and I were involved in a heated discussion about the recently released film *Return of the Jedi*. We'd seen it just a couple of days earlier and, at the time, it was a VERY BIG DEAL. The conversation wasn't heated because we disagreed with each other. It was heated because we all really, really hated it. It wasn't just a *bad* film, we unanimously proclaimed, it was an absolute *disgrace* – a flimsy, forgettable, merchandise-driven affront to the hallowed memory of the first two. It was much more than a disappointment. It was a betrayal!

Our list of complaints about the film was lengthy. Apart from the obvious things (poor script, wooden acting, no good lines for Chewy) there were two aspects that really stood out:

1. *The Emperor*

Was it just us, or were other people expecting the Emperor to be a bit tougher? After all, we're talking about the ultimate power in the universe here – the all-conquering overlord of darkness – the villain to whom even Darth Vadar bowed his head. Although he was hardly mentioned in the first film (and only made brief cameos as a hologram in the second) it was always made clear to us that he was The Man. If anyone was going to break heads, kick ass and fry a few good guys, it would be him, right? Wrong. Instead of a dynamic, invincible powerhouse of evil, what we got was this:

An old man, with bad teeth and a 'spooky' voice.
Doesn't quite cut it, does it?

2. *The Stormtroopers*

If there was ever an army in need of some basic training, it was the Imperial army. Although stormtroopers were well on their way to conquering the universe, they'd done so with the following impediments:

- they never got injured, they always got killed;
- they never hit anything, EVER; and
- they wore white, clunky spacesuits, specifically designed for getting shot through.

Amazingly enough, these things didn't bug us that much in the first two films. Sure, stormtroopers *seemed* incompetent, but maybe they were just unlucky? Maybe they were just good soldiers out of form? Yep, these excuses held up for a while, but when the galaxy's crack troops get knocked over by a bunch of teddy bears packing slings, you've really got to start asking questions.

These were just the main things that upset us about the film. There were countless others, of course (don't let me get started on the Ewoks), but none provoked the same passionate, effigy-burning fury as these two. How then, you might ask, did a negative film critique result in the destruction of my great mood? Well, it was like this. As the discussion drew to a close, Martin brought up the only good thing to come out of the film – the transformation of Princess Leia from sheet-wearing girl scout to aluminium bikini-clad goddess. After making this point (and giving us a detailed description of what *he* would have made her wear if he'd been Jabba the Hutt), Martin looked across at me and said something risky.

'You know, you sure can't beat girls with brown hair, can you, Daff?' He then winked and gave me an enthusiastic thumbs up. He was a good keeper of secrets, Martin. But sometimes, he liked to live dangerously.

Simon's reaction to all of this was as you might expect for a kid who was routinely left out of everything. He frowned, he made angry little snorting noises with his nose, and he demanded to know what was going on.

'What was that supposed to mean, Martin?'

'What was *what* supposed to mean? I was just asking Daff

here if he agreed that girls with brown hair were better looking than girls with blonde hair.'

'Yeah, but why Daff? Why didn't you say "You can't beat girls with brown hair, can you, *Simon*?"'

'Well,' Martin smiled, 'I reckon that's obvious, Sime.'

'Piss off. I know as much about girls as you two losers. There's one particular girl who's been after me all year. She's *desperate* for me!'

'You don't mean your cousin, "Gazelle", do you?' I cut in.

'Giselle! Her name's Giselle. And she's great and she's pretty and she's asked me to go with her *three times*!'

'You're *so* full of it, Simon,' Martin replied. 'If Gazelle's so great and so pretty, how come you keep saying no?'

'Well, you know. Because she's a relative. It'd be *wrong*.'

Simon's earnest, slightly bashful delivery of this last line provoked howls of laughter from his audience.

'Sorry, Sime,' Martin apologised, after regaining control of himself. 'I'm sure Gazelle – I mean *Giselle* – is lovely and everything and that you know tonnes about girls. It was just that Daff once said he liked girls better if they had dark hair and . . .' Then he froze mid-sentence. Turning slowly towards me with a look of horror in his eyes, he put his hand to his forehead and opened his mouth wide, as if he'd just remembered something terrible. 'Shit! Daff, um, could we have a word?'

'Sure,' I replied.

'In private?'

'Fucking hell!' Simon exclaimed. 'Fine, keep your stupid

secrets from me – see what I care. You know, I'm a lot more trustworthy than you guys think. You'll see, one day. You'll see!' He then paused for a couple of seconds (just to make sure no-one was listening) before storming off in a huff.

'Okay, what's the matter, Mart? You look like death.'

'I can't believe I forgot to tell you.'

'Tell me what?'

'I mean, I was *going* to tell you and then something must have come up. Something must have . . .'

'Tell me WHAT?'

Martin sighed heavily and looked me square in the eyes. 'You're not going to like it, Daff. You're not going to like it at all.' Then he placed his hands on top of his head and began to recount his horrific tale.

'It happened after cricket practice last week. It was a much longer practice than usual – on account of us getting beaten by Templestowe Valley – and Mr Bradbury said we had to keep running laps until we got the 'loser energy' out of us and . . .'

'The point, Martin – *the point*?'

'Sorry, I'm getting to it. Well, at the same time we were practising cricket, there was a group of girls practising next door on the basketball courts. They were playing that game they play with a ball – you know – what's it called?'

I shrugged helplessly.

'You know – like basketball, except you can't touch anyone.'

Martin then stood on tippy toes and waved his arms furiously in front of me.

'Netball?'

'Yeah, that's it – netball. Well, they finished at about the same time we did and we all walked off together, and then...' At this point, Martin lowered his voice and became frighteningly serious. '... And then, that Jenny girl – who you like...' My blood pressure made a sudden, dramatic increase. 'Came up to... (long pause)... *McEvoy* and...'

Oh my God...

'... Said some things.'

'*Things*? What do you mean *things*?'

'Orrr, you know, just this and that. Nothing important or anything. Just stuff you'd say to be polite – like she'd seen he was running for the SRC and that she wished him good luck and thought it'd be fun if he got on. Stuff like that.'

And with those innocently uttered words, my fantasy world came crashing to the ground. Jenny Hartnett wasn't in love with me. She was a two-timing well-wisher!

Seeing my ashen face, Martin moved to reassure me. Well, at least that's what he tried to do.

'Daff, don't worry about it. It was nothing. I haven't even got to the bad bit yet!'

Great. Fantastic. Sorry for jumping the gun with my misery.

'Anyway,' he continued, 'as she was walking off, McEvoy watched her go for a little while and then he turned to everyone and said... um... some stuff about her.'

'Stuff? *Stuff*? Why do you keep saying 'stuff' and 'things'? Why don't you just tell me what he said?'

'Because I can't remember,' he protested vehemently. 'It was last week!'

I looked into his eyes to assess the truth of this statement. He was lying, the bastard. He knew *exactly* what McEvoy had said about her, and could probably remember everything she'd said to him. He was just censoring the episode for my benefit, and I hated him for it.

'Look, Daff, the important part was this – McEvoy told everyone he liked Jenny and that . . . well . . . he planned to *kiss her*.'

Thwack! Martin landed the knockout punch. These words were so distressing, so incomprehensively awful, that I felt as if Muhammad Ali had just hit me with a wrench. For a second or two, I think I blacked out.

Sex, lies and videotape

Hate is a strong word. Well, at least that's what one of my aunties used to say.

'Do you really hate that person?' she used to chide me. 'Or do you just dislike them? Hate's a strong word you know, Christopher.'

The way Aunty Nance saw things, the world would have been a much better place if people stopped hating each other and just settled for 'strong dislikes'. In the days following Martin's revelation, however, I was in no mood for compromise. I didn't dislike Andrew McEvoy. I didn't disapprove of him either. And I didn't have an aversion to him in the same way that some people have an aversion to peas. I *hated* him.

It wouldn't have been so bad if he'd just said he liked her.

Or if he'd just mentioned that he planned to ask her out, or give her a present or something. But no – he had to go one step further. He had to give me a visual image! Every time I shut my eyes, I saw his hideous, smug face, planting itself on top of hers. It was unbearable. The news that Jenny had been wishing *all* the candidates good luck for the elections had been hard enough to stomach – but discovering that my most hated enemy had his sights set on 'pashing her' (to use the parlance of the times) was just too much for me to take. I became morose. If I wasn't moping around the yard skimming stones off concrete, I was picking the petals off daisies and humming *Yesterday* to myself; or lying on the grass pondering what might have been; or worst of all, engaging in one of those morbid, self-pitying fantasies, like the one where you kill yourself and then watch your relatives bawl their eyes out at your funeral. I was in bad shape. Fortunately, I didn't have to endure it for long. Before I knew it, the May holidays were upon me and it was time to crawl off and lick my wounds.

✳ ✳ ✳ ✳ ✳

The May holidays were a wonderful thing. Unlike holidays that are taken by adults, there was none of that ridiculous pressure to 'do things'. Nope, at that age, you felt it was your right – indeed, *your obligation* – to spend every second of your time doing as little as humanly possible. After all, you'd earned it. You'd put your head down during term one, turned up to school each day, handed in the occasional 300-word assignment on volcanoes, and now it was time to reap the rewards.

'Clean up my room? What are you – a *slave driver*? It's the holidays!'

There were literally millions of ways a kid could go about wasting his time. Being a boy, most of my favourite ones involved either sport or the mindless destruction of property. Falling within the latter category were such classics as:

- starting small fires;
- stealing letter boxes;
- setting up *Star Wars* figurines and then knocking them down with rocks; and
- placing those same figurines on top of the barbecue and watching them slowly melt.

These were the games that I enjoyed the most. The best part about them was that you could either play them on your own, or get together with other kids in your street and make an occasion of it.

One particular game I used to love playing with my neighbours involved the collection of spiders, bees, bull ants and other insects. Due to the inherent danger of being bitten or stung, it was left to Tom (a rather gung-ho kid from next door) to collect them. Tom claimed to have a special understanding with animals. This understanding apparently meant that no creature would injure or harm him – a claim that was neither plausible nor supported by the available evidence. Once Tom had finished collecting the bugs (and bathed his swollen hands in cold water), he'd place them in a jar and seal it up. Then we'd gather round, shake the jar like crazy, and try to make them fight each other in spectacular Insect Death Matches. My money was always on the bull ants. They were sturdy, they were resilient, and you could chop them into a million pieces without even denting their morale.

With activities like these to conduct, the May holidays were a blissfully carefree time. The days were long, the weather was mild, and you didn't have a responsibility in the world. Under normal circumstances, this would have been enough for me. But during these particular May holidays I found it difficult to get my mind off school. No matter how many toys I burnt or bug-bouts I witnessed, I just couldn't stop thinking about the dramas that lay ahead. Would I end up with Jenny? What had become of The Plan? How was I going to win the election, perform a play about *Dr Who*, and somehow destroy Andrew McEvoy in the process? I didn't know. What I needed was a diversion – some incredibly interesting and absorbing activity that was guaranteed to take my mind off my troubles. On the first Sunday of the holidays, I found one.

✳ ✳ ✳ ✳ ✳

The 22nd of May happened to be a particularly hectic day in the Daffey household, which suited me perfectly. Mum was busy making her famous Cherry Ripe slice; Carolyn was learning the guitar; Dad was fixing the roof; and Pop had come over to lend a hand.

'Maureen!' Dad shouted through the living room window as I sat watching TV. 'Tell your father to get down off the roof! It's ridiculous. The silly old bugger's going to get himself killed!'

'I'll try,' Mum replied from the kitchen. 'But he's not going to like it.'

My mother then wiped her hands on her apron, walked into the laundry and stuck her head outside the back door.

'Dad! What are you doing? Come down from there!'

'Eh?' came the distant, but clearly audible response.

'COME DOWN FROM THERE! YOU'LL HURT YOURSELF!'

'Naaaaaaah!' he yelled back. 'Don't be stupid – I'm almost done!'

This was followed by a loud noise, a terrible scraping sound and a series of roof tiles streaking past the window and shattering on the lawn.

'Mind yourself down there, Maur,' Pop yelled. 'I'm just clearing away some of the bad ones.'

He was a dogged individual, my grandfather. Age had certainly not wearied him, but good sense had packed up shop long ago.

It took the promise of a cup of tea and a slice of raisin bread to finally coax him down. He'd actually done a pretty good job with the roof, Dad admitted later. After all, his talents had never been called into question – just his ability to survive a five-metre drop. When he entered the living room, he gave me a big wave, quoted some random passages from Banjo Patterson's *Clancy of the Overflow* (as was his custom on entering a room) and sat himself down.

'Watcha watchin', Chrissy?' he asked.

'Music videos.'

'Eh?'

'*Music videos.* Videos with music!'

Pop put on his glasses and leaned closer to the television, but was driven back by the sight of Adam and the Ants. 'Baaah,' he said dismissively, rolling his eyes and waving an arm around. 'Don't know what's happened to music these days – all screaming and stupid costumes. Wasn't like that when I was a young man, you know. Ever listen to Al Bowlly?'

'Who?'

'Al Bowlly. The greatest singer of all time! That man had a voice as good as Sinatra's – better even. What was that song he used to sing? *Makin' Wickey Wackey Down at Waikiki.* Now there was a tune! He would have been more famous than Sinatra too, but they blew him up during the war.'

I placed my hands over my ears and tried to drown out the sound of Pop's voice. I was spared from further Al Bowlly anecdotes by the ring of the phone.

'Chris – it's for you,' came my mother's voice from the next room. I dashed out of the living room and gratefully accepted the call. It was Simon.

'Daff, it's Sime. Can you talk?'

'Ah, yeah, I guess so. What do you mean, *can I talk*?'

'I mean, is it safe? Can anyone hear you?'

'Um, hang on, I'll check,' I replied, casting a few bemused looks around the house to make sure no-one was listening. It wasn't often that I had to speak to my friends on 'secure lines'.

'There's no-one around, Sime. What's this all about?'

'Listen, Daff. I just got off the phone with Martin. He's on his way over. Get your mum to drop you round as soon as you can. Got it?'

'Hang on, slow down a sec. Why? What's going on?'

Simon paused for a moment and then whispered, 'Daff, I've got a video – a *RUDE* video!'

Click.

I put down the receiver and scratched the side of my head. A rude video, huh? This *was* going to be interesting!

※※※※※

Few things were as exciting to me and my friends as the prospect of seeing a rude video. To appreciate why this was, you have to understand the role such things played in a young boy's life. You see, the whole issue of sex (and all the things associated with it) was pretty damn intriguing when you were eleven. On one level, we were bombarded with it. Everyone discussed it, magazines were full of it, and there was a constant stream of late-night movies showing American kids clinking cups and vowing to 'do it before the prom'.

Closer to home, however, sex was nowhere to be seen. With the exception of known crackpots and compulsive liars, no-one at school claimed to be *having* sex – and at that age, the only other people we knew tended to be relatives. Technically speaking, there probably was some sex going on – right underneath our noses at home. But it would be many years before this possibility crossed our minds; and even then it was with a due sense of horror and disbelief. No, sex seemed both everywhere and nowhere. A foot away from our face and yet a mile away from our grasp. School was a hotbed of confusion, lies and wild speculation. Girls were sprouting breasts, guys were cracking stiffies and no-one had any idea what to do about it. Enter pornography.

For boys at least, pornography represented a valuable stepping stone into the unknown. We wanted to know about women, we wanted to know about sex, and *Playboy* and *Penthouse* appeared to be the best authorities around. Of course, adults tried to help us out occasionally. There was the much anticipated 'little talk' we had with our parents – a hideously embarrassing episode that was usually light on specifics and two years too late. Then there were sex education classes.

At our school at least, sex education seemed to be less

about informing children than it was about freaking them out. Where, for example, did they come up with all those frighteningly clinical terms?

> 'Today, class, we learn about ... *the spermatozoa!*'

I mean, are we talking about sex here, or some invading alien force?

> 'Greetings, Earthlings. My name is Zygote. These are my friends here, Uterus and Ovarian, and together we bring news from the planet Spermatozoa!'

It was scary. Not only was the terminology off-putting, but so were the illustrations. Did they ever put a decent-looking woman (or man for that matter) in a sex education book? I think not.

Deprived of any legitimate source of sexual paraphernalia, the three of us thus began a relentless search for illegitimate ones. The main stumbling block was, of course, that we were too young to buy anything ourselves. This meant we had to rely on older friends or the manipulation of our parents to get what we wanted. Take the video store, for example. Our parents had all the money, our parents had all the cards, and consequently, our parents called all the shots. To get the goods, you had to be smart.

One of the most common tactics used at the video store was a little ploy known as 'slippin' one through'. In short, this tactic relied on selecting a whole stack of videos in the hope that your parents wouldn't be bothered checking each one. It almost never worked.

'And what will it be tonight, Mr Daffey?'
'Well, I've got this pile of videos my son just handed me. Let's see, we've got *Rocky*, *Superman II*, *Ghostbusters*, *Ben Hur*, *The Ten Commandments*, *Kramer vs. Kramer*, and . . . SORORITY HOUSE SEX FEST? What the fuck?'

The second tactic involved careful selection of the video itself. Ideally, what you wanted was a video that you knew was full of sex, but which had a cover that suggested otherwise. Useful for this purpose were:

- foreign films;
- films involving medieval conflict (no barbarian film could be complete without naked female gladiators); and
- the so-called 'comedy' section.

Using these simple tactics, the three of us had been able to see our fair share of M-rated nudity. Judging by Simon's voice on the phone, however, we were about to see something much more exotic!

✳✳✳✳✳

Simon's house was ugly, in an expensive kind of way. It had two storeys, almost no garden and an architectural style that Pop always referred to as 'crazy roofs' (which meant that it had an odd-shaped roof with many segments and a variety of different angles). The interior of the house was a lot like what you find in a dental surgery or private hospital: muted colours, wide-open spaces, glossy prints of dolphins and rainforests on the walls, everything calm and serene so as not to scare the patients.

What the house lacked in atmosphere, however, it made up for in volume. Simon was one of the only kids I knew who had a dinky-di 'rumpus room' at home. He was also lucky enough to live in a house with a second TV *and* video. In those days, this was an almost unheard of luxury. It meant that everyone at school assumed your parents were some sort of royalty or business tycoons. After all, to a primary school student, multiple appliances were the absolute measure of wealth and privilege. No matter how rich a kid's parents actually were, no matter how many cars they drove, shares they bought or holiday houses they owned, nothing quite compared to the ability to watch *The Sullivans* in two different rooms of your house.

'My dad's the CEO of Microsoft!'
'Yeah? Well my dad owns *three TVs*!'

On this particular day, both the rumpus room and the spare electrical appliances were to come in handy. When I arrived at the house, I was greeted by Mrs Jackson. She was on her way out to do the shopping and so had to check with my mum whether it was okay to leave the three of us on our own. Mum said it was fine, they both laughed insanely at the phrase 'they're little men now', and I was left wondering what happened to people when they grew up.

I found my friends in the rumpus room lounging about on beanbags. They were both doing their best to appear casual.

'Has Mum gone yet?' Simon asked, as I walked in the door.

'Yeah, I think so. She went out shopping.'

'Are you sure? Is her car still there?' he said, leaping up from his beanbag and peering out the window.

'So what's the big deal? Where's this video?' I enquired.

'It's not *just* a video,' Martin replied, whipping a tape out from under his shirt. 'It's a *PORNO!*' He pushed the tape into my hands and I glanced down at it nervously.

'*Debbie Duz Dishes*? That doesn't sound like a porno.'

'Well it *is*,' said Simon defensively. 'It's X-rated!'

'X-rated? No way! Where did you get it?'

'I nicked it off my cousin. He's got tonnes of them!'

'Wow,' was all I could think of saying. 'So have you watched it yet?'

'Nope, we haven't had a chance. We've been waiting all morning for Mum to go out.'

Phew, I thought to myself, breathing a sigh of relief. There's nothing worse than watching a film with two guys who've already seen it. They might have given away the plot and everything!

'So let's go then. Let's put it on,' Martin commanded, clicking his fingers and gesturing towards the tape. Simon obeyed instinctively. Removing the video from my hands, he slid it into the recorder, switched on the TV, and together we stepped through the looking glass.

What the...? For the first few seconds, confusion reigned. Disco music blared through the speakers; limbs flew everywhere; somebody kept screaming 'dunk me'; nothing made any sense at all. The only thing I knew for sure was that we were witnessing some kind of 'close-up' – a close-up of what exactly, I had no idea.

Desperate to get a handle on things, the three of us screwed up our faces and peered closer at the screen, like old men trying to read a street map. It didn't help. Part of the problem was this: in our haste, we'd forgotten to rewind the tape. This meant that we'd been thrust directly into an action scene, with no warning, no build-up and no chance to get to know the characters. The other more significant part of the problem was that even *with* an appropriate build-up, we probably wouldn't have understood what was happening anyway. Sure, we had a rough idea what sex would look like, but seeing thirty people perform it simultaneously on a basketball court wasn't exactly what we had in mind.

It wasn't until the camera started panning back a bit that we were able to get some perspective. First we made out one person, and then another, and then another one after that. Pretty soon, a whole mob of them came into view. The scene reminded me of a group of kids playing in one of those inflatable, jumping castles. Except that they weren't kids. And they weren't wearing any clothes. And they weren't so much jumping up and down on a castle, as they were jumping up and down on each other. In fact, the more the camera panned back, the less and less I thought about the school fete.

Our reaction to all of this was as you might have expected. We were intrigued, but we were also appalled. You see, it was just too big a jump for us. Up until that point, our idea of 'porn' had consisted of women taking their tops off at the beach. If the video had have been about that, we would have been rapt. As it was, we were horrified. What we really wanted to see was *nakedness*, not a room full of people going hammer and tongs. It was like ordering a steak at a restaurant and having a cow dropped onto your table. It was too much, it was too soon, and it exposed some facts that we didn't really want to know.

We would have been much better off if Simon had just brought home a teen comedy – full of risqué, but at the same time 'hilarious' scenes such as:

- boy drills hole into girls' showers (only to have obese headmistress bathe in front of him); and
- college guy puts on a wig and some lippy, and somehow passes unnoticed in the girls' dormitory.

This was the Good Stuff. Crass, low-budget garbage with just the right amount of gratuitous nudity and lowbrow humour to impress an eleven-year-old. *Debbie Duz Dishes* showed us much more than we wanted to see.

As unimpressed as we all were, however, no-one wanted to let on. No matter how bad it got, no matter how many inexplicable zoom ins and stomach-turning close-ups we had to endure, the three of us just smiled, stared at the screen, and bobbed our heads up and down to the music. We did this for one simple reason: what if the only person hating the film was *you*? What if everyone else liked it? What if liking it meant you were normal, and *disliking* it meant you were some sort of freak? No-one was willing to take that chance. No-one was prepared to put up their hand and voice an opinion, lest they be labelled an outcast. That was, until one particularly memorable scene involving two fans and a so-called 'referee'. Just as the referee's strides came down and someone made an off-colour remark about 'blowing his whistle', Martin broke ranks.

'I don't care what anyone else thinks – this is just *gross*!'

And with these words, the gloves came off.

'You're so right, Martin. This film stinks!' Simon echoed.

'It's just plain disgusting,' I chipped in. 'I mean, what the hell does *that guy* think he's doing?'

The charade was over. *Debbie Duz Dishes* was in for some punishment.

We managed to keep up the abuse for almost the entire film. What had begun as a steamy sex romp quickly transformed itself into an uproarious comedy, aided greatly by Simon's liberal use of the fast-forward button (it's amazing how stupid sex looks at four times normal speed). We would have got through the whole thing had it not been for the unexpected return of Mrs Jackson. The instant we heard the front door open, there was a mad scramble to pull the tape out and slam in another one – a feat we accomplished just as she entered the room. Peering down at our guilt-ridden faces, she studied our expressions, looked at the telly, and said,

'*101 Dalmatians*? I didn't know you boys were into Disney?'

The closeness of this call prompted an immediate discussion about what to do with the tape now that we'd watched it. It was unanimously agreed that it shouldn't be thrown out. Simon had gone to a lot of trouble to steal it, and besides, even though we didn't like it now, maybe it was something we would 'grow into'. That settled, it was just a question of where to stash it.

Simon argued feverishly that his house wasn't safe. He claimed that Mrs Jackson had a 'nose for such things' and would sniff it out within weeks. I raised a similar objection and so all eyes turned to Martin. The Timms's household was the perfect place to hide the tape, Simon and I reasoned. They'd only recently moved in, so there'd be plenty of old boxes lying around, and Martin's dad was so cool that he might not even get mad if he found it. The only person who didn't see the logic in this was Martin himself. He dismissed our plan with an unusual degree of ferocity and said that we didn't know his father as well as we thought. Our friend had been in a strangely sullen mood all holidays, come to think of it, and neither Simon nor I could work out why. Whatever the reason, it was clear that his house was off-limits.

In the end, we decided to bury it with the rest of our stuff at the Log Fort. This was an insane decision in many ways, but at the time it seemed fair enough. Our old T-Bird hiding place hadn't been disturbed in a year and there was no reason to think that it ever would be. So long as we went to the school and buried it before the start of term two, we'd never be caught with it on us – and in the unlikely event that someone dug it up, they'd have no idea who it belonged to.

Satisfied that we'd thought things through, we agreed to meet again on the last day of the holidays and carry out our plan. And on Sunday the 29th of May, that's exactly what we did. We rode down to the school, we gathered at the Log Fort, and together we buried a small, pornographic time bomb. If we had listened carefully, we would have heard it ticking.

9

Stuart Lund's brain

STUART LUND WAS a child prodigy. I knew this because:

(a) he could do the Rubik's cube in under twenty seconds;
(b) he could spell 'phlegm'; and
(c) he had one of those enormous, pale heads that seem to go hand-in-hand with child genius.

Stuart's head was the price he paid for being so intelligent. Big, beige and bulbous, it sat on top of his skinny neck like a pumpkin squatting on a bean sprout. He looked more like an enormous embryo than he did a person, but if that were the case, he was one of the smartest embryos ever to pull on a pair of pants. Stuart Lund knew *everything*. Maths, science, history, geography, it was all second nature to the man they called 'The Brain'. Although Stuart was good at many things, his specialty was shapes. No-one knew their shapes better than Stuart Lund. He could tell a rhombus from a rectangle, a triangle from a trapezium, and he was on first-name terms with the entire quadrilateral family. Most impressive of all was his intricate knowledge of 'polygons'.

The word polygon just means a shape with many sides. The 'study' of polygons (and I use that term loosely) was one of the many pointless activities that made up grade six maths classes. Basically, all you had to do was remember what the different polygons were called. Most people are familiar with the first few: a triangle has three sides; a rectangle has four; a pentagon five; a hexagon six, and so on. It starts getting tougher when you reach number seven (the elusive 'heptagon'), steps back a notch with the well know octagon (which is the shape of Australian stop signs), and then heads into boffin territory with the comical sounding 'nonagon'. It was at this point that your average kid usually gave up. But not Stuart Lund.

Not only was Stuart well versed in the wiles and ways of the nonagon, he could also talk your ear off about the decagon, the hendecagon, and, the mother of all polygons, the twelve-sided dodecagon. Why Stuart knew all of this, and why, more importantly, our teachers thought it necessary to teach it to him, is a mystery. I mean, it didn't seem like much of a life skill. When, outside grade six geometry classes, would he ever be confronted with a twelve-sided, two-dimensional shape? What possible brain-taxing, high-powered job was Stuart being groomed for in later life?

'What do you make of it, Rodge? Pentagon? Heptagon? Parallelogram?'

'I'm not sure, Harry. Better get Lund in here fast!'

Despite the fact that almost everything he knew was useless, there was a great deal of hoopla surrounding Stuart Lund. For this reason, the teaching staff at Templestowe Heights had decided to make a film about him. It was called *Small Packages* and was designed both to celebrate Stuart's genius and to ostracise him from the rest of the school community. Although Stuart had the lead role, the film was also going to pay homage to a collection of 'lesser' prodigies. These kids wouldn't have speaking parts, but they'd get to hang around in the background and do clever stuff (like engage in fictional classroom discussions, or stand next to the blackboard pointing at formulas). They weren't glamorous roles, but they carried with them the recognition that you were Smart. To get into this film (and thereby fulfil item five of my Plan), I needed a gimmick. What I'd come up with was *doubling*.

With the obvious exception of Lund himself, I was Templestowe Heights' crown prince of doubling. Every Wednesday morning I'd blitz the field in Mr Weathershaw's weekly competition. 1, 2, 4, 8, 16, 32, 64, 128, 256, 512, 1024, 2048, 4096, 8192 . . . there was just no telling how high I could go. In the end, I got so good that the competition became a handicap event – like the Stawell Gift. Whereas everyone else in class got five full minutes to scribble down as many doubled figures as they could, I was held back until the third minute mark.

'Everybody here except Chris Daffey, pick up your pens, open your jotters, get ready, get set, and ... ... *GO!*'

While the rest of the field surged ahead, I'd lean back in my chair, yawn as loudly as I could, and bide my time. Then, with just two minutes to spare, I'd burst out of the blocks and mow the bastards down in the straight. It was one of my favourite parts of grade six. Fortunately, Stuart Lund wasn't in my class and so couldn't compete (it was rumoured that he could double into the billions) and so I was free to bask in the glory of being Templestowe Heights' undisputed doubling champion. This talent alone, I figured, should have been enough to get me into the video. I may not have been as good at maths as some of the other prodigies, but when it came to working stuff out on a calculator and then committing it to memory, I was an absolute *gun*.

Having come up with a gimmick, all I had to do was catch Mrs Newport's attention. This wasn't going to be easy. For one thing, I didn't want to *ask* to be in the video or make any overt attempt to get myself in. I wanted to be *discovered*. I wanted someone to stumble across my gift by accident, like the way they find geniuses in the movies. And so with these rather grandiose aims in mind, I went to work. Beginning the day after filming commenced, I made every conceivable effort to be 'accidentally' discovered. For the next few days, Mrs Newport could not enter a room, walk down a corridor or cross the yard without catching a glimpse of a diminutive, number-crunching psychopath. She didn't seem to take much notice at first, but it was just a matter of patience. In the meantime, I had plenty of other things to worry about.

✺✺✺✺✺

My return to Templestowe Heights had been a traumatic one. The May holidays may have taken my mind off things for a while, but my predicament was brought sharply back into focus the minute I walked through the front gate. My quest to win over Jenny was turning out to be harder than I'd anticipated. Back in January, when I'd first put pen to paper and sketched out The Plan, I'd thought it was just a matter of working at it. Put in some time, put in some effort, and hey presto, I'd have myself a girlfriend. It had never occurred to me that, despite my labours, despite my brave attempt to pull off a complete personality overhaul, she might not show much interest. It had also never occurred to me that the path to her heart might be strewn with so many unexpected obstacles. What had started out as a leisurely walk in the park, had turned into a *Deliverance*-style battle for survival.

- A competitor for Jenny's affections had arisen.
- That competitor looked set to thump me in July's must-win elections.
- Two weeks after that, I was going to be humiliated in an as yet unnamed and unplanned stage performance.

- And not one of objectives I'd set myself in The Plan had been successfully completed.

In summary, my back was against the wall and my front wasn't looking too good either. My only hope was to take a leaf out of the professional sportsman's coaching manual and take it 'one problem at a time'. First up was the act.

※※※※※

The breakthrough came in a Tuesday morning RE class. In primary school terminology, 'RE' stood for Religious Education in the same way that 'PE' stood for Physical Education. The similarities between these two subjects ended with their abbreviations. Being fit, healthy and good at sport was one of the key objectives of the Australian state school system. Believing in God was not. For this reason, PE had grown until it occupied almost a quarter of every school week, whereas RE had dwindled away to a one-hour chat about the importance of being 'nice'.

The person in charge of teaching us this message was called Mrs Casselopian. Our class delighted in testing the patience of Mrs Casselopian. Martin, Simon and I, for example, spent every RE period scouring the Bible for humorous or nonsensical passages. Every time we found one, we'd ask her to explain it.

As our teacher soon discovered, there was a lot of stuff in the Bible that really was *ridiculous*. Sure, there were the important bits – Genesis, the beginning of everything, Moses, the Ten

Commandments, the life and times of Jesus, Revelations, and so on. But nestled in amongst these key passages were some lesser known pronouncements, ranging from the trivial to the truly bizarre. Like:

- how to protect your home from mildew (Leviticus 14:36);
- what to do if your friend's donkey falls down (Deuteronomy 22:4); and
- why, if a man takes a second wife, his first wife should get the same amount of food (Exodus 21:10).

It was during one of our routine scans for such passages that Simon made a stunning discovery in his search for the perfect Act. We were sitting up the back and Martin had just stumbled across a piece of Old Testament gold.

'Hey, guys. Check this one out! Deuteronomy 25:11.'

Simon and I crowded close and peered down at the section he was pointing to.

'If two men are having a fight,' Martin read, 'and the wife of one tries to help her husband by grabbing hold of the other man's genitals, show her no mercy – cut off her hand!!!' We clutched our stomachs and laughed ourselves stupid.

'Hey, Sime – get out *your* Bible. It'll be even funnier in olden-days' language!'

Simon giggled with expectation and reached for his copy of the Good Book.

Simon's Bible was somewhat different from ours. Where

Martin and I owned the standard Good News version, Simon had possession of an ancient King James. It used to belong to his mother and was of the type given out when she was at school. It was small, it smelt of dust and, like any object that had passed through Simon's hands, it was covered in long purple labels marked 'PROPERTY OF SIMON'.

What made this Bible special was that it was full of expressions like 'ye shall', 'thou shouldest' and 'whosoever rebuketh'. Olde Worlde language like this made funny passages hilarious, and Deuteronomy 25:11 was no exception.

'Okay, okay, I've got it,' Simon said excitedly, opening up the leather-bound Bible and pushing it flat against the desk. 'When men strive together one with another, and the wife of the one draweth near for to deliver her husband out of the hand of him that smiteth him, and putteth forth her hand, and taketh him by the secrets . . .'

The *secrets*?!?!!? This was too much. The three of us collapsed into a fit of hysterics loud enough for the whole class to hear. Mrs Casselopian was not amused.

'Christopher – Martin – Simon. Do you have something you'd like to share with the class?'

'Yes!' we all cried in unison. 'Yes, we do, Mrs Casselopian. We'd like to know whether you think the rule in Deuteronomy 25:11 seems fair?'

Having gone through this routine with us before, Mrs Casselopian was naturally suspicious. While two girls sitting near us rolled their eyes at our childishness, she warily opened her Bible and perused the relevant section. She didn't have to study it for long.

'Actually, I don't think we should bother wasting the class's time with that passage. What do *you* think, boys?'

We smiled sheepishly.

'Instead, how about we have a reading from John, chapter ten, verse twenty-nine. Let's see, who shall we get to read it? How about, ummmmm . . . Terrance Wheldon?'

Terrance Wheldon (aka Spenda) had been happily doodling away on a jotter up until this point. As soon as Mrs Casselopian spoke, he jerked to attention and cast a wide-eyed look around the room (in the way a person does when their name comes out of nowhere). The rest of the class perked up a little too. After all, it was quite a treat to hear Terrance Wheldon read something.

'Terrance, we're looking at John, chapter ten, verse twenty-nine. Please open your Bible and read for the class.'

'Okay, Mussus Cussulopian,' Spenda replied, prompting the first of what would be many giggles. After spending a couple of seconds flicking through his Bible, he launched into a speech by Jesus.

'What my Father has guven me is greater than everythung, and no-one cun snutch thum away from the Father's care. The Father and I are one. (pause) Then the pupple pucked up stones to throw ut hum. And Jesus said to thum . . .'

'*COR BLIMEY, GUVNA!*' came a cry from the back of the class, prompting mass hysteria and the immediate cessation of Spenda's speech. It was a predictable gag, but a much loved one.

'Children! *Children!*' Mrs Casselopian barked in an attempt to regain order. 'That's quite enough. Jesus did not say anything of the sort. Now, when everyone's quite finished, Terrance will continue.'

It was just as Spenda was gearing up for another public shellacking that the thunderbolt hit Simon.

'That's it! That is IT!' he cried, grabbing Martin by the arm.

'What? What is it? Get the hell off me!'

'The act – that's what we'll do for the act. We'll get *Spenda* to play the Doctor!!!'

These words took a moment or two to sink in. At first, we just stared at our friend and raised our eyebrows dismissively. But then, as the potential of this idea dawned upon us, we opened our mouths slowly and turned to face each other, like a pair of those clowns you put ping-pong balls in at Luna Park.

'It's brilliant!' Martin exclaimed.

'Brilliant!' I repeated. 'The show is English. The Doctor is English. Spenda is English – well, sort of English. It can't fail! All we have to do is shove him on stage, make him say "Cor blimey, guvna", and then shoot him! It'll bring the house down!'

Simon nodded his head in enthusiastic agreement.

'There's just one problem with this plan,' I cautioned.

'What?'

'He'll never EVER do it.'

✳✳✳✳✳

Of course he wasn't going to do it. Why the hell would he? Who in their right mind would find the following offer attractive?

'Listen, Spenda. We've got this act that's desperately in need of a joke – and we'd like that joke to be *you*.'

Nope – it was a great idea for us, but there was precious little in it for Spenda. We couldn't think of one single reason why he should do it, but that didn't stop us bailing him up at lunchtime and telling him the exact opposite. His response was less than encouraging.

'I'll tell you what ya cun do wuth your Uct,' he said. 'You can stuck ut up your bum, thut's what!'

'But, Spenda . . .' Simon pleaded.

'But nuthin'! No-one un Unglund even *says* cor blimey, guvna!'

'Hey, that's not true,' I countered. 'What about in *Minder*? Or *The Sweeney*? They say it all the time!'

'Just because ut's on TV doesn't mean they say ut un real life, you *udiot*! Besides, they might say "guvna" sometimes, but I nuver heard unyone say "blimey".'

Martin, who'd taken a back seat in the negotiations thus far, picked this point to weigh in. He explained to Spenda that he had two choices. He could either do an act on his own and have the *audience* yell out cor blimey – or he could join up with us and get to say the line himself. Either way, people were going to laugh at him. But if he did it with us, at least he'd be in on it.

Spenda took a long while to respond to these words. He knew that Martin was right, but he didn't want to admit it.

'You don't know thut for sure,' he said finally. 'Maybe I'd do a good Uct.'

'Maybe you would,' Martin replied without any conviction. 'Maybe you would.'

Spenda paused for a second time, scratched his ear thoughtfully and then declared, 'Okay. I'll thunk about it.' Then he smiled glumly and turned to leave, before adding (by way of saving face), 'You know, back un Unglund, I was cuptain of the soccer team.'

A few moments later, he was gone.

'Can you believe it?' Simon screeched, as soon as Spenda had reached minimum safe distance. 'I can't believe he's even *thinking* about it!'

'I can,' said Martin. 'He's a smart kid. I'd do it if *I* was him too. What do you reckon, Daff?'

'1, 2, 4, 8 . . .'

'Daff?'

'16, 32, 64, 128 . . .'

'Daff? What the hell . . .'

But then he spotted her too. It was Mrs Newport at two o'clock and closing fast.

'Hello, boys!' she grinned, sweeping her arms around us and leaning down. 'I'm looking for a few strong men to help me shift some bags of tanbark.'

'Um. Sure. We'll do it,' said Martin.

'Yeah, just tell us where they go,' said Sime.

'256, 512, 1024,' came my reply.

'Christopher Daffey, what are you doing over there?'

'2048, 4096, 8192. Just doubling, Mrs Newport. Just doubling.'

'Gosh! You're getting very high. How often do you do this?'

'Um, pretty much all the time. That is, when I'm not *squaring*.'

Out of the corner of my eye, I saw Martin clap his hand across his forehead.

'Well, it's funny I should bump into you today, Chris. You may not be aware of this, but we're making a film about children with just those sort of gifts!'

'Really? You're kidding!' I said coyly.

'No. No, I'm not. It's about Stuart Lund, who I'm sure you must know. We're actually filming a scene for it tomorrow, where Stuart shows the class some of his polygon models. You wouldn't like to be in it by any chance, would you?'

Eureka!

✷✷✷✷✷

Settling on a format for our act marked an important turning point in my battle for Jenny's affections. All of a sudden, things started looking up. Two days after we approached him, Spenda officially accepted our offer. The day after that, we went into pre-production, and within a week, we'd sketched out one of the poxiest little screenplays ever to see the light of day. Martin was appointed director of the play, I put my hand up for scriptwriting duties, and Simon was given the rather elaborate title of 'executive producer'. It was a meaningless position, but it seemed to make him happy.

Although all four of us shared the acting roles, it was Spenda's portrayal of the Doctor that undoubtedly stole the show (and, considering the overall quality of the production, it was one of the easiest thefts in the history of theatre). Spenda *loved* playing the Doctor. Gone was the initial hesitation that saw him almost reject our offer, and in its place was a newfound and unbridled enthusiasm for self-mockery.

'Am I saying ut right?' he'd constantly ask us. 'Shud I beef up the blimey a but? Whut about muntioning thut I was born in New Zealund? Maybe I could ride un on a sheep or somethung?'

The kid was a consummate professional. If anyone was going to make fun of Terrance P. Wheldon, he'd obviously determined it was going to be *him*.

Not only was the act proceeding well, but I also started achieving success on a number of other fronts. True to her word, Mrs Newport included me in one of the key scenes of *Small Packages*. While Stuart dazzled onlookers with three-dimensional icypole-stick models, I got to stand in the background and scribble down numbers with a piece of chalk. It was a dream come true and I couldn't wait for the film to be finished. Last, but by no means least, was my unexpectedly impressive performance in the SRC campaign speeches.

The official campaign speeches were an integral part of the

SRC selection process. Although the candidates had already put up posters and given informal talks in front of class, this was the first chance they got to go head-to-head with the rest of the field. If you screwed up here, you were pretty much out of it.

Fear of failure (combined with a morbid dread of public speaking) led most candidates to err on the side of caution when delivering their speeches. No-one ever used the occasion to boost their chances or attack the opposition. It was just a matter of survival. For this reason, most candidates simply crept up to the microphone, read out a short, snappy summary of the bleeding obvious, and then scrambled off-stage before anyone had a chance to heckle. A typical speech went something like this.

'Hello, my name's Jeff Smith and I'm running for a seat on this year's SRC. I stand for more sport, less classes and the reintroduction of Ovalteenies at the canteen. I hope to get your vote. Thanks.'

Brevity was the name of the game, and if you could spit it all out in one continuous, rambling sentence, then all the better.

The first three speeches by this year's candidates followed the traditional format; each laying claim to its own particular brand of awful.

- Sandra Peterson spoke so quickly that her words became indistinguishable from a repetitive, high-pitched noise (something like 'bibble bibble bibble bibble bibble');

- Rachel Klimp got halfway through her maiden sentence before being struck down by an 'attack of the giggles' and having to retire; and
- Julie Greene boastfully sung her own praises for two and a half minutes before making the staggering claim that she was 'the JFK of student politics' (which was partly true, since half of grade six would have paid good money to see her assassinated).

The last of the female candidates to speak was, of course, my beloved Jenny. For three whole minutes she held me, and a smattering of others in the crowd, in the palm of her hand. She was eloquent, she was insightful and she was extremely organised. Her entire speech had been written out on tiny little cards, which she calmly leafed through as she outlined her points. Her voice was steady, her manner relaxed, and she was the only candidate thus far to attempt eye contact with the audience.

As for the content of the speech, I didn't really listen. There was something about waste disposal and doing our bit for the environment; a mention of bullies and making the playground safer; and then a bizarre, incomprehensible point about Australia's over-emphasis on sport. Although I took in little of what she was saying, I was captivated by the manner in which it was said. So commanding was her delivery, so mesmerising was her diction, that at one point Martin tapped me on the shoulder and said, 'Don't take this the wrong way, Daff, but I think I'm going to vote for *her*.'

I didn't take it the wrong way at all. The way things were going, I was probably going to vote for her myself.

When the speech finally came to an end and Jenny wrapped it up with the words, 'Friends, fellow students, vote with your conscience', Martin had to grab the back of my shirt to prevent me leaping to my feet and giving her a standing ovation. If I was infatuated with her before, I was in *awe* of her now.

Unfortunately, the end of Jenny's speech meant the beginning of the boys' efforts. I was scheduled to come in fourth, after Mitch Greenley (Scott Brenner's last-minute replacement, who was running on a 'save the Northern Bandicoot' platform) and Andrew McEvoy. I was nervous, of course, but not nearly as nervous as you might have expected. Sure, I was speaking in front of the whole of grade six. Granted, my potential girlfriend (and one of the twentieth century's most gifted orators) was sitting in the audience. But it was still just a speech. It wasn't like the act I was dreading later in the term. I was there to inform, not entertain. So long as I kept my head, spoke clearly, and moved my left hand up and down occasionally (to mimic authoritative body language) I'd be fine.

Stuart Lund was the first cab off the rank. Predictably, he played to his strengths: I'm smart, the others aren't, a vote for me is a vote for reason. Next up was Mitch Greenley, whose heartfelt plea for the protection of the Northern Bandicoot was met with a bemused but respectful silence. That is, until Stuart Lund pointed out that the animal wasn't even endangered and

Mitch's campaign came to a swift and humiliating end. Then there was McEvoy.

Andrew McEvoy wasn't known for his public speaking prowess. He was one of those kids whose confidence reigned supreme in the playground, but quickly evaporated when you put three kids and a microphone in front of him. The speech he gave that day was average at best. He squirmed, he stumbled, he kept forgetting where he was up to, and I lapped up every second of it. He still received a healthy ovation, however, but not because he'd done well. People just clapped him like they clap the Queen – because he was popular. When the applause died down, it was time for me.

Carefully unfolding a couple of handwritten A4 pages, I walked calmly to the microphone and did my best to exude an air of quiet confidence. So far so good. I reached the lectern without incident, laid out my pages and waited for Mrs Newport's introduction.

All things considered, I think I did pretty well. My voice held firm, my hands didn't shake, and I even managed the occasional glance up at the audience – just to show them that I wasn't scared. In terms of content, it was pretty standard stuff. I plagiarised part of Martin Luther King's famous speech and just changed a couple of words. The gist of it went something like this.

'Teachers, fellow students, I have a dream. I have a dream that one day this school will rise up and thrash Templestowe Valley on the inter-school sports day. I have a dream that children will one day go to a school where they won't be judged by the colour of their hair, but by the content of their character. I have a dream that school assembly will be held once a year, hot food will be served every day, and PE lessons will last as long as the day is young! Teachers, fellow students, I have a dream.'

(pause)

'Vote for me. Thanks.'

The ovation that followed wasn't exactly wild, but it beat the hell out of the receptions my competitors had received. Martin and Simon led the applause (clapping loudly above their heads), a handful of other kids joined in, and even Jenny herself gave me a warm, appreciative hand.

I was still a rank outsider in this race, of course, but at least I was fighting back. I just had to find a way of dealing with McEvoy!

10

Green, Green, you're my teAm!

A WEEK OUT from the elections and things were looking good. The rehearsals for the Act were going well, I'd jumped two points in the opinion polls, and Susan Spencer had invited me to her 'McDonald-land' birthday party.

McDonald's was the ultimate birthday party venue when you were a kid. Not only did you get to eat your favourite food, you got streamers, you got balloons, you got an ice-cream cake and, if you were lucky, Ronald himself would turn up. Ronald's routine (if you can call it that) was actually a pretty simple one. He'd arrive, say 'hi-ya kids', goof around a bit in his big pants, and then perform some rudimentary magic tricks – such as pulling plastic flowers out of his sleeve or making the vitamins disappear from all of his products. Even for children as young as six, there was something distinctly unimpressive about Ronald's skills as a clown. As a restaurateur, Ronald McDonald was something of a genius. As an entertainer, however, he wasn't much chop.

By the time you were eleven, the traditional McDonald's party format was considered a bit passé. For this reason, Susan Spencer had decided to make McDonald's only the first leg of her birthday extravaganza. We were there just to eat, and Ronald had been given strict instructions to stay away.

The party started well enough. We sat down, we gave Susan our presents, we gorged ourselves on burgers and chicken pieces, and then we retired to the playground to burn off the excess calories.

Most of the equipment in the playground was too young for us. The exception was a thing called the 'whirler'. The whirler was a large enclosed compartment that sat on top of a steel pole and was shaped like a giant Grimus (the obese, purple-coloured McDonald's character who'd obviously tucked into a few burgers himself). The whirler worked like this: you climbed inside, you sat with your back against the wall, and then you made the entire thing spin around by turning a steel disk faster and faster until everyone puked. It's hard to say whether the whirler's designers *intended* its passengers to throw up, but the circumstantial evidence was damning. If ever there were a sure-fire recipe for producing vomit, it would have to be this:

- take a group of young, excitable children;
- fill them full of fats, sugars and starches;
- and then place them into a centrifuge.

By the time Grimus had stopped spinning that day, half of Susan's guests had enjoyed a lunch they were never going to take home. Martin, Simon and myself were three of the first to go. As we sat on the sidelines scraping half-digested pickles off our T-shirts, our minds turned to the upcoming elections. You see, despite my successful campaign speech, I still had one major problem. I was coming second. Second was no good to me. If I wanted to win, I had to find some way of beating McEvoy. Simon, as always, claimed to have the answers.

'Listen, Daff – it's easy. We get a camera, we get McEvoy, and then we throw him into the girl's toilets. Reputation *destroyed*!'

Hmmm, I thought to myself. Devious, but impractical. No boy, no matter how popular, could stomach the indignity of being thrust two feet into the girls' dunnies. But how would we do it? How would it work?

'I'm just not sure it'd work, Sime.'

'Why not?'

'Well, for a start, we'd never get him in there. And even if we did, you could tell from the photo that he'd been chucked in. If you really wanted to get him, you'd need a shot of him going in on his own. Like he *wanted to*!'

My friend pondered this for a moment.

'Maybe we could drug him?' he suggested.

'What?'

'You know – put something in his Coke and then drag him inside.'

'I don't see how that helps.'

'Or what about this?' Simon continued, undaunted. 'We find someone who looks just *like* McEvoy and then get *him* to go into the toilets. Or better yet, get him to replace McEvoy completely!'

'Shut up, Simon,' said Martin.

'Hey, at least I'm thinking!' Simon shot back. 'Anyway, it's not such a bad idea. It's exactly what they did to Krystal on *Dynasty*.' This last revelation was met with a prolonged, disbelieving silence.

'You watch *DYNASTY*???'

'Um . . .' Simon stuttered, suddenly painfully aware that he'd been blathering on without thinking. 'No. Well, yes. Sometimes. My mum does!'

'Okay, that's it. From now on, you're not allowed to speak.'

'Shut up, Martin.'

'You just broke the law.'

'I said *shut up!* Daff, tell him to shut up.'

'I don't know, Sime. A law's a law.'

'Okay then, *don't!*' Simon snapped, enraged. 'I'm sick of talking to you two anyway. And I'm sick of everyone ignoring my ideas. If I'd been put in charge of this election like I asked, we would have already won. But no, we had to go with *Martin*.

Martin, you *suck* at stuff like this. If you want to beat someone like McEvoy, you've got to think dirty and go for the low blows. You've got to poke him in the eye and then kick him where it hurts. And if I was in charge, that's exactly what we would have done. Well, I've had enough! I'm sick of being ignored, I'm sick of being left out, and I'm sick of people keeping secrets from me!'

At the mention of the word 'secrets', I shot an uncomfortable glance at Martin – a glance that did not go unnoticed.

'Oh yes, Daff, I know you're keeping something from me,' Simon snarled, pointing an accusing finger. 'Well, from now on, I'm not going to take it! No-one trusts me to do anything, so I'm getting some new friends. Enjoy the rest of your lives, *losers*!'

Then he leapt to his feet, pitched a handful of McDonaldland cookies at us, and stomped away.

'Another go on the whirler, Daff?' Martin said, after a pause.
'Yeah, why not?'

*****

Simon's tantrum ended up lasting much longer than we anticipated. It took a full half hour before he abandoned his search for new mates and returned cheerfully to the fold. As for the topic of the elections and what to do about Andrew McEvoy, it never came up again. We were happy to leave the result to fate, secure in the knowledge that there was only a week to go and very little could happen in such a short space of time. How wrong we turned out to be! More was destined to happen in that one week than occurs in most years of an adult life. Fate, as it turned out, was about to do our dirty work for us, but not before giving us the biggest fright of our lives.

The scare occurred the very next day – on a Monday. It was no ordinary Monday, however. It was House Sports Monday. House sports were taken very seriously at Templestowe Heights Primary. Every child, from grade prep up, was allocated to one of four Houses, imaginatively titled 'Red House', 'Green House', 'Gold House' and 'Blue House.' These Houses competed against each other throughout the year for the honour of holding aloft the much coveted 'House Cup' (a supposedly ancient artifact with the words 'Doncaster Sports Pros' engraved on the handles). Central to this competition was the concept of the 'House point'.

House points were used by our teachers as a means of rewarding students who did well at things. If you did something good, your House received points, and the House with the most points at the end of the year won the House Cup. Points could be accumulated in any one of a million different ways. Chief amongst them were performing well in a test or winning an event on one of the House sports days. You could also pick up points for things like answering questions in class, mastering the complexities of the recorder (the instrument you played when you couldn't play an instrument), or learning to say 'My dog's name is Timmy' in a foreign language.

Even for kids who were pretty much crap at everything, teachers devised special categories of achievement so that they could earn their share of House points too. These took the form of some classic slap-in-the-face awards for those who overcame 'special difficulties' or who excelled at menial tasks, such as picking up litter or packing up their books the fastest at the end of the day.

On paper at least, the House points system was a wonderful educational tool. It provided teachers with an alternative rewards system to grades and gave each and every student the opportunity to be good at something. Unfortunately, the miracle that was House points had one fairly major practical flaw. No-one gave a shit about them.

I was a member of Green House. Despite the best efforts of my teachers to inject a bit of artificial rivalry into the House concept, I couldn't give a flying fuck about Green House, or its eleven-year Cup drought. If Gold House's domination of the school aths day continued into the next century, then good on them. If Blue House thrashed the hell out of us in the swimming sports, then hats off to them too. And if Red House broke into our trophy cabinet, torched our sacred house memorabilia and declared all of Green House dead and conquered, I'd be the first to pull on a red jersey and share a Coke with my new comrades. I just didn't give a stuff, and neither did anyone I knew.

Part of my apathy towards Green House stemmed from the fact that it was hard to feel much sentiment for an organisation named simply after a colour. It wasn't the sort of title you could get fired up about and scream out from the stands, 'Go, Green!', 'Get into it, Green!', *SOCK IT TO 'EM, GREEEEEN!*' It just didn't work.

Even if it had worked and I'd felt the slightest twinge of loyalty towards my House, I still wouldn't have lifted a finger to help it. This was because the House points system itself was a pretty shabby form of currency. The main problem was that there were no fixed House point values for doing particular things. It just depended on who the teacher was giving them out and how that teacher happened to be feeling on the day. The value of a House point was therefore forever shifting and often subject to periods of rampant inflation. Writing a good essay might be worth ten points one day, twenty the next, or two hundred if it happened to mention pixies and Mrs Newport was marking. For this reason, I felt towards House points the way that Russians must feel about roubles. One week you're set to retire on the four hundred you scraped together during aths week, and the next some loser grabs ten thousand for going a day without biting, and your nest egg's been devalued away to nothing.

For all of these reasons, I normally couldn't have cared about the annual aths carnival. That is, until *this* year. This year, I was absolutely *raring* to go. As I sat in Mr Weathershaw's morning class contemplating the day ahead, I reflected with pride on the rigorous training schedule I'd put myself through to be ready for the big day: Stratego games to sharpen the mind, ping-pong to improve the reflexes, swimming lessons for stamina, and countless hours spent sitting on my bed listening to inspirational music. I couldn't have been in better shape!

The point of all of this wasn't to *excel* on the day, but to demonstrate to Jenny that I was a robust physical specimen. You see, as much as women crap on about valuing brain over brawn in a prospective partner, one principle has remained true throughout the ages. *No-one likes a weed*. No matter how kind you are – or how funny – or sensitive – or smart – no matter how many poems you write, flowers you give or Jane Austen films you slog through – if a girl watches you collapse in a wheezing heap after sprinting fifty yards, she's going to start asking herself some serious questions. This was why I'd conditioned myself. This was why I'd done twenty star jumps and a handful of from-the-waist push-ups each day, every day for the past month. I was never going to look like Carl Lewis out there, but at least this way I'd look a little less like *Jerry* Lewis.

After the morning classes were over, everyone went to play lunch, and after that, the rest of the day was sports, sports, sports. It was during play lunch that the trouble began. Martin and I were engrossed in a particularly vitriolic game of downball when Simon came pelting across the basketball courts screaming blue murder.

'Daff, Mart, you'd better come quick. There's trouble at the Log Fort!'

'What do you mean?' Martin replied, deftly flicking the ball with one hand and gesticulating at Simon with the other.

'All our stuff. It's gone. Someone's trashed the place!'

They certainly had. When the three of us arrived breathless at the Fort, we found that the floor of our headquarters had been reduced to a veritable moonscape.

'Oh my God!' Martin exclaimed, dropping to his knees and frantically pawing through the dirt. 'We've been robbed! WE'VE BEEN ROBBED!'

'Forget it, Mart. I've already checked,' Simon assured him, placing a hand on his friend's shoulder. 'Let it go, mate. Let it go.'

But Martin wouldn't let it go. Our normally unflappable leader continued to burrow furiously into the earth, desperately clinging to the belief that our pornographic treasure chest would be found undisturbed. In the end, he had to be physically restrained.

'Who do you reckon took it?' he said finally, after calming down and picking the grit from his fingernails.

'Dunno,' I replied. 'Maybe kids from the Tech School. Maybe a kid from here. Maybe even a teacher!'

'A teacher? Shit! We'll be expelled!'

'No-one *ever* gets expelled,' Simon said authoritatively. 'No matter what you do or how you do it. It's *impossible*.'

'Do you think McEvoy could have done it?' I ventured hesitantly.

'Naaah,' Martin replied. 'How would he have known about it? He wouldn't even know that we hang out here, let alone that we buried a box.'

'Yeah, you're probably right. What about, ummmm...'

And then it hit me.

'Crowler!'

'What?'

'Julian Crowler – the bully. *He* took our stuff!'

'Hang on, Daff. I know he steals things, but why this? How would he have known where to look?'

'Don't you remember? We were in here talking about the act one time and he smashed a kid against the wall. We had the box out and he must have seen it through the window!'

'The *bastard*!' Martin exclaimed, pounding his fist into one of the many mounds of dirt he'd created. 'But why would he wait until now to nick it? That meeting was ages ago.'

'Dunno – the guy's a meathead. Who knows how a brain like that works.'

'Yeah, good point. So what do we do now? Ask him for our stuff back?'

'ARE YOU CRAZY?!' Simon shrieked. 'Go up to Julian Crowler, tell him he's a thief, and then say, "So how's about handing our tin back?" Yeah, that'll work. What do you want me to write *on your tombstones*?'

'C'mon, Sime. He's not *that* bad.'

'Are you kidding? He's the *ultimate* in bad. Remember Matt Pataki – the kid who scratched Julian's BMX? I heard Julian beat him to death with a branch and then buried him underneath the portable classrooms!'

'Mathew Pataki moved to *Perth*, Simon,' Martin said with disdain.

'Yeah, well I haven't got any postcards from him lately. Have *you*?'

With that absurd and yet somehow chilling statement hanging in the air, the three of us settled into an uneasy silence. Clearly, we were never going to ask Julian Crowler for anything. If he wanted to hang onto our porn collection, then he was welcome to it as far as I was concerned. The really frightening prospect was that Julian hadn't taken it at all. What if someone else had dug up our box? What if that same person had looked it over and then handed it in to a teacher? What if, at the very moment we were sitting there worrying about it, Principal Grace Dewhart was leafing through our lingerie catalogues and popping *Debbie Duz Dishes* into her VCR. The mind boggled.

The only thing that stood between me and a complete nervous breakdown was the fact that there was no way of tracing the stuff back to us – other than through fingerprints, of course – but who was going to bother dusting for prints? This was primary school, not *Colombo*. Nope, without any way of linking the contraband to its owners, the T-Birds were safe. It wasn't much of a consolation, but it enabled me to get through the day.

✳✳✳✳✳

Considering it was the middle of winter, the conditions were actually pretty good for a House sports day. The air was crisp, the ground was firm and the sight of all those kids competing was absolutely spectacular. Everywhere you looked there was a sea of colour and motion: blue skies above, green grass below and a multitude of brightly clothed combatants bustling in between.

The first few events were for the junior kids. While the rest of the school watched from the embankment, children as young as six tore around the oval for the glory of their House and the honour of wearing a ribbon. In the old days (i.e. when I was in grade two) only the first three place-getters received ribbons – a blue for first, a red for second, and a green one for finishing third. This was no longer the case. Nowadays, *everyone* received a ribbon, no matter how badly you performed and no matter how many people finished ahead of you.

The idea behind this change of policy must have been this: by awarding every competitor a ribbon, each child would walk away 'feeling like a winner'. Although I could see where teachers were coming from on this one, I have to say that they were sorely mistaken. You don't make a kid a feel like a winner by handing him a bunch of weird-coloured ribbons reminding him that he kept coming second last. Kids, you see, aren't stupid. They recognise that 'good' ribbons mean you are talented and 'bad' ribbons mean you are not. If someone walks by wearing the latter, eleven-year-olds don't think:

'There goes Charlie Watson, good on him for competing!'

They think:

'There goes Charlie Watson, what a frickin' reject!'

You couldn't disguise your ineptitude by stacking your chest with quantity rather than quality. If you were bad at sport, you were bad at sport, and no matter how many pink, puce, or aubergine-coloured ribbons you pasted to yourself, everyone still knew you were unco.

My quest for top-three finishes got off to a bad start. The discus was a disaster. I knew I was in trouble the moment the first competitor stepped up to take his throw. Much to my surprise, he put his hand over the top of the discus, spun around a couple of times and then somehow flicked it out of the back of his hand. I was *never* going to be able to do that. For some dumb reason, I'd always assumed that you held a discus between your thumb and forefinger and then tossed it like a frisbee. It was a horrendous miscalculation and it cost me any chance I might otherwise have had. In three tries, the best I could do was 2.8 metres. It wasn't nearly enough for a place, but it was more than sufficient to earn me a ribbon.

Thankfully, I fared better in the 4 x 100 relay. The key to my success was making sure that I ran the second leg. Not only did this involve the least pressure, but it was also located directly in front of the Blue House supporters, of which Jenny was one. By timing my run correctly, I managed to pour every scrap of energy I had into the thirty or so metres directly in front of her. It was brilliant showmanship! For those thirty metres, I was the fastest kid on the track. I overtook Red

House, I overtook Blue House, I made up some ground on Gold, and as soon as I was out of Jenny's field of vision, I collapsed in a panting heap. My team came last, of course, but what the hell did I care about the team?

As I was warming up for my final event – the high jump – Simon and Martin emerged from amongst a crowd of Red House supporters.

'You're not going to believe this, Daff!' Simon said by way of greeting. 'I just went inside to get a Prima from my bag, and when I got there, Oil Panic was gone!'

'What do you mean, *gone*?' I replied sceptically. 'You mean someone stole it? Are you sure you had it with you?'

'*Of course* I'm sure! I was playing with it this morning, and then I put it into my bag. It's been stolen, alright. Bloody Crowler! He must be cleaning out the whole school!'

'Don't worry, Sime,' Martin smirked. 'I'm sure he'll give it back as soon as he plays it.'

'Piss off, Martin! This is serious. That game was a *Christmas present*!'

Then, as quickly as he came, Simon dashed off to find the Principal, leaving Martin and I alone and shrugging our shoulders.

Once Martin had returned to his Red House buddies, I put Julian Crowler's crime spree out of my mind and concentrated on finding Jenny's face in the crowd. She'd been sitting with some friends while I was running, but I couldn't see her now. Maybe she was off competing in an event somewhere? She was pretty good at sport, I thought to myself, all things considered (and when I say 'all things', I mean considering that she was a girl). Knowing her, she'd probably entered a million different events, so my chances of spotting her amongst the throng were fairly remote. One face that didn't escape my attention, however, was Lucas Tordby's.

I hadn't laid eyes on Lucas since the Sheena Easton debacle. From what I understood, he'd been keeping a pretty low profile. When I saw him on this occasion, Lucas was lumbering down the embankment on his way to the shot-put competition (an event he qualified for automatically because of his size). As he made his way through the crowd, he attracted his usual share of whistles, catcalls and outright abuse. The main target of the mob appeared to be his attire. In addition to a rather figure-hugging Gold House T-shirt, Lucas was wearing one of the tightest pairs of shorts I'd ever seen. They were tiny, they were shrunken, and they'd ridden so far up his crotch, they'd almost disappeared. Leading the chorus of dissent were none other than Alex Trimble and Andrew McEvoy. As always, it was Trimble who did the insulting, while McEvoy just rocked back and laughed.

'Hey, Turd-boy!' he yelled. 'Don't look now, but I think your bum's eating your shorts!'

Lucas's cheeks reddened and the gallery went berserk. Just as Trimble prepared to fire off another salvo, McEvoy abruptly seized him by the arm and motioned for him to be silent. What was this, I thought to myself? Don't tell me Andrew McEvoy had suddenly developed a social conscience? Why would *he* feel sorry for Lucas? There had to be more to it. And there was. McEvoy's actions may have initially seemed confusing, but they made a whole lot more sense when Jenny strode into frame.

She was five metres away from McEvoy and closing fast, her long, brown hair pulled into a sporty ponytail and her royal blue T-shirt covered in an impressive array of ribbons. This was why the abuse had stopped. McEvoy wanted to show Jenny that he was all heart – that he didn't condone teasing or public displays of cruelty. He knew as well as I did that Jenny wouldn't approve of such things. Girls were much too nice for that. If a girl wanted to sledge someone, she wouldn't pick a stranger and she wouldn't do it in public. She'd pick one of her best friends and do it behind her back. Andrew McEvoy appreciated this distinction, and that's why he'd silenced his friend.

The moment Jenny drew level with McEvoy, I crossed my fingers and hoped she'd see through it. She was a smart girl, I reassured myself – smarter than me, and a lot smarter than Andrew McEvoy. She was certainly bright enough to see through a two-bit scam like this. Or was she? As I looked on intently and my fists involuntarily clenched, Jenny stopped, smiled and began what appeared to be a friendly conversation. So much for that theory.

'*You idiot!*' I screamed to myself. 'He's not a nice guy; he's a complete prick! He's evil, he's mean and *his team cheated in the tunnel ball!*'

But my silent raging went unheeded. No matter how much I swore, no matter how much I cursed, their conversation went on regardless. And every time she smiled, every time she giggled at one of his jokes or pushed her hair back behind her ear, in the way a girl does when she likes someone, a little piece of me died.

✷✷✷✷✷

It was with a heavy heart that I trudged off the field that day. My performance in the high jump hadn't been any better than my efforts in the first two events (though I did finish first amongst the kids still using the 'scissor kick'). All up, the day had been a bitter disappointment. I hadn't won any events, Jenny had been all over McEvoy, and I'd somehow injured my foot kicking a grapefruit at Simon. When I crawled into bed that night, the world seemed like a bleak, depressing place. But with the new dawn came new hope. The shit was about to hit the fan, and someone I knew was going to be standing right in front of it.

I realised something was up the moment I walked through the front gate. Everywhere I looked, kids were whispering to each other, gesturing excitedly, and then dashing off towards the back of the school. I didn't want to look like a sheep by rushing off after them. So instead, I walked quickly.

By the time I reached the basketball courts, a sizeable crowd had already developed. There must have been at least forty of them (mostly grade six kids) milling around the back entrance and chattering noisily. The main focus of their attention seemed to be the concrete stairway that led inside, the one that ran past the Principal's office. This could only mean one thing. Someone was in trouble – BIG trouble!

If you committed a misdemeanour at school, you were usually told off by your teacher. If you committed a more serious offence, you might have to stay back after class or write out lines. But the *Principal's office*! Well, that was reserved for crimes against humanity. Once you were inside that room, there was no telling what might happen to you. Violence was customary and human rights violations frequent. Or at least that's what people told me. Desperate to get a handle on things, I went in search of Matthew Hooper.

Matthew Hooper (or 'Hoops' as he liked to be called) was one of Templestowe Heights' most notorious informers. A diminutive, curly haired kid, he could be guaranteed to give you the scoop on almost anything – and if he didn't know the answers, he'd just make them up.

'Hey, Hoops – what's happening?' I said, when I found him chatting quietly with friends.

'It's Andrew McEvoy,' he replied. 'He's a dead man!'

McEvoy, I thought to myself. The Golden Boy? He'd never been in trouble in his life! This couldn't be right.

'Why's he in there? What did he do?'

'Well, you're not going to believe *this*. Yesterday afternoon while we were at the House sports, someone's Game 'n Watch got stolen.'

Yeah, that's right, I thought to myself. It was Simon's.

'And because so much stuff has been nicked lately,' Hoops continued, 'the teachers decided to search everyone's schoolbags to see who'd done it. Guess what they found in *McEvoy's*?'

'The game?'

'Nup! Even better. A *porno*!'

'A porno?' I repeated slowly, my blood turning to ice.

'Yep. He says it isn't his – but that's what they *all* say!'

One of Hoops's companions started chuckling at this point, and I felt as if I was going to be sick.

'So – um – what's going to happen to him?'

'You know – the usual stuff. They're going to send a letter home to his parents and make him write an essay about what he did. He also has to drop out of that SRC thing.'

'*WHAT?!?!*'

'You know – the SRC. That bunch of knobs who . . .'

But I wasn't listening. I was waving Hoops goodbye, clicking my heels together and dancing down the asphalt. This was too good to be true! Simon loses Oil Panic, *Debbie Duz Dishes* turns up in McEvoy's bag, and the end result is that *Daffey wins*! It was just too neat, too perfect, too impossible to believe. It was one of those occasions where you want to pinch yourself to make sure you're not dreaming. Except that I wouldn't have stopped at a pinch. I would have happily driven a nail through my foot, just to be sure.

I was about to skip off to class (and I mean literally *skip*) when the final act in the morning's drama played itself out.

Right on cue, Andrew McEvoy emerged from the office. He looked different from how he did normally. Gone was the arrogant winner I'd come to know so well, and in his place was a snivelling, puffy-eyed child, who'd clearly spent the last twenty minutes bawling his eyes out. Lowering his head and snarling menacingly, he pushed his way through the crowd and tried to make his escape.

The reaction of onlookers was one of respectful silence. No-one wanted to provoke McEvoy or show any sign that they found his predicament amusing. For my part, I managed to stave off laughter by pinching my palm really hard and thinking about *Police Academy*. This worked a treat until I caught sight of Lucas Tordby.

Lucas was skulking in the background looking as timid and innocuous as ever. But as soon as McEvoy had passed him, he smiled guiltily, looked around to make sure no-one was watching, and then dished out one of the most aggressive fingers I'd ever seen. It was too much for me and I burst out laughing almost directly in McEvoy's ear. He turned his head, his eyes met mine, and then all hell broke loose.

'You! You did this!' he shrieked, lunging forward and grabbing me by the shirt. 'I'll kill you. I'll kill you!'

A brief struggle ensued, one of my buttons flew off, and a group of kids had to prize us apart.

'If you had anything to do with this, Daffey – *anything*,' he bawled after me, as he beat his retreat, 'you'll pay! Do you hear me? You'll pay!'

'Yeah, well why don't you come *here* and say that!' I yelled after him (once he was safely out of earshot).

And that, as they say, was that. McEvoy disappeared from view, the crowd slowly dispersed, and a feeling of utter jubilation starting sweeping through my body. Nothing could stop me now! My greatest rival had been destroyed, disgraced, inexplicably wiped from the face of the earth by a stray porno and an angry Principal. He obviously hadn't stolen the tape himself (or else why would he blame me?) but that little fact wasn't going to help him. Somehow or other, it must have gone from Crowler to McEvoy. How or why this occurred, I had no idea; but I simply didn't care. All that mattered was that Chris Daffey was back on track! Next Monday, I'd blitz in the elections. The following week, I'd dazzle them with my acting skills. And some time after that, Jenny would see all the trouble I had gone to, and ask me to go out with her. That much I considered certain.

As I made my way to class, I recalled the wise words of my grandfather many years earlier. The old guy had been right after all. Just when things are at their worst and all looks lost – BAM! – something comes out of the blue and you're saved. If only I'd paid attention to what he'd said next. Because in two days time, I wouldn't be worth two bob.

It's time for a bit of a history lesson about Templestowe Heights' most fearsome character . . .

The mean streets of Lower Templestowe

JULIAN CROWLER WAS a large child. Not large enough to be considered fat, but fat enough to be considered large. At five feet three inches, he towered above your average sixth grader and represented the kind of shambling, slow-witted menace that no primary school could be without. As broad as a tumble dryer and with a personality to match, if you stuck shorts and a T-shirt on a sack of medicine balls and painted a lopsided smile somewhere near the top, even his own mother would struggle to pick him in a line-up. In a poll conducted at the beginning of grade six, Julian Crowler was voted the second most frightening sight in the playground. Julian Crowler eating a meat pie was voted the first.

Unfortunately for Julian, his intimidating combination of

graceless bulk and mind-numbing stupidity left him with very few vocational options in primary school society. He was too chunky for an athlete and lacked the necessary hand–eye coordination for the sporting set. He didn't have the smouldering good looks or social graces to gain entry into the popular crowd, and lacked the style and imagination to pull off brooding rebel. He was about ninety IQ points shy of hanging out with the school intelligentsia and, since his idea of humour centred around watching big bugs eat small bugs, 'class funnyman' was also out of the question. If schoolyard occupations were advertised in the classifieds section, Julian would have to thumb his way through a great number of pages before stumbling across something he was qualified to do. It is easy to imagine his stubby little fingers pawing their way through the paper for hours, before finally circling the following ad in red texta:

WANTED – FIGUREHEAD OF MENACE
If you're sick of people calling you names and you'd like to make money out of hurting them, THIS IS THE JOB FOR YOU!

Starved of career opportunities, hamstrung by some of the bleakest genetic material to find its way into a homo sapiens, Julian Crowler had little choice but to become a bully.

Life as a bully was not a difficult one for Julian. If he wanted something, he'd just ask for it. If he didn't get it, he'd punch you in the face and then take it. If Julian had grown up in a Sicilian village, he would have been known as the 'Simple Don'.

For the victims of Julian's standover regime, there was precious little they could do. In a long list of useless remedial measures, parental advice was easily the worst. Mothers in particular held an insane belief that bullies (being troubled children in need of understanding) could simply be reasoned with. This little theory ignored one, fairly obvious, fact – that bullies probably wouldn't have become bullies in the first place if they'd favoured 'talking things out' as their preferred dispute resolution mechanism. It is quite possible that no child in history has staved off an impending blow by putting up his hands and saying, 'Listen, we can talk about this.'

Television, a dubious source of information at the best of times, was equally misleading when it came to dealing with bullies. If TV taught us anything, it was that bullies are all hot air and bluster and that one good punch on the nose or other show of defiance would instantly transform them into repentant, blubbing cowards. How untrue this was. As far as I could tell, bullies only got to be bullies because they were strong, relatively fearless and pretty handy with a Totem Tennis racquet. On the rare occasions that someone summoned up the courage to fling an ungainly blow in Julian's direction, he would exclaim,

'Oooo, we got us a fighter,'

and then systematically kick the shit out of them.

For most of his time at primary school, Julian was the lone wolf of the bullying world. Suspicious and distrusting of everyone, he kept entirely to himself, except for occasional forays into the playground to drum up business. Although he seemed content enough with the pleasure of his own company, he must have secretly longed for just one friend – someone with whom he could share the highs, the lows, and the other lows of being a social pariah. A companion, a soul mate, a compatriot. As Julian embarked on his grade five year, that compatriot presented itself in the form of Nathan Hathaway.

Nathan was known at school as 'the Gibbon', in part for his resemblance to a small woodlands ape, but mostly for the time he painted his arse red and mooned Mrs Kaufman. The Gibbon was a wiry, energetic creature with an unrivalled capacity to annoy and a penchant for torturing insects. They met one afternoon when Julian bent down to observe the Gibbon roasting a community of slaters with a magnifying glass. Intrigued by the senseless carnage, Julian sank down on his haunches and settled in for the show. As four generations of slaters were fast-tracked to that big collection of rocks in the sky, a bond of some description began to develop. Within a week, they were inseparable.

With his boundless energy and ability to form complete sentences, the Gibbon was the perfect choice as Julian's right-hand man. His first major initiative was to modernise and streamline Julian's entire operation. He quickly put an end to the ad hoc targeting of victims and drew up a comprehensive list of easily intimidated children. He then convinced Julian that it would be better to minimise the need for actual violence. Drawing upon tactics he'd seen employed by door-knocking Mormons, the Gibbon decided that he would do all the talking and 'negotiating', while Julian would stand silently in the foreground and play the part of 'mute threat'.

The final step in reorganising Julian's business was to acknowledge the fact that Julian and the Gibbon were now a team. In much the same way as bikers who suddenly feel the need to buy themselves a clubhouse and splash out on matching monogrammed jackets, Julian and the Gibbon decided to become a 'gang'. They named themselves the 'Jubbins' and adopted the slogan 'give us all your money or we'll rip your fuckin' nuts off'. It wasn't exactly catchy, but it had the desired effect.

The Jubbins were the first recognised gang to hit Templestowe Heights Primary. As such, they were accorded a type of celebrity status and whipped up a considerable amount of enthusiasm for the whole 'gang' concept. So much so that it suddenly became vogue to be a gang member. The birth of the Jubbins spawned an enormous collection of ridiculously unnecessary organisations, such as:

- the 'Pencils' (for people who liked drawing);
- the 'Footies' (a bunch of guys who played football); and
- the 'Mr Eds' (a group of girls who braided each other's hair and traded pictures of horses).

Last, and quite possibly least, came the 'T-Birds'.

The T-birds were born on the third day of June in our grade five year. Our first meeting was held inside the Log Fort. Within minutes of officially opening the meeting, Martin elected himself leader, I was awarded the post of second-in-command, and Simon was designated as 'rank and file'. In a stroke of genius, Martin invented the concept of 'limited membership' and immediately applied it to Simon. In a nutshell, it meant that Simon couldn't qualify as a full member of his own friendship group until he'd completed a series of humiliating and often dangerous initiation tasks.

It is an everlasting credit to Simon that he managed to avoid being killed during the first month of the T-Birds' existence. In addition to a demanding public performance schedule involving a great deal of singing and a fair amount of nakedness, Simon was often required to demonstrate his T-Bird-worthiness by climbing on top of tall structures and then hanging off them upside-down. This little manoeuvre was popularly known as a 'roast turkey'. For twenty successive lunchtimes, Simon performed countless roast turkeys and other death-defying feats for the amusement of his peers and in the hope of earning full membership. Initially, Martin and I had no real intention of ever granting him that right. We figured it'd be more entertaining to just keep raising the level of the bar until he gave up or died trying. But even for children with a seemingly endless capacity for cruelty, there came a time where we simply ran out of ideas. Exactly thirty-two days after the T-Birds came into being, Simon Bartholomew Jackson became its third fully-fledged member. It was a mistake we would live to regret.

Once the golden age of Simon's initiation was over, the T-Birds struggled to find themselves a purpose. Other than occasionally whipping out compasses and scratching our motif (a big 'T') onto desks, there were precious few gang-related activities to conduct. Morale was low, membership was stagnant and Simon's ill-conceived 'Trixie Belden' stand at the school fete had decimated what was left of our tough-guy image.

For a time, we dabbled with the idea of revitalising the gang through the adoption of an aggressive motto, such as 'death from above'. This seemed to help for about two days. During that time we repeatedly climbed onto tables, screamed out 'death from above' to disinterested passers-by, and then leapt onto the ground brandishing hot dogs. It soon became obvious that the only people we were scaring were ourselves.

Bored, restless and dispirited, the T-Birds appeared destined to fade into obscurity. That is, until a sunny July afternoon almost a year later – when a vintage example of Simon's incompetence breathed new life into its ranks.

✳ ✳ ✳ ✳ ✳

The three of us were sitting on a bench enjoying our cut lunches. It was a glorious day for the middle of winter and we were all in glorious moods. Two days had passed since McEvoy had withdrawn from the elections, and my friends were as excited about his demise as I was. Simon, in particular, had received the news well. When I'd first told him about it, he'd leapt around the place shouting and hollering as if he'd just won Tattslotto. Then, for some odd reason, his mood changed. He still looked happy – there was no doubt about that. But he also looked worried – extremely worried. At the time, I put it down to superstition. A good thing had happened, so Simon was naturally concerned that a bad thing was just around the corner.

If my friend was worried, he certainly wasn't showing it on this particular day. The reason had to do with a girl. Simon, as was his custom, had arbitrarily determined that he was in love with Kylie Hewitt. Kylie was a tall, striking, blonde girl who was, to put it mildly, way out of Simon's dating league. This was no real disincentive to my friend, since *every* girl he'd ever liked was way out of his dating league.

Simon's preferred method of alienating women he was infatuated with was to perform a ritualistic 'love dance' around them during lunchtime. Although this tactic had never worked in the past, he was keen to try his hand with Kylie. He spotted her strolling with a group of friends along the northern basketball courts. Within a blink of the eye, he was up off the bench, fifty metres away, and launching himself into one of his routines. It was agonising to watch. As Kylie held her face in her hands and begged him to go away, Simon performed an impressively complex little jig around her while continuously chanting the words,

'Kylie, Kylie, why wontcha go with me, Kylie?'

In a less tolerant, more heavily armed society, someone would have shot him.

Simon's dance that day was identical in virtually all respects to every other woefully embarrassing dance he'd performed over the years – with one catastrophic exception. As his act wound its way to its frightening climax (in which Simon would shriek his victim's name one final time and then drop to his knees), Simon became dizzy, span out of control and then trod on the Gibbon. And with that one hopelessly incompetent act, he dragged us all into Templestowe Heights' first, and last, gangland war.

'Geez! What happened to *you*?' Martin exclaimed, when a tearful, dishevelled Simon returned to the bench some ten minutes later.

'D . . . didn't you see?' he replied feebly.

'See what? Your stupid dance? Yeah, we saw it. I don't know what goes through your head when you do stuff like that, Simon. I really don't.'

'No – not the dance,' Simon stuttered. 'The bit after it.'

'Nup. What happened? And how come you're all messed up? What's the matter?'

'Well,' he began glumly, wiping his nose with the back of his arm and sniffing loudly, 'it was going okay at first and I think Kylie was really into it. But then I tripped and fell over. And when I hit the ground, I crashed into (sniff) . . . I crashed into *the Gibbon*!'

'Shit!' Martin and I exclaimed in unison. 'Did you say sorry?' 'Was Crowler there?' 'Did he accept your apology?'

Our questions poured out in a rush. Simon didn't answer them at first. He just stood there nodding and shaking his head in the exact opposite order we were hoping for.

'Bloody hell, Sime!' I said finally. 'So what did they say? What are they going to do to you?'

'Um, well, at first I tried to look really tough and everything,' he spluttered, 'you know, in front of Kylie. But then Julian picked me up off the ground, and I panicked!'

'So did he hit you? Are they going to beat you up?'

Simon looked particularly sheepish when asked this question. Lowering his head and looking up at us with guilty eyes, he replied, 'The Gibbon said I was going to have to pay for what I'd done. He said that the Jubbins didn't like clumsy people, and that clumsy people had to fight them in the sandpit. He said they'd be waiting for me tomorrow at lunchtime, and if I didn't turn up, they'd come and get me!' This dramatic admission was followed by a lengthy pause. 'And then he asked . . . if I had any friends or was part of a gang who could help in the fight.'

And suddenly Simon's problem was *our* problem.

'And what did you say, Sime?' Martin demanded, leaping to his feet. 'You said no, right? You said you were a pathetic, useless loser who had no mates at all and wasn't part of any gang. Didn't you, Sime? Tell us that's what you said, Sime!'

If we'd been sitting in an American courtroom, Simon Jackson would have pleaded the Fifth. He quivered, he trembled and then he whispered in the smallest, most timid voice imaginable:

'*I said I was a T-Bird.*'

There. He'd done it. He'd damned us all.

Martin and I were understandably horrified. As far as we were concerned, the T-Birds were only a 'gang' in the sense that the Salvation Army was an 'army'. We looked like a gang, we spoke like a gang, we claimed to *be* a gang, but at the end of the day fighting just wasn't our business. Concerned about what might happen to us, we called an emergency meeting to discuss a means of averting the crisis.

At first, we considered simply expelling Simon from the T-Birds and trying to avoid conflict that way. This idea was dismissed on the basis that, while this tactic might be enough to confuse Julian (who, after all, was often perplexed by the sight of his own reflection), the Gibbon couldn't be duped quite so easily.

We then gave serious consideration to beating Simon up ourselves and throwing him into the sandpit as a kind of 'peace offering'. We were all set to go with this plan until I pointed out that attacking one of our own members in order to save ourselves might, if you looked at it from a certain angle, appear cowardly. Though it pained him to do so, Martin reluctantly agreed. It suddenly became obvious to all three of us that there were no quick fixes to our dilemma – no ingenious short cuts, no easy answers.

'There's nothing else for it,' Martin said defiantly. '*We*

fight!' Then he drove a stick into the ground, pushed out his chin and crossed his arms manfully, before adding, 'Or even better, we quit school.'

Quitting school was a great plan on paper. We'd never see a teacher again, never have to worry about homework and we wouldn't get killed tomorrow. When you looked at it like that, it was hard to mount an argument against it. Amazingly enough, our parents managed to.

We tried to persuade them that the educations we were receiving were pretty ordinary anyway, and that we'd be better off tossing them in and forming a roving band of freelance detectives (who'd travel the country solving mysteries, in much the same way that Scooby Doo did). Although they didn't object much to the first part of this analysis, it was the second half of the plan that proved the real sticking point. With the Scooby solution effectively scuttled, our only option was to fess up and tell our parents about the fight. In other words, we had no options.

As we crawled into bed that night, we could only hope that God would see fit to intervene and save us from certain death. Given our track record in RE, the smart money was on God shafting us.

✶✶✶✶✶

The next day began like any other for the T-Birds. We got up, we ate sugar balls masquerading as some type of wheat derivative, and we prepared ourselves for the car ride to school. Unlike most days, however, that preparation involved throwing a few left jabs at the mirror, the endless repetition of motivational phrases such as 'fear is your best friend, Rocky', and the placement of cricket boxes in our underpants (in case the Jubbins went for the nurries). It wasn't exactly a world title fight standard build-up, but it was the best we could do.

On a morning that otherwise didn't show a lot of promise, there was at least one pleasant surprise awaiting us at school. As we gingerly entered the front gate, we noticed that students from all walks of primary school life seemed to be smiling at us or giving us the thumbs up. Apparently, the grade six rumour mill had been working overtime and everyone now knew about our upcoming clash with the Jubbins. In the space of twenty-four hours, we'd become schoolyard celebrities and achieved a level of fame not seen since mad John Distasio coated himself in Clag and tried to glue himself to the Principal. Throughout the morning, guys and girls came up to us, shook our hands and passed on heartfelt words of encouragement. At first, we were a little embarrassed by all the attention, but after a while we really began to suck it up. Like puffed-up miniature Churchills, we strode around the school pumping our little fists and flashing V for victory signals. If we didn't deserve to get beaten up before, we certainly did now.

Somehow or other we'd become symbols of hope and courage in the face of oppressive tyranny. We were heroes; we were icons; we were brave warriors fighting the good fight against overwhelming odds – we were none of these things and worse, but we lapped it up anyway. By the time the bell rang signalling lunchtime, all three of us had started to believe our own press. It was time to get out there and strike a blow for the little guy.

✻✻✻✻✻

'Are we going to die, Mart?' I asked, as we strode our way to the sandpit. 'I mean, they couldn't kill us, could they? They'd be expelled for sure!'

'I dunno, Daff. Remember what happened to Matthew Pataki?'

'I thought you said he moved to Perth?'

'Yeah. Well, now I'm not so sure.'

'If something did happen to you, Daff,' Simon interjected, 'and don't take this the wrong way or anything, what would happen to your Atari?'

Martin and I turned around to face our friend and glared at him angrily.

'Hey, I was just asking!'

As we neared the pit's entrance, Simon peeled off to take his place amongst the assembled throng of onlookers. We had, of course, made the decision to exclude Simon from the fight on the grounds of gross ineptitude. At first, Martin and I had argued about the merits of having him in the pit with us. Martin thought he might be of some value if we sent him in first. He explained that it was just like sending in a nightwatchman in cricket. In all likelihood he would be dealt with harshly and dismissed quickly, but if he landed a few punches or tired them out in the process, it'd be a bonus. In the end, we scrapped the idea because we were afraid that the sight of Simon getting comprehensively flogged might embarrass us in front of our fans. Besides, there was the distinct possibility that he would fall down in front of the Jubbins and blub for mercy, and we couldn't have that. If anyone was going to shamelessly plead for our lives, it would be us.

When we arrived at the sandpit, Martin and I took a few moments to take in the scene. The school actually had a number of sandpits, but when someone mentioned THE sandpit in the context of violent confrontation, everyone knew which one they were talking about. It was about ten feet wide and twenty feet long and was surrounded by jagged walls made out of rock. You could see the structure from the other side of the school and you could smell it from twice that distance. Not known for its pleasing aroma, it was dubbed the 'stink pit' by many in recognition of the fact that more people pissed in it each day than would visit the toilet block in a week.

In terms of its suitability as a sporting stadium, the pit was low on player comforts but high on spectator amenities. Fightgoers could perch themselves on top of its stone walls and enjoy their cut lunches, while combatants beat the crap out of each other in the pungent arena below. The enclosed, thunderdome-esque shape of the pit gave it a terrifying, biblical feel. If the

Christians ever came up against the lions in a modern gladiatorial league, this venue would surely be chosen for an away game.

I had always hoped to make it through primary school without ever having to front up to the pit. As Martin and I walked through its arched entrance to the hysterical applause of our supporters, I kissed that dream goodbye.

'You know, Daff, I've always thought of you as my best mate,' Martin said, as we stepped inside.

'Gee, thanks, Mart. Same here. Um, why did you bring that up now?'

'No reason,' he said. 'No reason.'

The Jubbins were there to greet us as we entered. Relaxed and seemingly blasé about the whole thing, they leaned against the opposite wall of the pit and waved at us with a mindless cheer that reminded me of teenagers in Coke ads. Despite the casual demeanour of the Jubbins, the overall atmosphere in the pit was eerily similar to that of a WWF wrestling bout. A self-nominated referee-cum-ringmaster began by introducing the competitors and reciting a brief summation of their brawling credentials. If that little comparison wasn't demoralising enough, each team was then given the opportunity to address the crowd and engage in a bit of pre-match posturing.

Martin pulled off a great impression of a brave person and spouted some crap about appearing on behalf of everyone to defend the T-Bird name. It was pretty ballsy stuff really – especially considering that the T-Bird name was about to be torn into little pieces and rammed up our respective arses.

In response to Martin's bold but hollow words, the Gibbon told us both to fuck off, gave everyone the finger, and then handed the spotlight over to Julian. Like a performing orangutan, Julian loped along the walls of the pit flexing his blubber at everyone and making a series of threatening gestures. Once he'd completed a couple of laps, he returned to his end of the pit, pointed a flabby finger in our direction, and then farted at us. He was quite the showman.

The preliminaries now complete, the referee called the crowd to order and officially pronounced the fight open. Martin and I had no real idea of what to do at that point and just stood there staring at our opponents, like guppy fish waiting to be harvested. The Jubbins, on the other hand, knew exactly what they were doing. Adhering to their standard fight procedure, the Gibbon came at us first, while Julian stayed back and threw scabs at the crowd.

The Gibbon wasn't much of a fighter. His basic methodology was to deliver a wild flurry of blows in all directions in the hope that he'd occasionally hit something. It never worked, but it didn't have to. No matter how poorly the Gibbon performed in the opening minutes, the Jubbins could always rely on the sixty-two kilogram insurance policy waiting in the wings.

'I'll take him head on,' Martin barked, as the Gibbon came out punching. 'You try and flank him.'

'Righto,' I said, putting up my dukes and inching sideways along the wall.

Martin and the Gibbon met in the centre of the sandpit. It was a violent clash, but not a skilful one. As the Gibbon rained down a series of ineffectual blows, Martin shielded himself with his arms and waited for his chance. When he sensed his opponent was tiring, he struck.

The punch that felled the Gibbon that day wasn't even a great one. In fact, it wasn't even a punch. It was a *slap*. A clumsy, open-handed wallop that caught the Gibbon on the hop and sent him sprawling to the ground. Martin was shocked, the crowd was ecstatic, and I finished off the job by jumping on top of him and ramming his face into the sand. At the exact moment that the Gibbon's head met earth, our audience went strangely silent. Julian Crowler had stirred, and Armageddon was upon us.

Recognising that I wasn't much of a threat, Julian decided to deal with Martin first and began to advance in his direction. Martin responded by bringing his hands up in front of his face and adopting a classic karate stance. This was a bold and dangerous ploy. Feigning knowledge of martial arts was a tactic usually employed by weak children in the hope of intimidating more powerful adversaries. As far as I knew, it only ever resulted in a volley of abuse along the lines of,

'No, stop it – you're scaring me, Mr Miyagi!',

followed by a severe beating using conventional means. On this occasion, Julian decided to dispense with the insults and go straight for the beating.

Martin, however, was ready for him. In line with our pre-determined battle plans, Martin threw his left hand high in the air to distract his adversary, while his right fist made a beeline for Julian's testes. All our plans hinged on this decisive blow. As Martin's clenched hand plowed into Julian's crotch, I heard a noise that will haunt me for the rest of my life – the dull, lifeless thud of flesh against plastic. My jaw dropped and Martin's eyes nearly popped out of their sockets. We weren't the only ones who'd thought of cricket boxes!

That was pretty much it for us really. We never planned beyond disabling Julian with a well-timed ball-burster, and with his nurries tucked safely away, there wasn't much we could do to hurt him. Julian found the whole thing hilarious and began to laugh in Martin's face. It was deep, resonant 'MAW HAW HAW' kind of laughter, and I began to wonder whether it was the school bully we were fighting, or the bad guy from *Inspector Gadget*.

Once his mirth had subsided, Julian grabbed Martin by the hair, muttered, 'Bye bye, Birdy', and then punched his nose off. Well, not quite all the way off – but it was suddenly a lot closer to his left ear than it had been moments before. As Martin's hands ranged across his face to make sure he still had one, the crowd 'ooooed' with a disturbing blend of horror and amusement.

Afraid that Martin was about to be killed, I released the Gibbon and jumped at Julian's back, hoping somehow to pull him to the ground – but he heard me coming, and sent me careering off into a wall with a well-executed sweep of his arm. It was at this point I discovered just how fickle fans can be. Whereas moments ago the crowd was at least *trying* to hide its excitement, the sight of my body flying through the air like a hookey ring prompted a full-on round of applause. The Jubbins may have been the bad guys, but they were also gifted entertainers!

With the wind knocked out of me and showing no signs of returning any time soon, I could do little more than watch as Julian casually dispensed with Martin and began lumbering towards me. He paused for a moment to step over the Gibbon (who was still lying on the ground picking sand out of his nose) before launching himself gleefully into the air and crashing heavily onto my chest. The crowd hushed in anticipation and a number of our former backers yelled out, 'Finish him!' It was at this precise moment that a miracle almost occurred. Displaying courage that was as much a mystery to himself as it was to those who knew him, Simon pushed his way through the cheering masses on top of the wall, screamed out, 'DEATH FROM ABOVE!' and prepared to leap to our rescue.

It should have been a crowning achievement in an otherwise unremarkable life. It should have been one of those fabled 'nerd proves his mettle in a time of crisis' moments. It should have been Simon Bartholomew Jackson's coup de grâce. But when God takes a newborn in his arms and stamps 'screw up' on its forehead, a child's fate is sealed. As our would-be saviour propelled himself into the air, his foot caught on Brett

Thompson's Family Tree House and he stumbled headfirst towards the sand below.

In terms of manufacturing a safe and successful landing, Houston never had a problem as big as this one. Despite flailing his arms wildly, Simon did little to alter his pin-drop trajectory and ploughed skull first into the ground at a frightening speed. It was death from above, but not in the way that he might have hoped. Our rescue bid foiled and Simon presumed dead or dying, Julian returned to the task of terminating my life.

Things at this point looked pretty grim. Martin had been beaten up, Simon had beaten himself up, and I was *about* to be beaten up. It was not a flattering scorecard. I was almost ready to resign myself to death, having lived a long, rich and fulfilling life, when it occurred to me that none of those things were the least bit true. I'd lived a short, poor and empty life, in which the highlights so far were getting Castle Greyskull for Christmas and seeing Andrea Scarper's underpants. There had to be more than that. They were good underpants, but there had to be more. Summoning all of my remaining energy and whatever strength I could muster, I drew my fist back and punched Julian as hard as I could in the throat. He responded by opening his eyes wide, making a hideous gurgling sound, and then collapsing like an old person on a hot day.

It would have been neater if the skirmish had ended there. If the curtains had closed on the sight of yet another Goliath biting the dust at the hands of an unlikely and fairly unethical

David. But like every cheap horror film ever made, the Jubbins had at least one surprise comeback left in them. After Julian hit the ground frothing and the initial euphoria surrounding his demise had died down, I leaned close to his contorted face and asked him if he was alright.

Schoolyard etiquette dictated that such a question had to be asked whenever someone was hurt, no matter how severe the injury, and no matter how rhetorical the question seemed. If a child was beaten senseless, sliced in half, squashed flat, scraped off the ground, pushed through a cheese grater and then set on fire, you'd still get a group of twenty children clustered around the resultant substance anxiously inquiring whether it was okay.

It was in this spirit that my question was delivered – more out of robotic habit than genuine concern. When Julian heard me, he decided that the question was best answered by giving me a very accurate picture of how he was feeling. As my face drew near to his, his left arm shot out, wrapped itself around my neck and began throttling me to death! If he couldn't win the fight, he was at least going to get himself a nil-all draw.

For the next few moments, my life hung in the balance. Julian squeezed my neck like he was trying to wring water from a chicken, and the only response I could think of was to choke him right back. Normally, I would have easily lost such a contest. But Julian was not himself. The blow to his throat was clearly troubling him and the tighter I held him, the less strength he seemed to have. Just as I reached the point where

I felt I could go on no longer, Julian did something completely unexpected. He started to plead. Although I may have been hallucinating (and considering my brain hadn't tasted oxygen for at least two minutes, that's not entirely out of the question), I could have sworn that his beady little eyes were begging for mercy.

At first, I just ignored him. You don't get to Number One Primary School Headkicker without a few tricks up your sleeve, I reasoned. This was obviously one of them. But as the seconds ticked by and I moved dangerously close to passing out, two distinct thoughts occurred to me:

(1) Mercy was preferable to suicide; and
(2) Maybe Julian was more afraid of losing this fight than I was.

From my perspective, a loss wouldn't mean much at all. I'd still walk away from the contest a hero, having weathered the Jubbins storm and even scored a surprise knockdown with an illegal blow to the larynx. For Julian, however, a loss would be catastrophic. Beating people up was this kid's claim to fame. If he couldn't knock over a couple of lightweights like Martin and myself, what sort of a bully was he? That was the question everyone would be asking as soon as the fight was over. Julian Crowler *had* to win. This was his job, his livelihood, his very reason for existence. Looking down at his gasping face, he didn't even look that mean anymore – just a chunky, frightened child who was about to lose everything he had. There was nothing else for it. I was going to have to let him go.

Relaxing my hands slightly, I pulled away a bit and waited for his reaction. He didn't respond immediately, but after a second or two, I got the reply I was looking for. He smiled! It wasn't much of a smile, mind you. More of a twisted grimace, really. But it was a smile nonetheless, and it signified that Julian Crowler was grateful! Happy, relieved, and satisfied that I'd done the right thing, I relaxed my hold completely and smiled back. Just long enough for him to punch me in the teeth.

Crime and punishment

THERE WAS SOMETHING really exciting about being in trouble at school. There was something exhilarating about knowing that you'd done a bad thing, and that other people were upset about it. Or at least there was when you were in grade six. When you were that age, getting in trouble was like a badge of honour. Falling foul of the authorities was a way of proving your courage, of testing your nerve, of introducing yourself to the school community:

> 'Hi. My name's Chris. I'm the guy who wrote "dick" on the blackboard.'

Since my friends and I didn't actually *get* into that much trouble at school, we had to make the most of the opportunities that came our way. We had to bask in the glory of rebelliousness while we had the chance. And that's precisely what Martin, Simon and I were doing on the morning after the fight. Sitting on a bench outside the Principal's office, we did our best to savour the moment.

※ ※ ※ ※ ※

The bench was a kind of 'parking bay' for children awaiting punishment. If the Principal wasn't ready to shout at you yet, you were given fifteen or so minutes to sit in the corridor and reflect on your crimes. The three of us hadn't been doing much in the way of reflection since we'd arrived. This was because we didn't expect to get punished. We were, after all, the Good Guys in this conflict. If anyone deserved to be punished, it was the Jubbins. They were the ones who'd arranged the whole thing. They were the guys with the reputation for fighting, stealing, and making rude noises during the national anthem. We were just innocent victims.

Although we weren't feeling the least bit repentant (in fact, quite the opposite), we were doing our best to make it look that way. The Principal's office was only three doors up from the staffroom. This meant there was a steady stream of teachers moving past us on their way to get coffees and bitch about their day. In that sort of environment, it paid to look remorseful. If we appeared the least bit blasé, if we showed even the slightest sign that sitting outside the Principal's office wasn't the harrowing experience it was supposed to be, someone might take offence. That was the last thing we needed. So instead of relaxing, we tried hard to look concerned. We stared at the floor, we ran our fingers through our hair, and Simon rubbed spit into his eyes to make it look like he'd been crying.

Not surprisingly, this got pretty boring after a while, so to pass the time, we focused our minds on different things. For me, it was cartoons. Cartoons were a big part of my life in grade six. Although I was past the age where 6 a.m. starts to catch reruns of *The Hair Bear Bunch* were the norm, I still got up early on Saturday mornings to watch the children's show marathons. There were millions of different cartoons I watched during these marathons, ranging from the great, to the average, to the downright terrible. As I sat there waiting for the Principal, I had a think about all three.

The first thing that popped into my head was how much I hated *The Smurfs*. I didn't mind the figurines so much (which you could buy with a tank of petrol from BP service stations) but I hated the show. *The Smurfs* fell into a category I liked to think of as 'girls' cartoons' – fluffy, insubstantial pieces of nonsense, with no genuine conflict and no fistfights with space mutants. A typical plot of a girl's cartoon like *The Smurfs* went something like this:

'Oh no! Someone's stolen the enchanted turnip! However shall we get it back?'

It was scintillating stuff.

The most annoying aspect of *The Smurfs*, however, wasn't the plots. It was the dialogue. For some dumb reason, the characters spoke in their own special 'smurf language'. This language happened to be identical to English, except for one minor detail: every now and then, and for no apparent reason, they'd replace a normal word with the word 'smurf', like:

'The car's broken down. I think there's a problem with the smurf.'

or

'Bill went out smurfing last night, and I think he's got a smurfover.'

It's hard to explain just how much this annoyed me. In some ways, however, I viewed it as a missed opportunity. With a little bit of tinkering, *The Smurfs* could have been my favourite show on TV. All they had to do was chuck out all the boring dialogue they normally used, and replace it with something that *all* kids found funny – swearing! If only Papa Smurf had said things like:

'Get smurfed!'

'Smurf off!'

or

'Why don't you ram it up your smurf, you mother-smurfing smurfhole!'

Now *there* was a program with potential.

One rung up from girls' cartoons were a group of programs that can loosely be described as 'comedies' (loosely, in the sense that, although they weren't funny, I can't think of any other point to them). These shows typically revolved around 'zany' families or talking animals; shows like *Secret Squirell*, *Magilla Gorilla*, *Quickdraw McGraw* or *The Jetsons*. I didn't think much of programs like these, though I did have a soft spot for *Wacky Races*.

So I didn't like girls' shows and I didn't like comedies. What I did like, however, was superheroes. Superman, Spiderman, Space Ghost, G-Force, Blue Falcon and the Dynomutt Dog Wonder – I watched them all. The great thing about these characters was that there were no limits to the creators' imaginations. They could dream up any old superhero, with all sorts of ridiculous abilities and powers, and kids like me would swallow it. Take Birdman for example.

Birdman was a winged, hawk-like superhero who could fly, shoot lasers, and who drew all his energy from the 'power of the yellow sun'. Helping Birdman out in his adventures was a giant eagle named 'Avenger', who was famous for going '*rarrk!*'

Although I worshipped this show with a passion, it did have its flaws. Since Birdman relied on direct sunlight for his powers, he suffered from the same sort of limitations as a solar-powered calculator. When it was sunny, he was good. When it was overcast, he was average. All the bad guys had to do to knock him out completely was drag him indoors or throw a tarpaulin over him. As soon as the lights went out, so did Birdman.

Largely because of these limitations, the plot of each episode tended to be exactly the same:

1. Birdman confronts villain.
2. Villain deprives Birdman of sunlight.
3. Birdman summons Avenger, who yells 'rarrk!' and then drags his master back into the sun.
4. Birdman kicks arse.

Which begs the question, why didn't the bad guys just wait until it was dark, and then beat the crap out of him?

Birdman was just one of many ridiculous superheroes that populated my cartoon world. And as I sat there that morning (waiting for the Principal to finish doing whatever it is that Principals do in their offices), I thought about them all. I considered them, I analysed them, I weighed and I ranked them, until finally I found that I was boring even myself. Just as I was about to move on to big-screen adaptations, a voice shattered the calm.

'The Principal's ready to see you now, boys,' one of the office staff said.

Gulp. Now I really *was* nervous.

※※※※※

Grace Dewhart had been the Principal of Templestowe Heights for as long as anyone could remember. She was a good Principal, most people seemed to agree: relaxed, patient, friendly almost, in an authoritarian kind of way. She must have been in her forties by the time I was in grade six, but it was hard to tell. Like many educators, she had a strange 'ageless' quality about her, which placed her anywhere between thirty-eight and five hundred. She wasn't a tall woman, but she wasn't particularly short either. She had warm, pleasant features, wore warm, pleasant clothes, and did her hair up in one of those permanent, 'can't be budged' perms (designed to survive anything from a thermo-nuclear blast down). I hadn't had much to do with Mrs Dewhart in my years at school. What I had seen, however, gave me hope for a fair hearing.

She was sitting at her desk when we entered, calmly sifting through some papers and arranging a pile in front of her.

'Thanks for coming to see me, boys' she said without looking up. 'I presume the three of you have some idea why I've called you here?'

'Yes, Mrs Dewhart,' we murmured together, before Martin cleared his throat and took over.

'We got into a fight yesterday with Julian Crowler and Nathan Hathaway, and we expect you want to see us about that.'

'Hmmm,' said Mrs Dewhart, looking at each of us in turn and then studying one of the pieces of paper.

'Yes, that's right. I've already spoken to the other boys about it. Julian didn't say much, but Nathan was quite forthcoming. He claims, among other things,' she said, pausing and reading from her notes, 'that the fight occurred because of an incident earlier in the week between Simon and Nathan. That Simon approached Nathan, started teasing him, and then attacked him for no reason . . .'

'*What?*' Simon gasped.

'... that the three of you are members of a gang; that this gang is known for brutalising other students; that you are Neo-Nazis; that you carry knives; and that Martin here knows karate. Is any of this true?'

Incredulous, open-mouthed silence was quickly followed by an angry rush of denials:

'That's bullcrap!' Simon spat.

'Complete bullcrap!' I repeated.

'He's a lying little ... he's a *liar*!' spluttered Martin, unable to come up with a G-rated term of derision.

Mrs Dewhart regarded us sternly and searched our faces for the truth.

'I expected as much,' she said finally, screwing up her notes and tossing them into a wastepaper basket.

'Nathan has a certain – er, how shall I put this – *reputation* when it comes to making such claims. You're not the first group of Neo-Nazis that Nathan has been attacked by – if you get my meaning.'

We nodded our heads with relief.

'Nevertheless,' she continued, 'no matter who started it, or how it came about, you should never resort to fighting. I won't have people using violence to settle disputes at my school. Is that clear?'

'Yes, Mrs Dewhart,' we said dutifully.

It was at about this point that all worries left me. Everything was going exactly as I'd expected. The truth had come out, the bad guys had been identified, and we'd received a crappy little lecture about the evils of using your fists (which, by the sounds of it, *Mrs Dewhart* didn't even believe). We'd got into what you might call the 'perfect' amount of trouble: just enough to give us some much needed street-cred, but not quite enough to attract any real consequences. It was turning out so well, I started to wish I'd been beaten up *earlier* in the year.

So confident was I that the danger period has passed, that it came as quite a shock when Mrs Dewhart said, 'Now, had this fight of yours been an isolated incident, I think I would have let you off lightly. Unfortunately, that is not the case.'

I stopped congratulating myself and bit down hard on my swollen lower lip.

'Christopher,' she said, 'I had a visit yesterday from Mrs Kaufman, your art teacher.'

Uh oh.

'She explained to me that since the beginning of term three last year, you've refused to bring your smock to class and have resisted all reasonable attempts to persuade you to do so. Is this true?'

'I can explain, Mrs Dewhart,' I replied instinctively.

'Good,' she said, crossing her arms. 'Let's hear it.'

I couldn't explain, of course. What possible reason was there? I don't have one? My dog ate it? The wearing of smocks offends my religious principles? None of these was going to wash.

'I, um . . .' I stuttered, hoping that an explanation would present itself halfway through the sentence, '. . . keep forgetting it.'

'Right. That's it? That's your explanation?'

'Yes. Yes, it is.'

'Well, I'm afraid that's not quite good enough, Chris. Of itself, refusing to wear a smock is a small thing. But when you combine it with this fighting incident and, er, certain other matters, it begins to add up. Which brings me to the main reason you're here.'

Main reason? You mean punching and half-choking a kid to death in full view of the entire school wasn't the *main* reason we were there? Shit!

'What I'm really concerned about is *this*,' she said ominously, pulling a book-sized object out of a drawer and waving it accusingly in our faces.

And there it was. Jangling around only a few feet from our noses was *Debbie Duz Dishes*: the porno that had been stolen from the Log Fort; the time bomb that had been ticking away for months; 120 minutes of pure, unadulterated expulsion.

I tried to keep calm, but my nerves betrayed me. Trembling like a leaf and struggling to retain control of my facial muscles, I shot a glance at my friends to see if they were faring any better. They weren't. Martin was rapidly turning eleven different shades of green, and Simon looked like he'd just swallowed an elk. They weren't going to need a polygraph for this one.

'As you may be aware,' Mrs Dewhart continued, placing the

tape on the desk in front of us, 'this tape was found in Andrew McEvoy's schoolbag a few days ago, along with a cigarette lighter and some cigarettes. At first, he denied that any of these things were his, but later admitted to owning everything but the tape. For this offence alone, I sent a letter home to his parents, got him to stay back after class, and asked him to withdraw his nomination for the SRC. I also, at the time, presumed that the tape was his. That is, until I made a certain discovery yesterday afternoon.'

She paused momentarily to let this last fact sink in.

'Now, I'm going to ask you a question and I expect an honest answer. Do any of you know anything about this tape?'

Silence.

'Christopher? Simon? Martin? I'll ask you a second time. DO ANY OF YOU KNOW ANYTHING ABOUT THIS TAPE?'

'No, Mrs Dewhart,' we murmured guiltily.

'Really?' she said, sighing, 'Well how do you explain this?'

Picking up the tape again, she slipped it out of its cardboard sleeve and then pulled the mouth of the sleeve open, so we could see inside. Sure enough, running along the back of the sleeve, in a darkened place you could only just make out, was a long, purple label marked:

'PROPERTY OF SIMON, MARTIN AND DAFF.'

This was going to be hard to come back from.

'*You labelled it?!?*' Martin screamed at Simon, before he could stop himself. '*You IDIOT!*'

I wheeled around and glared at my friend, demanding an explanation. But Simon just looked away and stared at his feet.

'I guess that answers that then,' Mrs Dewhart observed grimly.

I guess it did.

The rest of the meeting was an absolute horror show. Mrs Dewhart explained to us that she didn't care how the tape got into Andrew's bag; that she didn't care whether we'd put it there, whether he'd taken it from us, or whether we were all in cahoots together. What she *did* care about was that the tape was originally ours and that we lied about it. In light of this, and taking into account our part in the brawl and the whole smock saga, Judge Dewhart handed down the following sentence:

1. that letters would be sent home to our parents;
2. that we would have to sit apart in class;
3. that my nomination for the SRC would be withdrawn; and
4. that our performance next week would be cancelled, in favour of individual acts at the beginning of next term. (The last thing she wanted to do was risk the three of us 'on stage together'.)

When I protested that the last of these measures was particularly harsh, and that we'd put a lot of work into our act and would never think of another one, she said simply, 'That's easily fixed. Martin, you can do a talk. Simon, you can read out a poem. And Chris . . . why don't you have a go at a song.'

Great. Glad I asked.

As utterly devastating as these punishments were, it should be said that Mrs Dewhart wasn't a cruel woman. She couldn't have known that she was systematically destroying two terms' worth of work. She could never have guessed that by punishing me in this way, she was effectively tearing out my heart and then slapping me in the face with it. In her mind, she was just being fair. When a group of kids starts misbehaving and getting into fights, teachers always do the same thing. They send a letter to home to their parents and then they separate them as much as they can. This was all she'd done. Which isn't to say I didn't hate her for it. Thanks to her, my parents were going to kill me, I was out of the elections, and the rest of grade six was going to be exposed to my vocal chords. The nightmare that had been stalking me all year was now only a hair's breath away. Lucas Tordby, here I come.

*****

The remainder of term two was just one kick in the nuts after another. First, there was my parent's response to the letter. When I told Dad that I'd been in a fight, his reaction was the same as any typical Australian father. He frowned, he told me off, and then he asked if I got any good shots in. When he read that I'd been kicked out of the SRC for bringing an X-rated movie to school, he was a little less accommodating.

'What? Is this right? Did *you* do this? *What the hell do you have to say for yourself, Son?!?*'

There was no point beating around the bush with someone like Dad. I had to be adult about it. The situation demanded nothing less than a full and frank confession.

'It wasn't mine and I didn't have anything to do with it. It was *Simon!*'

Pointing the finger at my friend took a little bit of the edge off Dad's anger, but it didn't do much for Mum's. For weeks afterward, she badgered me about the incident and kept repeating how shocked and disappointed she was. Even Pop tried to get his two cents in (or should I say, 'two farthings') when he found out I was in trouble. He told me that fighting should be reserved for animals and Liberal backbenchers, and that no decent human being should have any part of it. No-one told him about the video, of course. Pop and the subject of pornography were two things that should never exist together in the same room – like matter and anti-matter. If someone had raised the topic with him, I think he would have just blipped out of existence. There'd be a bang, a blinding flash, and then all you'd have left would be a puff of smoke and a pair of hearing aids.

Simon seemed to fare similarly in the punishment stakes, but it was Martin who really seemed to suffer. He said that his mum burst into tears when he told her and didn't speak to him for days. When we asked how his dad reacted, Martin just looked really sad and turned away. We took this to mean he reacted badly.

After all the fuss at home came the elections. In true, democratic fashion, all votes for the SRC were cast by 'secret ballot' (which meant that you wrote it down on a piece of paper, placed it in a special, tamper-proof box, and then told as many people you could think of who you just voted for). Even before the results were announced, I had a fair idea who was going to win.

Jenny romped away with the top spot, polling the most number of votes overall, and Rachel Klimp managed to hang on to second. In something of a boilover, the third position went to Mitch Greenley, who (in a clever piece of spin doctoring) had changed his campaign slogan from '*Save* the Northern Bandicoot!' to '*Long live* the Northern Bandicoot!' It was champagne politics, and the electorate was obviously impressed.

Hearing Mitch's name read out at assembly was hard to stomach. If it hadn't have been for *Debbie Duz Dishes*, it might have been *my* name that was up in lights. Then again, if we hadn't brought the tape to school in the first place, Andrew McEvoy would have remained in the race – and he would have kicked *both* of our arses.

No-one was more acutely aware of this fact than Andrew himself. When the winning candidates were announced, he eyeballed me from the second row and made threatening gestures with his hands. Evidently, he still blamed me for his disqualification. He probably also blamed me for losing his chance with Jenny (who now seemed to regard him as some sort of sex-craved pervert). All this blame was based on suspicion alone, of course. He didn't *know* that the tape had originally belonged to the T-Birds. He wasn't aware that Julian Crowler had stolen it from us and then inexplicably dumped it into his schoolbag. He just knew that *someone* had planted it on him and that the most likely candidate was *me*. Thankfully, Mrs Dewhart hadn't gone public with the details of the tape's ownership. As far as anyone knew, I'd been forced out of the elections for my part in the brawl. This suited me fine. If the truth ever did come out, Jenny would loathe me instead of McEvoy, and McEvoy's suspicions would harden into stone-cold certainty. That prospect didn't bear thinking about.

If I felt slightly robbed when Mitch took my place in the SRC, then I felt absolutely fleeced when Terrance Wheldon took Broadway by storm with his hilarious play about *Dr Who*.

When Simon, Martin and I were told to abandon our act and prepare for individual performances at the beginning of next term, Spenda was left out in the cold. As the innocent party in all of this, he was given the option of postponing his act as well, or going ahead with it as scheduled. He chose the latter option. He chose to take our idea, tweak it a little bit, and turn it into a Liza Minelli-esque, all-singing, all-dancing, one-man show in celebration of himself. It was brilliant!

The key idea he latched onto was that there was no funnier topic at school than *him*. Although his act was loosely based around *Dr Who*, the real focus was self-ridicule. He made fun of New Zealanders, he gently mocked the English, and for the first time in his life, the masses embraced him. They giggled at his costume, they roared when he said 'Cor blimey!', and they went absolutely *mad* when he rode in on a foam sheep, yelling,

'Tally ho, chups – let's blast these buggers to Blighty!'

I have no doubt that the first words to come out of Spenda's mouth when he eventually returned to England would have been, 'Back in Australia, I was the funniest kud in school!'

For once, he might actually have had a point.

The only vaguely positive thing to come out of the end of term two was that the Jubbins didn't kill us. Once the fall-out from the fight was over, I was afraid that my enemies would simply lie low for a day or two and then finish the job they'd started. To my grateful surprise, the Jubbins instead decided to view the outcome of the brawl as a type of 'honourable draw'. Rather than regarding us as a continuing threat to their supremacy in need of urgent quashing, we were accorded the status of 'worthy and brave opponents'.

This outlook stemmed largely from the fact that the brawl had actually enhanced Julian's status as a fighter. Although his ability to crush opponents had never been called into question, no-one had seen how he'd react when the chips were down. Many had even speculated that maybe – just maybe – TV was right after all, and that one good punch in the throat would be the end of him. Our fight put a stop to all that. It proved once and for all that Julian was (to quote from the Gibbon's post-match press conference) 'A fierce, never-say-die warrior, who'd prefer to pass out choking his enemies, than to lose in a sandpit showdown!'

A few days and some treatment for a bruised larynx later, it was business as usual for the Jubbins.

I had cause to reflect on all of this as I stood near the bag racks on the last day of term. I'd just stormed out of the multi-purpose room in disgust, having witnessed the first screening of Stuart Lund's bio-epic, *Small Packages*. The scene I was supposed to be in had been cut at the last minute and replaced with a still-screen shot of Stuart playing backgammon.

'If that doesn't just take the cake,' I muttered to myself angrily, pulling open my schoolbag and venting my frustrations on a Cheestik. I'd just managed to tear the stick into six separate cheddar portions when the rest of grade six started exiting the room. Leading the way was Jenny.

She looked almost regal that afternoon – with her hair pulled back and an SRC badge pinned proudly to her chest – and I felt humbled in her presence. As she passed by, our eyes met briefly and she shot me one of those 'hello, person I recognise' smiles. It wasn't a great smile by any standards. Certainly not a patch on the one that had bewitched me almost a year ago. But it was enough to remind me of what was at stake.

Sure, I'd been kicked out of the elections. Granted, my act had been stolen, the school bully had punched me out, and my theatrical debut had ended up on the cutting-room floor. But so what? What did it matter if I had to sing in front of the entire school? Who cared if Andrew McEvoy thought I'd framed him and would stop at nothing to get even? They were small things, all of them – minor setbacks in the pursuit of a much greater goal.

I still had one term left, and plenty of time to win back that smile.

Mr Dribbles Goes Bananas

TERM THREE BEGAN full of promise. The sun was out, the weather was warming up, and the September holidays had been an absolute ripper (Number One Highlight: my next-door neighbour, Tom 'friend to the animals' Sharkey, was bitten by a red-back spider and had to spend two days in hospital; which wouldn't have been too funny if he'd died, but was pretty funny given that he didn't). If this wasn't reason enough for joy, I still had one more treat left in store. On the first day of term, my mum was on canteen.

The canteen was a wondrous institution when you were eleven. It was staffed by mothers and sold a variety of things that you could buy with your pocket money. In summer, you could get stuff like fruit and sandwiches, and in winter you could buy hot food, like pies and sausage rolls.

The one thing you couldn't get much of at the canteen was snack food. Snack food had been driven from the canteen shelves by government initiatives such as the 'Munch 'n' Crunch' campaign. Like many similar initiatives, the Munch 'n' Crunch campaign was dedicated to convincing kids that healthy food was just as nice as junk food and, more importantly, *just as cool*. So, instead of a little box with the word 'sultanas' on it, they'd have a little box with a *picture* of a sultana on it. And then they'd put a little hat on the sultana; and then give him a little cane; and then have him dance all over the box shouting slogans like 'Hey dude!', 'What's happenin' man?' and 'Sultanas rock!' Just how dumb did they think kids were?

Having said all that, there were *some* nice things you could get at the canteen. In the 'so close to lollies they may as well have been' department, you had things like honey logs and apricot squares, as well as the classic primary school snack food – the Sunny Boy (along with its lesser known cousins, the Funny Face and the Zooper Dooper). There was also a full range of Samboy potato chips, including my all-time favourite flavour, Samboy Gold – an extra-salty variety that came in a shiny gold packet and which I don't think exists anymore.

The one downside of being able to buy all these treats was what happened when you tried to eat them. The moment your food came out, so did the 'scummers'. Scummers were the scourge of the schoolyard. They were sly, they were devious, they usually hunted in packs, and they were *always* after your chips.

'Caaarn, how about a chip? Give us a chip. Just a couple of chips? How 'bout a Bacon Ring? C'mon, *just one little Bacon Ring?*'

It wouldn't have been so bad if the scummers were actually in need of food or didn't have their own snacks. But they did – they just ate them before you did or hid them for later. The only proven defence against the scummer was to rip open your packet of chips and spit all over them. This, however, was something of a 'scorched earth' policy. Saliva-drenched snacks were only marginally more appetising to the owner of the spit than they were to the scummer. But like many things in life, it was a matter of principle.

On this particular day, my friends and I managed to evade the scummers. We purchased our food, we moved away quickly, and then we raced to the Log Fort (where we were safe from prying eyes). Once there, we sat down on the clay floor and enjoyed our bounty in silence; until Simon complained that he'd found a real piece of apricot in his apricot square.

'Hey, guys! Check this out!' he said with disgust, pulling a fibrous piece of fruit from an otherwise homogenous lump of sugar. 'Bloody Munch 'n' Crunch campaign!'

'You reckon *that's* gross,' Martin countered. 'Yesterday Dave Turnball found a whole mouse head in his pie!'

'You're kidding?' I exclaimed. '*Another one!* That's unbelievable.'

A little too unbelievable, I think. If primary school kids were to be believed, Australian pie companies spent more time catching mice to put in their pies than they did on any other corporate activity. Every second day you'd get some kid swearing black and blue that he'd found such-and-such piece of vermin floating in amongst the gravy. You never saw the evidence, of course. But each story was believed without question.

Once we'd scoffed our meals, we abandoned the Log Fort and ventured out into the sunshine, taking up places as extra fielders in a bat-for-ball cricket game. When Simon put down one of the easiest catches I've ever seen (causing him to lose his temper and everyone else to laugh their heads off), Martin turned to me and said, 'We'd better enjoy this game while we can, Daff – 'cause you know what we've got after lunch.'

I shuddered at the thought of it. On the other side of the lunchtime bell was the terrifying Mrs Quong.

*****

Mrs Quong, it's fair to say, was a tyrant. She was about two feet high (give or take my ability to exaggerate), weighed about eight grams and had a voice that could bore through steel. In peacetime, she worked as a part-time dance instructor whose job it was to prepare students for their end of year balls. In wartime, however, I'm convinced she would have been one of those insane, scream-in-your-face drill sergeants (like the guy who made Richard Gere's life hell in *An Officer and a Gentleman*). I can just picture her standing on my toes and shrieking,

> 'YOU – USELESS – PIECE – OF – NO – GOOD – SCUM, DAFFEY! You call that a twirl? Now get down on the floor and give me fifty!'

Everyone was afraid of her. Even the teachers. Mr Weathershaw had a particular aversion to her, which was compounded by the fact that she insisted on referring to him as 'Mr Wilberforce' (no matter how clearly he introduced himself, and no matter how many times he corrected her).

Mrs Quong's classes weren't so much about the art of dance as they were about military precision. Students were paired up, given some tightly choreographed moves, and then forced to parade up and down in front of her, like Russians celebrating May Day. We may not have scored too many points in the grace department, but we were ready to invade Czechoslovakia at a moment's notice.

As frightening as Mrs Quong was, she wasn't the worst aspect of dancing classes. The worst aspect was having a *partner*. Up until then, the only dancing any of us had done was in Mrs Newport's discos. This type of dancing involved neither skill nor interaction with others. In my case, for example, it just meant standing on my own and 'slow-motion jogging' (a style which served me well for the next twenty years). Dancing with a girl was a whole different ball game. For a start, you had to hold hands. This was bad enough in the best of circumstances, but was particularly humiliating if the girl you were partnered with was:

(a) some sort of 'loser' (which meant that touching her was considered shameful); or
(b) really attractive and popular (in which case, it was her embarrassment at having to touch you that did the damage).

Which brings me to biggest issue of all – the selection of partners.

At this early stage, the selection process was random. Each lesson, you danced with a different girl, and sometimes, you danced with more than one girl during the same class. Sooner or later, however, these random partners would be replaced by permanent ones. These were the people that you'd dance with at the end of year Ball. These were the girls you'd have to practice with, week in, week out, for the rest of term three. Given the gravity of the situation, the selection process was always going to be tricky.

You obviously couldn't let kids choose their own partners. This would be just like picking cricket teams all over again, except much worse. Nor could you use standard selection procedures, such as numbering off or standing people in lines. These measures were open to abuse, and the last thing you wanted was twenty-five kids all swearing they were 'number two'. To avoid problems like this, teachers went with height, pure and simple. If you were 130 centimetres tall and Debbie 'no, it's a beauty spot' Watson was 130.1, then the odds were Debbie was your woman.

The height system was designed to reduce prejudice and prevent kids from being cruel. Predictably, it didn't. As soon as the scheme was announced, there was a rash of enquiries about the proportions of Templestowe Heights' least eligible singles. How tall was this girl? How tall was that girl? Would you mind turning round and standing back-to-back with me? Everyone at school was obsessed with who they might get, and my friends and I were no exception. The moment Mrs Quong gave us a break from dancing, this was where our conversation turned.

'This system's *so* unfair!' Simon moaned, as he leant against the multi-purpose room wall. 'I mean, it's not right that you just get stuck with someone. What if I get a girl that *you* really want, Daff, and you get a girl that *I* really want? We should be able to trade 'em. Like footy cards!'

'Maybe we could flick them as well?' I replied, laughing to myself and imagining a group of boys tossing their dates against a wall to see who got closest.

'Daff, do you promise that if I get someone I don't want, you'll swap with me?'

'No, I don't promise.'

'But what if I get someone really awful? Like Tabatha Grobtook?'

'What makes you think *I'd* want her? Anyway, there's much worse than Tabatha Grobtook.'

'Yeah, like who?'

'Like Julie Greene for a start.'

'God, yeah.'

'Or Arli Jones.'

'Shit!'

'Or Tiffany Chilvers. Or Sally Cousins. Or that girl from Queensland who only eats eggs!'

'Stop it, Daff. You're scaring me!' Simon shrieked.

'Hang on, boys,' Martin interrupted. 'I've got one for you. How'd you like to wrap your arms around... DONNA GOBBO?'

'GROSSSSSSSS!' we exclaimed together, clutching our stomachs and feigning illness.

Funnily enough, it never occurred to us that these girls might feel the same way; that at the precise moment we were discussing *them*, they were probably having exactly the same discussion about *us*.

'Imagine getting Martin Timms!'

'Or Simon Jackson!'

'Or what about that dork, *Chris Daffey*? God, I think I'd puke!'

We just always assumed that we were the Good Catches, swimming around in a sea full of bad ones.

*****

As daunting as dancing classes were, they were quickly overshadowed by a far greater menace. After six months of worrying about it, my act was finally upon me.

A good deal of my September holidays had been spent agonising over song selection. Just what is a kid supposed to sing when he can't hum a bar or hold a tune and has to impress both his girlfriend and a merciless, bloodthirsty mob? Not *Old Man River*, that's for goddamn sure! Serious songs and tear-jerking ballads were definitely off the list; as were contemporary hits and hard-rock classics. What was needed was a song that wasn't a song at all; something I could basically speak my way through and get away with; a tune that was both simple and yet somehow entertaining. Finding such a song wasn't going to be easy.

For a time, I toyed with the idea of singing a medley of popular schoolyard rhymes. I could open with the classic –

Jingle bells,

Batman smells,

Robin flew away,

Wonder Woman lost her bosoms,

Flying TAA.

Oi!

Follow this up with the amusing but cautionary tale of Nick and his forty-foot dick –

My friend Nick

Had a forty-foot dick,

He showed it to the girl next door,

> She thought it was a snake,
> Hit it with a rake,
> Now it's only four foot four!

And then bring it all home with a rousing rendition of *Popeye the Sailor Man* –

> I'm Popeye the sailor man,
> I live in a dunny can,
> There's a hole in the middle,
> Where I do my piddle,
> I'm Popeye the sailor man,
> *Toot toot!*

It was a wonderful idea, but to be honest, I just didn't have the balls. I was in enough trouble already with the whole *Debbie Duz Dishes* thing, and the last thing I needed was controversy.

It wasn't until the end of the holidays that the idea finally hit me – television theme songs! It was the perfect combination of cornball pop culture and recognisable tune. And what more recognisable tune was there than *Gilligan's Island*? It was short, it was punchy, it didn't have any challenging notes, and it would convey the distinct impression that I wasn't taking my singing career too seriously. It couldn't lose. Or could it? I certainly didn't think so at the time. After two weeks of religiously practising it, I went to Martin's house to record the backing track.

✸✸✸✸✸

Martin's house was located only a couple of streets away from the school. It was a smallish house, with a big, open-air garage and a massive grevillea right out the front. They'd only been in it for six months, having moved from what I always thought was a much better house a few blocks up the road. There were five Timms in all: Martin, his dad, his mum, an older sister who I almost never saw, and an enormous, red-eyed bloodhound called 'Mr Dribbles' (named for his two-litre a day drooling habit). When I arrived, the first thing we did was play with the dog.

'Watch this, Daff,' Martin enthused, dancing around Mr Dribbles and waving a long, metal tube in his face. 'He hates the bike pump!'

Martin demonstrated this point by raising the pump above his head and squirting it furiously. Mr Dribbles responded with a series of loud, cavernous barks and a frenzied attempt to drown Martin's sneakers.

'He doesn't like any type of machine at all, Mr Dribbles,' Martin said earnestly. 'Doesn't like the noises they make. Mum says he has really sensitive ears.'

Mr Dribbles barked approvingly.

'They're a weird breed, the bloodhound,' Martin continued. 'Did you know that in Switzerland they tie these special barrels around their necks? And when people get lost in the snow, the dogs dig them up and bring them beers!'

I crinkled my face up sceptically. 'Really? I thought that was St Bernards?'

'No,' Martin replied, shaking his head. 'It's definitely the bloodhound.'

The two of us reflected on this thought for a moment, before tossing the pump onto the couch and switching on the TV.

The reason I'd gone to Martin's house to get the music was that he was one of the few people I knew who had a tape machine you could record with. It wasn't much to look at, but it had a microphone that you could plug into the side and speak into. Just before *Gilligan's Island* was due to come on, we sticky-taped the microphone to the TV and pressed play/record.

'The quality's going to be shocking, Daff,' Martin observed, as the theme song started up.

'That's okay, Mart. So's my singing.'

With the tape recorder happily whirring away, the two of us left the living room and headed for the backyard. There were still a couple of hours of light left, and my friend was keen to try out his new Tim the Bird.

Tim the Bird was the single best toy I ever played with at school. It was the only toy I can remember that not only *lived up to*, but actually *exceeded* the claims made on the box. My childhood was filled with the bitter memories of toys that promised big but delivered small – water pistols that were guaranteed to shoot twenty metres, but that barely got past the length of your arm; motorised four-wheel drives that not only couldn't cross rivers, but failed to negotiate plush-pile carpet; rubber-tipped darts that had more chance of earning a law degree than sticking to a cardboard target. Tim the Bird was different. He actually worked.

To look at, Tim wasn't that special. He was about a foot long, made of white plastic, and had a pair of flimsy, paper-thin wings (which you could get in black, blue, or red and yellow). Although his appearance was unspectacular, Tim's internal workings must have been one of the modern wonders of the world. All you had to do was wind this key thing on the side and the little champion *actually flew*! And not just a few feet, either. If you turned the key hard enough, Tim would soar into the air and flap around for ages.

Tim's mastery of the sky made him a must-buy toy – but it also spelt his downfall. The problem was that Tim the Bird worked *too* well. You'd wind him up, launch him into the air, and then watch him arc majestically across the yard, over the fence and out of your life. I must have gone through at least fifty Tim the Birds during my childhood – each one sent on an epic journey from which he never returned. The funny thing was, though, no matter how many birds my friends and I sent hurtling out of our yards, none ever found their way back. They simply disappeared. Like pens, sunglasses and umbrellas, everyone seemed to lose them and yet no-one seemed to find them.

I didn't give this phenomenon much thought at first – but as my losses started racking up, I began to have my suspicions. I started to believe that Tim the Bird was a much more sophisticated toy than I'd ever imagined, that whoever constructed this toy, secretly programmed him to fly up into the air, away from his owner, and all the way back to the Mattel factory – to be re-boxed, relabelled and sold to another unsuspecting child. I know it sounds insane, but if I'm wrong, then where the hell did they all go?

Martin's new Tim the Bird was no more resilient than the others. He wound it up, he let it go, and then he watched it sail off towards the coast. Once the two of us were satisfied that he was definitely lost, we kicked a soccer ball around for a while and then trudged back inside.

'You'd better check to see if the tape worked,' Martin said gloomily, as he sat himself down on the couch. I rewound the cassette and hit play. The first grainy bars of *Gilligan's Island* filled the room.

'Bingo!' I exclaimed, hitting the stop button.

'Aren't you going to make sure that it worked all the way through? You wouldn't want it to cut out in the middle.'

'Yeah, you're right. Good point.'

I fast forwarded the tape for a while and pressed play, just in time to catch the words '... the Professor and Mary AAAAnn ...'

'Done!' I said with finality, ejecting the tape and slipping it into my pocket.

Having successfully completed my backing track, I started looking around the room for something else to do. Just as my eyes fell upon an old copy of Scrabble, I heard the sound of a car pulling up.

'Hey, Mart. Someone's home,' I said cheerfully. 'Will that be your mum or your dad?'

'That'll be Mum,' Martin replied, peering out the window and looking unusually anxious.

'Well, when your dad gets home, promise that you'll ask for a ride in his new car. You've been saying that you would for ages and he's never . . .'

'WOULD YOU STOP HASSLING ME ABOUT THAT, DAFF!' Martin exploded suddenly. 'Go for a ride in your *own* dad's car, why don't you!'

I stared at my friend in shock. Martin *never* got angry with me!

'Anyway,' he continued, in a slightly friendlier tone, 'isn't your mum supposed to pick you up soon?'

I pulled up my sleeve and looked at my watch.

'Yeah, you're right. I'll go call her.'

❋❋❋❋❋

For the first few weeks of term three, I remained convinced that I was on a winner with *Gilligan's Island*. Despite a strange, nagging voice in the back of my head and the occasional misgivings of friends, I didn't doubt myself once. *My act was going to succeed!* I learnt the words, practised it in the shower and looked forward to the day that I'd unleash it on the world. So confident was I that the song would do well that I never once bothered rehearsing it with the backing track. The tune was easy to remember, after all, and I didn't want my performance to sound 'stale'.

Martin's and Simon's acts slipped by without incident (Martin giving a talk about horseracing and Simon bumbling his way through a poem) and this only increased my confidence. In fact, I continued to think that *Gilligan's Island* was a brilliant idea right up until the moment I stepped onto the stage; right up until the exact second that I took the microphone in my hand, saw the crowd looking up at me, and realised what I was about to do. It was at this point that the nagging voice piped up and said,

'Nice one, loser. What the *fuck* were you thinking?'

All of grade six had gathered in the multi-purpose room that day – just as they'd done six months before, when Lucas Tordby had disgraced himself. Memories of that event flashed through my mind as I stood there waiting for the music. My predicament had suddenly become very clear. I was standing in front of my peers and about to sing a terrible, goofy rhyme about a show that almost everyone hated. I wasn't going to succeed. I was going to suck, and suck *big time*!

'Okay, children, a bit of shush please,' Mrs Newport instructed, as I took my place behind her.

'Please put your hands together and show your appreciation for today's act – *Christopher Daffey*!'

Lukewarm applause filled the room and a sea of eyes alighted upon my terrified face.

I caught sight of Jenny sitting somewhere near the back

and I felt myself wince. I didn't want her to see this. I didn't want *anyone* to see this. As the first muffled notes of *Gilligan's Island* rang out across the room, I opened my mouth and hoped for a miracle.

'Just sit right back . . .'

A look of surprise crossed the faces of the audience.

'And you'll hear a tale . . .'

Surprise turned to bewilderment and bewilderment to concern.

'A tale of a fateful trip . . .'

Concern was swiftly replaced by an expression that looked like the beginnings of laughter. They held back for the moment, however. They smiled, they beamed, they grinned and they smirked, but no-one actually giggled. I had no idea why this was, and it somehow made it more frightening. What were they waiting for? Why weren't they laughing yet? Couldn't they just put me out of my misery? And then it hit me. Oh my God, I thought to myself. They're waiting for the punchline. They're waiting for the joke. Everyone thinks this is a send up, and they're waiting for me to say something funny!

'The mate was a . . .'

This, apparently, was the audience's signal to give up hope. There wasn't any punchline. There wasn't any joke. I hadn't changed the lyrics or done anything clever. I hadn't somehow tweaked the words to make it more interesting. I had, in fact, chosen to sing the song exactly as it had been written – without change, without embellishment, and without any attempt to reduce its corniness. I saw Jenny trying to suppress a giggle. I saw Andrew McEvoy trying to suppress nothing. I saw Simon cover his ears, Martin cover his eyes, and Lucas Tordby quivering in the corner like a bowl of jelly. I saw it all.

Under the pressure of imminent laughter, my voice began to crack. Where once there was a steady, if somewhat toneless, patter, there was now a shrill and unpleasant squeak. It had almost trailed away to nothing when something entirely unexpected happened. Just as the SS *Minnow* was about to hit rough seas, the backing tape exploded into a maelstrom of growls and static. At first I thought it was broken, but then the music returned. Then it went away again; and then it returned. What the hell was going on? Some strange and incredibly loud noise was blaring over the top of my backing track – a noise that was at once totally foreign, and yet at the same time oddly familiar. I flubbed my way through the next line before realising what was wrong. I knew what that sound was. It was Mr Dribbles!

The stupid dog must have gone berserk at the noise of the tape recorder and barked the whole way through! As soon as the audience cottoned onto the fact that it was a dog barking (and not some boring, technical problem), the laughs came thick and fast. I was a goner.

I tried to keep singing, but it was virtually impossible. My voice was now competing with one hundred hysterical children and the world's angriest bloodhound. My eyes darted frantically around the room searching for some sort of escape hatch, and I began to wish I had one of those cyanide pills they hand out to spies. Then I spotted Martin.

Unlike the rest of the crowd, Martin wasn't laughing. He was gesticulating wildly with his hands and mouthing words at me. It was hard to make out what he was saying, but it looked like he wanted me to do something. He was... he was... telling me to laugh!

In hindsight, it was this inspirational piece of quick thinking that saved me from utter annihilation – that spared me from having to switch schools or change my name or wear some sort of disguise. Without Martin's last-ditch intervention, my childhood would have been permanently marred.

It didn't come easily at first. I was confused, I was scared, and the last thing I felt like doing was having a good hard cack. As the seconds ticked by, however, I began to see the sense of it: laugh along; go with the crowd; pretend I'm in on it! It was brilliant. By the time the castaways had hit the beach, I was laughing as hard as any of them.

In the end, it was left to Mr Dribbles to finish off the vocals. When the song hit its final triumphant note, Martin's dog actually started to howl, and I leapt from the stage like a man who'd just beaten death row.

'Great song, Daff,' someone said, as I sat myself down on the carpet.

'You sucked me in bad,' said another. 'For a moment there, I thought you were serious!'

It was hard to believe that people actually thought I was in on it. After all, what sort of person plans to walk on stage, sing the *Gilligan's Island* theme, and then have it deliberately ruined by the sound of a barking dog? Sounds nuts, doesn't it? Well, it does until you consider the alternative. What sort of person plans to walk on stage, sing the *Gilligan's Island* theme, and then *not* have it deliberately ruined by the sound of a barking dog? Me, obviously. But who'd have believed it?

14

It's ALL about hAiR

THE LIST OF dancing partners was posted in the multi-purpose room on the fifth Friday of term. Getting near enough to read it was damn near impossible. Packed between the doorway and the noticeboard was a writhing mass of students, all struggling against each other in a desperate battle to discover their fate. Standing anxiously on the periphery of this crush were Martin, Simon and me.

'I'm not sure I can do it,' I shouted above the noise. 'I mean, it's so sudden death!'

'I know what you mean, Daff,' said Martin. 'That's why *you guys* are going first. Buzz third!'

'Buzz second!' I blurted out.

'Buzz se . . . ! Oh, come on, no way!' Simon protested. 'I wasn't ready. It's not fair. I don't want to go first!'

Martin and I shrugged our shoulders and pointed towards

the noticeboard. No matter how much Simon bitched about it, there was just no getting round the International Rules of Buzz.

If either Martin or myself had tried to push our way to the front, it would have taken us ages. Simon Jackson, on the other hand, knew neither shame nor social convention. Launching himself into the throng, he began nudging, pushing, pulling, bumping and hacking his way through the crowd like a Russian matriarch scrapping for the last fish at market. He knocked into Matt Stein; he elbowed Graeme Koop; and when he got near the front, he placed his hands in the small of Michelle Smart's back and then shoved her aside like a sack of cement. When Michelle regained her footing and looked around for the perpetrator, my friend shook his head sympathetically and gestured towards Robert Frank. He was a hard kid to like, Simon Jackson. But you had to respect him.

Once he'd arrived at the board, Simon began a ridiculous process of elimination. Moving his head rapidly from side to side, he scoured the girls' names for his list of 'worst cases' and then mentally started ticking them off. It took a full five minutes before he worked up the courage to scan for his own name. Running his finger down the E–K section, he mouthed the word 'Jackson' over and over again until his finger finally stopped dead. *This* was the moment of truth.

Martin and I craned our heads forward to gauge his reaction. At first, he hardly seemed to move at all, but then his fists slowly clenched in triumph.

'Yes!' he said to no-one in particular. '*YES!* Nadine Fawkner! I got Nadine Fawkner!'

Nadine Fawkner, I should point out, was the prettiest, most 'glamorous' girl at school.

'Jackson shoots . . . he *scooooooooooores!*' Simon screamed, throwing his arms up in the air and dancing around like an idiot.

A few feet away, Nadine Fawkner put her face in her hands and was comforted by friends.

'Okay, you next, Daff,' Martin enthused, pushing a finger into my back and prodding me towards the board.

My journey to the noticeboard took a good deal longer than Simon's had (though with a lot fewer casualties). By the time I got there, the crowd was starting to thin out and my heart was beating like a jack hammer. I couldn't afford a controversial partner. If I was the toughest or most popular kid at school, I could have carried a dud – I could have laughed off the smears, the taunts, and the guilt by association. But I wasn't strong enough for that. I was weak – weak and selfish. *Just gimme someone DECENT,* I pleaded, crossing my fingers and scanning the list.

I found my name almost immediately (the word 'Daffey' having a certain 'leap out' quality to it) and then panned across to see who I'd got. My partner was . . . my partner was . . . *Virginia Smith!*

Brown-haired, freckle-faced, furry-animal-loving Virginia Smith. Quiet, kindly, wouldn't catch your attention in a room, but wouldn't give you a fright either, Virginia Smith. Bland, colourless, dependable, *inoffensive* Virginia Smith. *God bless you*, Virginia Smith!

I turned around and gave a big thumbs up to my friends. 'I'm okay,' I yelled cheerfully. 'Virginia Smith!'

With Simon and myself out of the way, all eyes now turned to Martin. As he itched his palms and prepared to wade through the crowd, I wondered whether he was thinking the same thing I was – Simon had done well, I'd done well, now would it be a case of third time unlucky? We couldn't all go through unscathed, surely? And if we couldn't, what monster would God serve up to balance out our fortunes? Only time would tell.

Nervous though he undoubtedly was, Martin strode to the board like the fearless leader we'd come to love. He went straight to his name, checked out his partner and then marched back to base.

'So who do you have?' Simon demanded, when his friend didn't immediately proffer this information.

'Donna Gobbo,' Martin said stiffly. 'I have Donna Gobbo.'

Then he looked us both in the eye, raised a cautionary finger and stormed out of the room.

Donna Gobbo – one of the cruellest, most spiteful girls ever to walk through Templestowe Heights' gates, one half of the evil Gobbo twins who'd cut me apart in the breezeway so many months ago. If I had to define hell in less than ten words,

I would say: *Donna Gobbo in a ballgown*. Martin Timms had drawn the short straw.

✷✷✷✷✷

With all the drama surrounding our partner selection, I was reminded just how close the end of year Ball actually was. It seemed like only yesterday that term three had begun full of promise; that the sun had been shining, the birds had been singing, and the air had been filled with the sweet smell of hope. Now, it was almost a third of the way through. Grade six was slipping away from me and time was running out. If I wanted to achieve my goal of dancing with Jenny at the Ball (the last two dances of the night being reserved for 'free choice') I was going to have to get my skates on. The first step, however, was to find myself some skates.

The problem (if I can simplify it to just one) was that I was out of ideas. I'd had a bash at each and every task I'd set myself in The Plan and I'd come up short. Sure, there'd been some minor victories: a good act; a better than average campaign speech; a great second leg in the 4 x 100 relay; but by and large, I was losing the war. It seemed that there was more to getting a girlfriend than just being average on paper. If I wanted to win Jenny over, I had to get in her face more! I had to speak to her, hang out with her, get to know her friends. I had to listen to her stories, laugh at her jokes, feign interest in her games and hobbies, do everything I could to show that I liked her, while at the same time leaving enough ambiguity so that she couldn't be sure. In short, I had to turn her into a friend first, and then worry about turning her into a girlfriend later. The only question left was when to make my move.

Naturally, I couldn't do it in the playground. The only people I mixed with at school were *guys*, and if I suddenly started hanging out with Jenny and the hopscotch crowd, people would start asking questions. I needed an environment where *nothing* would seem out of the ordinary. A place where right was wrong, black was white, and the normal rules of primary school society were replaced by anarchy and the law of the jungle. I needed school camp!

*****

According to my friends, not all primary schools *had* camps. I think that's a real shame. If it hadn't have been for school camp, I wouldn't have learnt about billies, damper, knot-tying, and the sound a kid makes when he's hung off a bridge by his ankles. School camps were entertaining, informative and *brutal* affairs. There was something about the combination of fresh air and wide-open spaces that sent kids feral. Give a boy a map, a compass and twenty minutes to enjoy the peace and tranquility of the Australian bush, and the first thing he'll do is punch the kid next to him. For anyone who's read *Lord of the Flies* and thought it was a little 'over the top', all I can say is this: the only thing unrealistic about that book is that Piggy lasted as long as he did. At my school, he would have been dead in the first twenty minutes.

The year before we'd been to a place called the Blue Hill Pioneer Settlement, a historical township located on the Murray River, near the New South Wales – Victorian border. According to the brochures, the settlement faithfully recreated Blue Hill, as it was in the 1850s. If this is true, the 1850s were an ugly time indeed. The sun was hot, the streets were made of dirt, and the only entertainment on offer was visiting the local post office or buying boiled lollies from men with fake beards. The most significant memory I retained from that camp was deciding whether to buy a novelty poster that said:

'Chris Daffey – WANTED for sheep rustling'
or a novelty poster of Mona Lisa picking her nose. I went with Mona Lisa and have regretted it ever since.

This year we were off to Phillip Island. Phillip Island was renowned for its penguins, who swam ashore each night and waddled up the beach on the way to their burrows. I was looking forward to this camp because I loved animals and I'd heard that the penguin show was grouse. On a hot and blustery October morning, we gathered in the St Marks' church car park and bid farewell to our mothers.

'Now, are you sure you've packed enough socks?' Mum pestered, as I struggled towards the bus.

'Yes. I have enough socks.'

'What about underpants? You can never have enough . . .'

'*MUM! For God's sake!*'

'Sorry,' she said smiling. 'You're all grown up now, aren't you? Goodbye then. I'll miss you!'

'Goodbye,' I said.

Then I pulled myself loose, evaded a kiss, and made a mad dash for freedom.

The drive to Phillip Island was a long and arduous one. Martin and I amused ourselves during the early part of the trip by putting our seats back as far as we could and jamming chewing gum into the ashtrays. When this started wearing thin, we began talking up the prospects of a good camp.

'Do you think it'll be a good one?' Martin asked with enthusiasm.

'Yeah, for sure,' I replied.

'Better than last year's?'

'God, I hope so.'

'Yeah. Same here. I mean, I'm into history and stuff. But what was with all those paddle steamers? This is the biggest paddle steamer, this is the oldest paddle steamer, this is the first paddle steamer powered by steam? I mean, *I* don't care. Why the hell should I care?'

I laughed at the memory of it and then shuddered at the prospect of it happening again.

'I heard there's a flying fox at the campsite,' Martin continued.

'No way!'

'Yep. A huge one too. And trampolines, and a playground, and some of the cabins even have *bunk beds*!'

Ah, the lure of the bunk bed. Take a normal bed, make it infinitely less comfortable, and then raise it five feet in the air, and you've got every eleven-year-old kid's idea of heaven.

'Who'll be on top?' I ventured hesitantly.

'Well, let's see,' Martin began. 'There'll be three of us in our cabin and two sets of bunk beds. That means two of us will get to sleep on top, and one of us will have to sleep on the bottom.'

We smiled at each other guiltily and looked across at Simon, who was listening to his Walkman on the other side of the bus.

'Shall we buzz for it, Daff?'

'Yeah. Why not.'

If we had driven straight to Phillip Island we would have arrived there by noon. That is, if we hadn't stopped at every crappy tourist attraction between Templestowe Heights and the coast. The worst of these attractions were of the 'demonstration' variety: 'this is how we make butter'; 'this is how we milk cows'; 'this is how we keep our farm afloat – charging idiots like you two dollars a pop to watch us do our chores'. By the time our buses crossed the bridge separating the island from the mainland, I'd seen enough primary production to put me off the countryside for life.

The campsite was located on the far end of the island, in a town called Cowes. It was everything that Martin had promised. There were trampolines, there was a flying fox, there was a playground, and yes, there were bunk beds. Having spent the better part of eight hours cooped up in the bus, everyone was desperate to get outside and *do* something. Unfortunately, there wasn't enough light left in the day. We were given a quick tour of the grounds, shown into the dining hall for dinner (where some of us confronted vegetables for the first time in years) and then packed off to bed. The great outdoors were going to have to wait.

*****

When I woke the next morning it was still dark: dark and *freezing*. A quick check of my feature-packed digital watch (the kind with a million useless functions that was popular back then) showed that the time in Barbados was 3.17 p.m. A further check revealed that November 9 was 'Iqbal Day' in Pakistan, and a final, frenzied punching of its tiny buttons seemed to indicate that local time was 5.17 a.m. Shit. It was early.

'Is anyone else awake?' I whispered from the top of my bunk.

Silence.

'Martin, *Simon*,' I hissed, 'are you awake?'

There was no response from Simon, but Martin rolled over and made a grunting sound.

'Geez, Daff,' he croaked, as a pinprick of light illuminated his watch on the other side of the room. 'Do you know what time it is? What are you doing up?'

'Dunno,' I replied. 'I think I heard noises.'

'What do you mean? What kind of noises?'

'Not sure. Animals or something.'

'Don't be stupid, Daff. They don't keep any animals here. Now go back to sleep.'

I placed my head back on the pillow and shut my eyes.

'What about *native* animals?' I suggested, after a pause. 'You know, like wombats and things. Koalas maybe?'

'You're kidding aren't you, Daff?' Martin scoffed. 'Koalas don't even *make* noises. You're not telling me you're scared of a fucking koala, are you?'

'I didn't say I was scared. I just said I heard noises.'

'Whatever.'

'Besides,' I continued, 'koalas *do so* make noises. I saw this episode of *The Leyland Brothers* once where Mike tried to pull one out of a tree, and . . .'

'Daff!' Martin said suddenly, tearing off his doona and sitting bolt upright. 'Shut *UP*! How am I supposed to get back to sleep?'

'Sorry,' I said quietly. 'Guess I'm just nervous.'

I left this comment hanging in the air for a while, as Martin thrashed about in his bed and tried to rediscover sleep.

'Okay,' he said finally, propping up on his elbows and resigning himself to a long conversation. 'What is it?'

I smiled and opened my eyes. He was good like that, Martin. Whenever you needed him and no matter how dumb your problem was, he was always there to help.

'Well,' I began, feeling suddenly embarrassed, 'it's about Je . . . I mean *Jart*.'

'Jart', in case you were wondering, was the ingenious code

name we'd invented for Jenny so that Simon wouldn't know who we were talking about. Jenny Hartnett – 'Jart'. Get it? Well, we thought it was clever.

'Yeah. What about her?'

I sucked in a deep breath and began telling him about my plan to talk with Jenny.

'Hmmm,' Martin said when I was finished. 'Sounds pretty solid, Daff. You want to get to know her, so you've decided to talk to her. Smart move.'

'That's what I thought,' I said proudly.

'So what are you going to talk about?'

'Talk about? I don't know. Just stuff. Like the things *we* talk about.'

Martin hesitated for a second, before asking, in a carefully measured tone, 'Are you *sure* about that, Daff?'

I scratched the back of my neck and made a quick mental list of the last three conversations I'd had with my friend.

(1) If you took away the Iron Sheik's camel crush, would he be a better wrestler than George the Animal Steele?
(2) Do snails have mouths?
(3) Are silent farts actually smellier than loud ones – or does it just seem that way?

Okay, maybe he had a point.

'Actually, Mart, I'm not too sure.'

'Let me give you a tip,' my friend said, deepening his voice and drawing upon twelve years of experience of not having a girlfriend. 'If you want to win over a girl, there's just one thing you have to do.'

'What? What is it?' I asked, leaning out of my bed in anticipation.

'All you have to do, Daff, is talk about their hair.'

'Their *hair*?'

'Yep. It's all about hair.'

'What do you mean?' I said, stunned. 'What would I say?'

'Anything. Doesn't matter. Just so long as it's about hair. I like your hair. What have you done to your hair? Am I just imagining things, or is there something different about your hair? They love it, Daff. They *LOVE IT!*'

I lay back on my bed and marvelled at the simplicity of it. Her hair. All I had to do was talk about her hair. This was going to be easier than I'd thought.

✳✳✳✳✳

The activities for the following day (and in fact, the entire camp) were set out in a special camp booklet. The booklet was an A4-sized document with a yellow cover and a picture of the school emblem on the front (a circle containing two hills and a little sun). The opening pages of the booklet contained a list of camp rules, a sketch of the campsite, and a mercifully brief history of Phillip Island itself. The remainder of the booklet was divided into three segments:

1. a 'notes' area where you could record your thoughts and sketch pictures of the local wildlife;
2. a timetable and list of activities; and
3. a bizarre section marked 'autographs' (just in case you bumped into Burt Reynolds at the Coal Creek historical farm).

The most important of these segments was number two.

If you include the day we drove down, our trip to Phillip Island was exactly five days long. The activities for each of those days were set out in the timetable. Since there were too many of us to all do the same thing at once, we'd been divided up into six groups, each named after a species of local wildlife: the Penguins, the Sharks, the Seagulls, the Seals, the Koalas and the Mutton-birds (guess which one was unpopular?). Simon and I were Penguins, Martin was a Shark, and Jenny had been designated as a Seagull. This last piece of information was crucial to my plans. Since Jenny and I weren't in the same group, it was going to be a while before we did anything together. This was annoying, but at least it gave me time to think.

The first activity for the Penguins was 'beach collage with Mrs Newport', which (if this is possible) proved to be even worse that it sounded. Next up was 'blindfold trailing with Mr Linny'. This was much better. For this exercise, we were led out into the bush and divided up into pairs. One person in each pair was told to put a blindfold on, and the other had to guide them around an obstacle course using verbal instructions only.

The point of the exercise was to demonstrate the value of teamwork and cooperation. For most of us, however, it just meant spinning our partners around, pointing them in the direction of the nearest tree, and yelling,

'Forward, forward, forward, forward, forward, forward, forward, BANG!'

It was great fun for a while, but in the end, no-one would keep their blindfolds on.

Although blindfold trailing had its moments, it wasn't until late afternoon that we really got into the good stuff – the trampolines and the flying fox.

For these activities, the Penguins were joined by the Mutton-birds. While Mr Thompson supervised one half of the group on the flying fox, the rest of us gathered around the trampolines. Since there were just two of them, only a couple of kids bounced at a time and the others waited for their turn and watched. At first, we watched in silence, but after a while we began to cheer the bouncers on – whistles for knee-drops; awed gasps for high bounces; polite applause for those who did somersaults or tricks. Some kids wilt under this sort of pressure. Others flourish.

Falling into the latter category was a kid called Reece Burton. Mediocre in all other aspects of life, Reece was a wizard on the trampoline. He had style, he had grace, he had flair, and he had an unbelievable willingness to do the bidding of the crowd. When we asked him to bounce harder, he bounced harder. When we begged him to fly higher, he flew higher. And when we got to our feet and demanded something special, he didn't let us down! He tumbled, he piked, he twisted, he turned, he Rudolphed and he Randolphed (they're real terms, you know – look them up), and then came back to earth, landed neatly between two springs, and broke both his legs.

Reece Burton took no further part in Camp Cowes. After some urgent medical attention from Matt Bradbury ('I think they're just dislocated, I can pop them back in!') he was rushed by car to a mainland hospital. Although he was gone, Reece was certainly not forgotten. In order to commemorate his achievements and honour the Burton name, a proud tradition developed. From that moment on, any incident resulting in a broken bone or other serious injury became known as 'doing a Reecey'. He may not have been there to hear it, but I'm sure he would have been chuffed.

*****

It wasn't until Day Three that the Penguins finally got together with the Seagulls. Both groups were scheduled to take the Eastern Passage Tour at ten o'clock in the morning. The Eastern Passage Tour was a bus drive through the east of the island towards Newhaven and San Remo. My mission on the trip was to stick to Jenny like glue and wait for a conversational opportunity to present itself. When I caught sight of her boarding the bus, I felt my first pang of nerves. She looked sensational! Two days of sunshine had tanned her already olive skin to a light, chocolatey brown, and her face shone with the kind of wholesome, robust vitality that models have in home gym ads. I licked my palm, flattened down the back of my hair, and straightened my America's Cup T-shirt. If I was to have any chance with a girl like that, I needed to look my best.

Our first stop was at a historic chicory kiln. Chicory, as I soon discovered, was a stringy, flowering plant, the root of which, if you roasted it, treated it and then ground it up with spices, still tasted like shit. A lady showed us a film about chicory and then gave us a talk. According to her, there were a million different uses for chicory, including as a pipe-filler, as an additive to pet food, and as a substitute for coffee (presumably, for those to whom coffee was fatal). I didn't pay much attention to this talk. This was partly because it was hard to get fired up about chicory, and partly because I spent the entire time staring at Jenny's neck and marvelling at how nice it was. Occasionally, Jenny would sense my eyes boring into her and turn around, at which point I'd snap my head sideways and stare intently at the chicory woman – so intently that she mistook my stares for interest and directed almost all of her spiel to me.

The chicory kiln was a wasteland in terms of conversational opportunities. The next stop was much better. At twelve noon, our bus rolled into the Phillip Island Koala Reserve. I felt much more comfortable here. I had a lot to say about animals, and most if it (at least in my own opinion) was interesting.

My favourite topic for discussion was the fact that

Australian animals, while cute, adorable and much beloved by Japanese tourists, were boring. Like any eleven-year-old boy, I liked *tough* animals – the kind with big teeth, razor-sharp claws, and the ability to tear other animals to pieces. Australian animals had none of these qualities. Millions of years ago, when the continents starting breaking away from each other, all of the world's wussiest animals had somehow conspired to be on the same boat. Sure, we had some pretty nasty spiders and snakes. But those aside, name one Australian species you'd be afraid to be locked in a room with. The kangaroo? The wombat? The quokka? The malley fowl? I mean, *come on*.

Having discussed this issue many times with my friends, I considered myself a bit of an authority on the subject and was keen to share my wisdom with Jenny. All I had to do was work up the courage to approach her.

My first attempt was at the start of a talk given by our koala guide. I sidled up behind Jenny, opened my mouth to say something, and then choked under the pressure. My second attempt was much like the first, except that I didn't open my mouth, and my third consisted of taking one step towards her and then fiddling self-consciously with a stick. As my efforts became more and more pathetic, I learnt a fact that would remain true for the rest of my life. I was no pick-up artist.

It wasn't until I almost crashed into her in the gift shop, that I was jolted into conversation.

'What did you think of the koalas?' I blurted out quickly, before I had a chance to change my mind.

'Um, hello,' she said, smiling. 'The koalas? I thought they were cute.'

'Yeah – same here,' I nodded, happy to have gotten past first base. 'Could be a bit tougher though.'

'.'

'Well, you know. They don't really *do* much, do they? Sit around, hold onto trees, chew leaves ... I mean, what's the point of that?'

'I don't think there has to *be* a point,' Jenny said sensibly. 'It's just how they are.'

'Yeah, sure, I know. But wouldn't it be better if they were much bigger? Or really vicious? Or when you walked under one of their trees, they'd jump down on top of you and bite off your face?'

'Ummm ... I'm not sure about that. Why would I want them to bite off my face?'

'No, well, you wouldn't, would you? But it'd make 'em more interesting animals.'

Jenny stared at me blankly for a moment, before picking up a boomerang and checking for a price tag. This wasn't working out as well as I'd hoped. If I'd been talking to Simon or Martin, they would have known exactly what I meant. They would have said,

'Yeah, you're right, Daff. What about huge wings, an extra head, or a retractable arm that shoots explosive gum leaves?'

They would have unanimously agreed that koalas could have

done with some toughening up. But Jenny seemed clueless. I didn't know what girls talked about normally, but it clearly wasn't this.

'What I meant to say,' I continued hopefully, 'was that Australian animals are all so . . . I don't know, *useless*. And small! I don't think there's one large animal in the whole country. Except maybe for horses. And they're not even Australian!'

'No, they're not,' Jenny said absently. 'They were brought here by settlers. I *love* horses.'

Then she took out a tiny red purse, snapped open its clasp and turned on her way to the counter. *Damn it*, I thought to myself. I was losing her! I'd thought up a great topic, given it my best shot, and all I'd managed to do was *bore* the girl! This was the biggest disaster of all. This was my most shameful episode yet. Unless, unless . . .

'*I* have a horse,' I said without blinking.

'*Really*?' Jenny exclaimed, spinning around and almost blinding me with her ponytail. 'You're kidding? That's fantastic! What sort is it?'

Sort? Horses came in sorts?

'A brown one,' I said unconvincingly. 'With a white mane. Like a Shetland pony, but bigger.'

'Wow!' Jenny gushed. 'It sounds gorgeous! What's it called?'

'Barney.'

'And where do you keep him?'

'On a farm. My parents own one.'

'Really? You are *soooo* lucky! Can I see it sometime?'

'Yeah. Sure. Maybe.'

And as the questions rolled on, my lies became more elaborate, and the smile on Jenny's face grew broader and broader. When I'd run out of things to make up and Jenny's grin had no further room to expand, I decided it was time to play my trump card.

'Um, you haven't, like, done something to your hair, have you?'

Jenny's grin disappeared. The sparkle in her eyes winked out and her brows knitted together in an expression that appeared to be somewhere between confusion and rage. *Fuck. Dumb question. Thanks a lot, MARTIN!*

'Well, actually,' she said, flushing furiously and folding her arms across her chest, 'I normally wear it straight down, but today, it's up in a bobble!'

I couldn't believe it. I was in!

✱✱✱✱✱

The Koala Reserve gift shop was the start of a beautiful friendship between Jenny and I. It wasn't the kind of friendship you have when you're an adult. There were no long walks, cosy dinners or comforting shoulders to cry on when you busted up with someone else. There was, however, visual recognition, the occasional pleasantry, and various animated conversations about Barney, the amazing trick-performing pony. (I was really milking that one for everything it was worth.)

The key to maintaining this relationship was making sure I had something interesting to relate each time I saw her. I didn't yet trust my ability to ad-lib or impress off the cuff, so instead, I racked my brain for bizarre or fascinating facts – like that tastebuds have a lifespan of ten days, or that 'pogonophobia' is the fear of beards. It was hard to tell if Jenny liked that sort of stuff. But at least it gave me something to say.

The hardest part of my new friendship was keeping track of what I'd told her. Not only did I not want to double up on trivia, but it was also important to recall every not-quite-true detail I'd passed on about myself. For example, on the second last morning of camp, Jenny asked me how my grandfather was doing. I was halfway through telling her that he'd just finished paving our driveway and re-stumping his house, when I remembered that he was supposed to be a bedridden cripple. Slip-ups like this were never far away. There were a whole host of things to keep in mind and the effort became increasingly burdensome. I had to remember about Pop. I had to remember that I had a horse. I had to remember what the horse's name was; what he looked like; where he lived; the tricks he could do; where our farm was; what my parents did; and that my family had appeared in (and won) an episode of *Family Feud*. It was exhausting work.

At first, I trusted the good old Daffey brain to keep abreast of things. But after a while, I started putting it all down in my diary. I hadn't written a single word in the diary since tossing it under my bed in February, after missing out on the First Eleven. Like every diary I'd ever owned, it was completely blank, except for a few boring entries in January and a single line whinge a month later. On a nice fresh page in the middle of October, I jotted down the relevant facts: who I was, the pets I owned, and what imaginary illnesses my relatives were suffering from. I also wrote a brief summary of the year to date, including my failure to make the SRC, the T-Birds' showdown with the Jubbins, the great *Gilligan's Island* escape, and how McEvoy had been blown out of the water by our porno. Mostly, however, I wrote about Jenny. I wrote about how much I liked her and how beautiful she was compared to the other girls. I wrote about how I loved to make her laugh and how her lips curled up at the sides when she giggled. I even spent three hours alone in my cabin sketching a tiny, detailed portrait of her (which ended up bearing an unhappy resemblance to Ace Freeley from Kiss and having to be scribbled out with a texta). And when all this was done, I closed my diary, put it back in my bag, and resolved that one day soon, I would tell her how I felt.

*****

Not much else happened on camp. There were the usual brawls, fights, and heated disagreements over whose torch had the strongest beam. Jeremy Ng fell off the flying fox, Lucas Tordby got tied to a sheep, and some of the cooler kids took part in a game of strip poker (which ended abruptly when Justin Cobb cracked a stiffy and the rest of the participants fled in terror). Other than that, it was pretty uneventful.

The penguins were great, of course. We saw them on our last night away and they waddled clumsily ashore to the delighted gasps of their audience and the heartfelt thanks of Tourism Victoria. Once the last straggler had clambered its way up the beach, we were herded onto the buses and shipped back to camp.

Given that it was our last night, most of us were expecting some sort of special meal or 'end of camp feast'. What greeted us in the dining hall was a tad disappointing. In my experience, there were two categories of food in life: good food, and the type you serve with ladles. The semi-solid mush being dolloped onto our plates fell clearly into the latter category. The label on the drum they were serving it from said 'beef stew', but I found that hard to believe. If it *was* beef stew, then the recipe for producing it must have looked something like this:

> Take a side of beef. Carefully remove all of the choice cuts, the standard cuts, the budget cuts, and every morsel of edible meat. Then place all of this to one side and serve the rest of the animal with gravy.

It was *gross*. The only person who didn't seem to think so was Julian Crowler. When it came to his turn with the ladle, he piled it so high on his plate that it looked like an organic witch's hat (which made you wonder what the hell they fed him back home). Unluckily for Julian, he was destined to wear more of this meal than he was to eat. He took two steps towards his table, tripped over a sports bag, and came crashing catastrophically to the ground.

The sight of a kid lying arse-up in a lake of gravy would normally have brought the house down, but since it was Julian Crowler, no-one dared make a sound. That is, until Andrew McEvoy whispered something behind his hand, and the rest of his table erupted in mirth. Bruised, filthy and humiliated, Julian struggled to his feet and glared at his accusers – and for a moment, I thought he was going to attack McEvoy with a fork. But even the meanest kid in school thinks twice before messing with the most popular.

Once dinner was out of the way, a representative from the SRC thanked our hosts for their hospitality and our teachers led us in a series of rowdy singalongs. After that, everyone was given two hours of free time, and we roamed around trying to get each other to sign our camp booklets.

As with most pursuits in my young life, my ambition was to collect *the set*. I didn't just want the autographs of my friends or those I knew well. I wanted *everyone* – whether they were friend, foe, or complete and utter stranger. The autograph section of my booklet had fallen off, so I used the back of my diary to record the signatures. After half an hour of collecting, I had all but one of the ninety-seven names required, including Jenny, her friends, the Gobbo twins, Spenda, Trimble, Marty Goldbloom, Alex Milano, Jeremy Ng, Lucas Tordby, Virginia

Smith, Martin, Simon, the Gibbon and Julian Crowler (who I'd expected to sign with a cross, but actually had quite an elegant signature). The only one I hadn't got was McEvoy.

Part of me didn't want to get Mc Evoy's signature because I couldn't bear the thought of asking him. This faction, however, was overruled by the one that wanted the set, and so I went out in search of my prey. I found him sitting under a gum tree in the fading light, not far from the trampolines.

'Hello, arse-face,' he said by way of greeting.

'Hello, Andrew,' I replied. 'I was wondering whether you'd like to sign my diary here?'

I pushed the book into his hands and pointed at all the signatures.

'Yeah, why not,' he said, fumbling around for a pen. 'I'd do anything for a fan.'

Chuckling to himself, he put pen to paper and was about to sign his name, when there was a crash, a shriek, and an inhuman cry of pain.

'Hey, Daff – come quick!' Simon yelled from the trampolines. 'Someone's just done a Reecey!!!'

I grinned to myself and dashed off to join the festivities, leaving my diary, and every secret I'd ever had, in the hands of my worst enemy.

The race-tuned, VH SS Group Three Holden

It was a beautiful machine. It had sleek lines and a luscious blood-red duco. It had eight cylinders and a 5.0 litre engine. It had mag wheels, race-tuned suspension, rear spoilers, colour-coded bumpers, bucket seats, and a strange curvy thing in the middle of the bonnet (which may have had something to do with wind resistance). It was the type of car that sports' fans love and environmentalists love to hate. It was the kind of vehicle that came with three settings on the gear-stick: forward, reverse and 'doughnut.' If it's true what they say about guys, cars and their penises, the VH SS Group Three Holden was my first erection.

I first sighted the car during the Christmas holidays at the end of grade five, when Martin got picked up from my house by his dad. The two of us were sitting in the living room playing Ms Pacman on the Atari (a girl-friendly version of the game in which Pacman wore a little bow) when the walls started to shake and the air filled with the sound of rolling thunder. The Commodore had arrived.

I'd been bugging Martin for a ride in it ever since, but to no avail. Initially, he'd seemed quite keen on the idea, even arranging a drive down to the country just for Simon and myself. This trip, however, was eventually cancelled; as was the next one, and the next one, and the one after that. By the time it got to halfway through the year, I was beginning to wonder whether something was wrong. Why was Martin being so stingy with his father's car? When were *we* going to get a go in it? Were we to be left to the tedium of our own family sedans? Surely not. Admittedly, Simon's parents owned a BMW, but foreign-built cars were considered crap at our school. You drove a Ford, you drove a Holden, or you drove rubbish.

I began to think that something had happened to the car; that Martin's dad had sold it, or crashed it, or traded it in for something else. This suspicion seemed confirmed when invitations to Martin's new house were not forthcoming. The Timmses moved in during April but Simon and I didn't get a look in until June. Even then, it was only for a moment, and I wasn't asked back until September (when I went over to record the *Gilligan's Island* soundtrack). Clearly, he was trying to hide the car's absence. He was trying to cover up the fact that his macho father now drove something small and feminine that turned on a ten-cent piece and got ninety miles to the gallon. But then, on a rainy afternoon a week after camp, I saw it! Waiting to pick Martin up after school was Mr Timms and his beloved Commodore – still rugged, still manly, and still gleaming like a shiny new button. Mr Timms hadn't sold it after all. Martin was just being a tight-arse.

With a positive sighting of the car under my belt, I started badgering Martin afresh. I hassled him, I needled him, I pestered and I harassed, until finally, only a few weeks from the end of term, he caved in. Martin agreed that on the last day of the year, when Simon and I were at home getting ready for the big dance, Mr Timms would pick us up and drive us to the Ball in style! I couldn't wait. We'd be the toast of the town if we arrived in a car like that. Boys would whisper, girls would swoon, and our dance cards would be filled for the rest of the evening.

I'd like to say that Martin was happy about the whole thing, but he wasn't. Almost from the moment the deal was hammered out, he seemed in an unusually glum mood. Talking about the Ball bugged him. Talking about dancing classes bugged him. And a mere mention of the car was enough to send him into a fit. To my mind, there could only be one reason for all of this. That reason was Donna Gobbo.

Martin's experiences with Donna hadn't been at all like we'd expected. When he'd first told us that Donna was his partner, we'd imagined a kind of 'Bambi meets Godzilla' scenario.

Martin would be polite, Martin would be considerate, and then Martin would have his head ripped off and kicked down the street. We couldn't have been more wrong.

In over four weeks of dancing classes, Donno Gobbo hadn't hurt our friend once. In fact, she'd taken a real shine to him. Donna's budding affection for our friend was obvious to everyone who saw them dance together. As soon as classes commenced, she'd wrap herself around him like an anaconda and stare directly into his eyes – eyes that darted frantically from side to side searching for an avenue of escape. Not surprisingly, Martin was terrified by this development, and Simon and I had been forbidden from discussing it.

My relationship with Virginia Smith was much less controversial. She was polite to me, I was polite to her, and neither of us bothered to hide our relief that we hadn't got someone worse. Whether or not Simon was getting along with *his* partner (the stunning Ms Fawkner) depended on who you believed. There was Simon's version of things:

'She loves me. She loves me. She is *sooooooooo* desperate for me.'

versus what we could see with our own eyes:

She wouldn't touch him, she wouldn't talk to him, and Mrs Quong had to physically *push* them together in order to dance.

Simon put no stock in this, however, and explained that Nadine was simply playing 'hard to get'. He was so convinced that she was after him, that he made all sorts of elaborate plans about what they'd do once they were going steady: hang out at his house; play Game of Life together; go bowling; go fishing; go up north to visit the Big Pineapple; and even (if Martin and I were lucky) help fix us up with some of her friends.

The one thing that did concern Simon was getting the last two dances at the Ball. Since Nadine had no option but to dance with him until then, it was the free choice section that was crucial. If she chose him, he'd be vindicated. If she chose someone else, he'd look foolish. As the end of the year inched closer and closer, Simon started getting edgy.

'She'll pick me, won't she, Daff?' he asked anxiously one Thursday afternoon.

'Course she will, Sime,' I replied diplomatically.

'Good. That's what I think too. I mean, she'd be *crazy* if she didn't. Have you seen the way she looks at me? I'm telling you, Daff, that girl's after a bit of the old Jackson magic!'

I clamped my lips together and managed to keep a straight face. The only magic trick I'd ever seen Simon perform was to make girls hate him.

'I know what you're thinking, Daff,' he said. 'You're thinking that she doesn't even like me. Well, you're wrong! I told my dad about it and he explained the whole thing. You see, girls aren't like us, Daff. If they're after someone, they don't just walk up to them and tell them! They're much trickier than that. If they like you, they pretend they *don't* like you. And if they *really* like you, they pretend they hate your guts. Get it?'

I nodded my head. 'She must really, really, *really* like you then, Sime.'

'You're telling me!' he grinned proudly. 'So, Daff, who are you going to ask? Or are you just going to sit on the sidelines and watch, like the rest of the chickens?'

I squirmed uncomfortably. I knew damn well who I was going to ask (or who I was hoping would ask me) but I wasn't about to tell Simon 'it's safe as houses' Jackson.

'Um, dunno. Haven't really thought about it.'

'Aw, come on, Daff. There must be *someone*!' he repeated, in an almost pleading tone.

For a second or two, I came close to relenting. *Stuff it*, I thought to myself. I'd been keeping it from him all year, why not tell him now? The poor kid was always left out of everything, and he must have overheard a billion cryptic references to a person called 'Jart'. Why shouldn't I tell him?

This feeling lasted about as long as it took me to remember the last time I told Simon a secret. It was grade four, I'd just accidentally killed our class's pet terrapin, and I told Simon to hush it up while my mother shopped around for a replacement. When I arrived at school the next day ready to switch the new 'Terry' for the lifeless one at the bottom of the tank, I was confronted by a mob of weeping girls and the words, 'There he is – the terrapin murderer!'

Nope, Simon Jackson couldn't be trusted. If Jenny found out that I liked her before I had a chance to tell her myself, the game would be up. Like any primary school kid worth his salt,

I'd have to deny it. And if the allegation persisted, I'd have to deny it aggressively. No-one wanted that. So despite Simon's insistence, despite his need to feel included and his pleading eyes, I decided it would be best to lie. If primary school had taught me anything, it was that leopards never, ever changed their spots. Once a blabber-mouth, *always* a blabber-mouth.

'Seriously, Sime, there isn't anyone. I'd tell you if there was.'

'Oh,' he replied dejectedly.

And that was it.

※※※※※

With our ride to the Ball worked out and my secret safe from Simon, it was time to get on with the main event – The Plan. My relationship with Jenny wasn't exactly hurtling along, but it was at least comfortably chugging. The superficial friendship that we'd struck up at camp had blossomed into a superficial friendship that we continued at school. I was still very discreet about it. I rarely, if ever, approached her during lunchtime, preferring instead to orchestrate 'chance' meetings at the end of the day.

Although I probably spoke to her at least once a week, I wasn't any closer to getting to know her. Not in any real sense, anyway. This didn't overly concern me. When you're that age, relationships aren't about finding a soul mate or a companion – they're just about having one. All of the key things I needed to know about Jenny I already knew. She was pretty, she was well liked, and she wasn't openly hostile to my advances.

Jenny, too, would have had a hard time discovering who *I* really was. Mainly because I kept it hidden from her. What she would have seen instead was a ceaselessly changing facade of a person who reinvented himself daily in an attempt to come up with a version she liked. There was nothing I wouldn't have said, done, or tried to *be* in order to curry Jenny's favour. More than anything, I just wanted to be agreeable. She could have said:

> 'Chris, I'm a mentally disturbed, borderline psychotic, white supremacist, who believes in crop circles, racial purity and arranged marriages,'

and I would have simply said –

'Great. Same here!'

This tendency to hide my own personality and go in search of another, more pleasing one made it hard to know if Jenny was actually interested. Did she like *me*, or did she like my imaginary horse? I couldn't tell.

Not knowing whether Jenny liked the real Chris Daffey, or the delicate web of lies I'd woven in his place, made it difficult to progress the relationship. I'd been hoping that our conversations would reach some sort of 'critical mass of intimacy', and that romance would automatically spring forth. This hadn't happened. Instead, I was forced to contemplate more extreme measures – like telling her how I felt, or making a sudden lunge at her and trying to kiss her (something I'd been practising with a beanbag for quite some time). The thing that stopped me from doing this was fear of rejection. As much as I liked

Jenny, as keen as I was to bring things to a head, I just couldn't bear the thought of her turning me down. I *wanted* to tell her, I *wanted* to go the lunge, but cowardice held me in check.

Gradually, and not even consciously at first, I began pinning all of my hopes on the end of year Ball. On that last school night, in that strange and heady atmosphere, I hoped that things would just 'happen'. And if I screwed it up, at least I'd never see her again.

✼✼✼✼✼

Focusing on the Ball like this made the end of term a daunting prospect. As the last weeks of my primary school existence ebbed away, I felt a growing sense of unease. It wasn't just the spectre of the dance, either. It was something else – something I couldn't quite put my finger on. Just like with the *Gilligan's Island* song, a little voice in the back of my brain was quietly muttering ill tidings. It was telling me that I'd done something bad. That somehow, somewhere, sometime, I'd made a terrible mistake that had left me vulnerable and exposed. On the first Monday of December, it hit me.

I was sitting in one of Mr Weathershaw's capital cities classes and Alex Milano had just been busted for swearing in a foreign language. Apparently, Mr Weathershaw had been tipped off by our part-time Italian teacher, Miss Di Stasio, who'd given him a list of key words and phrases to watch out for. Our teacher thought he heard one, the offender was summoned to the front of class, and Alex ended up apologising in both English and Italian.

'I'm sorry, Mr Weathershaw,'
followed by,
'*Mi dispiace, signore testa di minchia.*' ('I'm sorry, Mr Dickhead.')

While all this was going on, I was happily sketching a second, more detailed portrait of Jenny, complete with love hearts, little arrows, and a set of my initials carved into her forehead. It was so much better than the aborted Ace Freeley version that I resolved to cut it out with a pair of scissors and paste it in my diary when I got home. It was at the precise moment I had this thought that I experienced an incredible sinking feeling. My stomach lurched, my chest began to cramp, and my intestines felt like they were wrestling each other. At a loss to explain its cause, I gripped the desk firmly and tried to remember where I'd last left the diary. It wasn't under my bed anymore because I'd taken it away on camp – but I couldn't remember what I'd done with it once I'd got home. In fact, I couldn't remember bringing it home at all.

The whereabouts of my diary plagued me for the rest of class. The harder I thought about it, the worse my stomach seemed. I had no idea why I felt this way. After all, what did it matter if I'd misplaced the diary? It'd turn up. Besides, I hardly ever used the thing.

It wasn't until lunchtime, as I was walking away from the canteen clutching an ice-cold Razz, that the penny dropped.

I was halfway through retracing my steps (in the way that you do when you lose something) when I began zeroing in on my diary's last known movements. I *definitely* took it to camp, I said to myself. I knew that for sure because I remembered drawing Jenny's face in it. I also remembered writing a rather schmaltzy entry about how much I loved her – an entry which, three weeks on, made me cringe with embarrassment. After that, I wasn't so sure. I put it back in the bag under my bunk, and then . . . and then . . . *That's right!* I used it to collect signatures! I got the whole set too, including that knob-end McEvoy, who I snared at the last minute by the trampolines. It was just before that kid did a Reecey and . . . and . . .

OH – MY – *GOD*!!!!!!

The Razz slipped through my fingers and crashed to the ground, symbolically bleeding raspberry all over my shoes.

I'd left my diary with *Andrew McEvoy*! I'd handed it to him, I'd run off to see the Reecey, and then I'd left it behind. My most private thoughts, my most intimate confessions, two and a half paragraphs of love-sick blather, all in the possession of the Dark Prince of Smug. I took a few deep breaths and dashed off to find Mrs Newport.

I found her in the staffroom lunching with the other teachers. While I waited at the door for someone to retrieve her, my mind filled with unspeakable horrors. The main image was that of McEvoy, standing atop a chair at lunchtime, with my diary in one hand and the assembled crowd in the palm of the other.

'My beloved Jenny!' he read in a silly, high-pitched voice.
'I love you more than my Scalectrix racing set! I love you
more than a hot pie on a cold day! I love you so much that
I'd even pretend to have a big farm, and a fake horse, and
a whole bunch of other crap, just to make you like me!'

I shuddered and tried to cast the image aside. The mere *prospect* of something like that happening to me was enough to chill my bones. But if McEvoy had the diary, why hadn't he nailed me already? Camp was more than three weeks ago, and he'd had ample opportunities since then. Perhaps he was just biding his time? Perhaps he was waiting until the Ball, or some other pre-determined moment, to whip it out and blow my plans to hell.

Or maybe he didn't have it at all? Maybe he'd just left it on the ground or handed it in to lost property without reading it? After all, it was mostly empty, and a person could have been forgiven for thinking it was blank. These possibilities bounced around in my head until Mrs Newport appeared in the doorway.

'Hello there, Master Daffey,' she said. 'To what do I owe this pleasure?'

'I can't find something, Mrs Newport, and I need to check lost property.'

'Sure. Okay then. But can't it wait until after lunch?'

'No, it can't, Mrs Newport. It really can't!'

The lost property bin was located two doors down from the Principal's office. While I looked on anxiously, Mrs Newport rummaged through the contents of a musty cardboard box.

'What was it you said you'd lost?'

'It's a book – I mean a diary,' I said, making a small, squarish shape with my hands.

'Is this it?' she asked, holding up a large, green hardcover, entitled *Mr Pinkwhistle's Extraordinary Hat*. I screwed up my face and shook my head from side to side. *What the hell was wrong with this woman?*

'How about either of these?' she continued cheerfully, waving around a tatty exercise book and a copy of *James and the Giant Peach*.

'No, not those either. I'm looking for a *diary*,' I repeated.

'Oh yes, a diary,' she said.

Over the next ten minutes, Mrs Newport pulled out all manner of book-sized objects, none of which could possibly have been a diary, including a notepad, two jotters, a Bible, an atlas and a surprising number of the *Biggles* series.

'Well, that's it for the books I'm afraid. Maybe you should check with Mr Weathershaw or Mr Bradbury in case they . . .'

I was out of the door before she could finish her sentence.

I caught up with Mr Weathershaw during yard duty. He wasn't very helpful. He disclaimed any knowledge of lost property, said it was all Mrs Newport's department, and then made me pick up chip wrappers for the next twenty minutes. Mr Bradbury was even worse. Mistaking me for someone else, he gave me a brief medical examination and then demanded to know why I hadn't been turning up to footy practice. Depressed, rattled and running out of options, I sought out the wise counsel of Martin.

'Martin,' I said breathlessly, when I found him on the basketball courts, 'you have to help me. Something terrible's happened!'

My friend regarded me with an interested but slightly mopey expression (prompting me to wonder, briefly, what on earth was the matter with him these days).

'What's up, Daff? What's the problem?' he said.

I took a deep breath and then blasted out the details at a hundred miles an hour.

'Big deal,' Martin said dismissively, when I'd finished. 'Don't worry about it, Daff. He probably doesn't even have it.'

I stared at my friend in disbelief, stunned by his blasé dismissal of this crisis.

'What do you mean *big deal*? I'm dead, Martin. Don't you understand – *dead*! We've got to get it off him somehow. Maybe even kill him!'

'Geez, Daff. Take it easy. You're cracking up!'

'No, I'm not, Martin. This is *serious*. If you just knew how bad the stuff was in the diary. There's this mushy part about how much I love her; plus a whole big list of lies that I've told – like that I have a horse and that Pop's a cripple. He's going to bring it out at the Ball. I just know it!'

Martin didn't even respond this time, and just stared vacantly around the playground.

'Are you even *listening*, Martin?' I demanded angrily.

'Yeah, you're worried he'll use it at the Ball. About the Ball, Daff. There's something I've been meaning to tell you.'

'What? I don't want to talk about the Ball *now*!'

'It's the car,' he said slowly. 'You see . . .'

'Not the car *AGAIN*!' I exploded. 'What excuse have you got this time? It's broken? It ran away? Your dad took it down to the carwash and it won't be back for a month? If you don't want us to have a ride in it, Martin, *just say so*!'

I was furious now. This behaviour was very unlike Martin. Here I was with big, *BIG* problems, and all he could do was think about himself. I'd never thought of our leader as selfish, but I was beginning to have my doubts.

'There is no car,' he said suddenly, meeting my eyes for a moment and then looking away.

'What do you mean? I saw it two weeks ago. Your dad picked you up from school in it.'

Martin didn't say anything.

'*Martin*? What are you talking about? I saw it. I *saw* it!'

My friend remained silent and for the first time I noticed his face. His jaw was set forward, the muscles in his cheeks were tense, and his eyes were squinty and bloodshot. If I'd ever seen Martin close to tears before, I might have known what this expression meant. As it was, I was simply confused.

'He wasn't picking me up,' he said stiffly. 'I mean, not to take me home. He doesn't live with us anymore, Daff. He's gone.'

Then he turned away from me completely, and I was left staring at his back.

✱✱✱✱✱

The next few weeks were difficult ones for Martin and me. He seldom mentioned his father again, except to impart the barest of details – that he'd left six months ago, that he still visited occasionally, and that the rest of the family had been forced to move house.

You would have thought that the knowledge of these things would have brought us closer together – that by revealing that his life wasn't nearly as perfect as I had always supposed it to be, Martin would have somehow 'let me inside' – but the opposite was true. A distance grew between us, an unspoken recognition that one of us had been through things the other couldn't possibly hope to understand. A few kids at school had parents that were separated, but not many, and I wasn't close to any of them. At that stage of our lives, it was still a rarity; an event that happened only to strangers – not the commonplace phenomenon that ended up claiming a third of all the parents I knew (including, eventually, my own).

Martin had always seemed older than me, and now he seemed *much* older. It was as if, in sharing his secret, he'd admitted that we were different – that while he'd appeared just like me for the past year, he'd actually gone off and grown up behind my back. It was only a subtle thing, mind you. On the surface, things remained pretty much the same. We played together, we prepared for the upcoming Ball, and Simon was informed that the Commodore had been sold. But the difference was there, nonetheless.

'It's okay, you know,' Martin said one day, 'living with

Mum. She takes us out, lets us watch TV, and we get to eat Kentucky Fried whenever we want.'

Looking at his face, it was hard to know if Martin actually believed these things, but there was one thing I knew for sure. He didn't want to talk about it.

In all other respects, the year drew to a close in a predictable fashion. Gold House won its fourth successive House Cup, the SRC declared the school grounds a 'nuclear-free zone' (meaning that American warships could no longer dock in High Street), and a piece of tinsel was draped around the canteen in readiness for the festive season.

Jenny and I continued to speak occasionally, but I approached these conversations with more caution than ever. Each time I saw her, I was terrified it would be my last – that the next time I laid eyes upon her, she'd march right up to me, slap me across the face and yell, 'There *is* no Barney!'

My paranoia that McEvoy had my diary only increased as the Ball got closer. I studied his every move to try and work out if he had it; but if he did, he wasn't giving anything away. Many times I considered asking him outright, but baulked for fear of getting the wrong answer. If he did have it, and he planned to use it, and my question did nothing more than reveal these things, then life would not be worth living. I was in no hurry to get this news. So instead, I put it off, and off, and off, and off, and off. That is, until the very last day of term, when the need to know became unbearable.

In order to mark the occasion of our last day at school, all three grade six classes had been decked out in party mode. There were streamers, balloons, chips, Cheezels, soft drink, toffees, chocolate crackles, and my own personal favourite, *fairy bread*. Naturally, there were no lessons. Children were free to do what they pleased, and wandered happily from one classroom to the next, signing each other's T-shirts and chatting about the evening's Ball.

We were all pretty excited about the end of school, but there was also a touch of trepidation. It had taken us seven long years to climb to the top of this particular dung-heap, and we weren't too rapt with the prospect of having to start again. Primary school had been our whole lives for as long as any of us could remember and we were about to leave it behind. This was a thrilling notion, but also a frightening one, and it was hard to know which way to feel.

I found McEvoy sitting up the back of Mrs Newport's class. He had a large bowl of lollies in his lap and was tossing them carefully across the room and into his mate Trimble's waiting mouth. When I walked in, Trimble turned his head to look at me and was hit in the eye with a liquorice allsort.

'What's up, Ducky?' McEvoy sneered, as his friend hopped around gripping his face. 'Lost one of your eggs?'

I clutched my sides to mimic laughter. 'Good one.'

As Trimble wiped his eye with his sleeve and began lumbering towards us, I studied McEvoy's face for any indication that he had my diary. He definitely looked smug enough. He also looked like he had something over me; that it was within his power to snuff out my miserable existence whenever it took his fancy. The problem was, he *always* looked like that. Was I witnessing an *especially* conceited look, or just the same, run-of-the-mill, up-himself expression that he normally wore twenty-four hours a day? That was the question I had to answer. Summoning up all of my courage, I cleared my throat and popped the question.

'Listen, I want to ask you something. On camp, I got you to sign this d . . . I mean, book. And – um – you see, I've lost it!'

I looked straight into McEvoy's eyes to gauge his reaction. His brow wrinkled and his face went completely blank. Thank God!

'Book? What book?' he said. 'Oh, you mean the *diary*. Yeah, I've got it. It's at home. My mum keeps telling me to give it back.'

I opened and closed my mouth wordlessly.

'Don't know why you'd care, though. There's nothing in it – except some boring crap at the start about what you got for Christmas. Poor old Ducky didn't get Test Match, huh?'

I stared at him dumbfounded. He had it alright – but the stupid prick hadn't bothered to read it through!

'I'll bring it tonight, if it'll make you happy.'

'.'

'Ducky? *Ducky?*'

'Yeah, tonight. Great. Sure. Whatever,' I babbled, backing out of the room as if the whole place was laced with mines.

16

The Ball

No-one under the age of sixteen should be allowed to wear a tie. It should be illegal, like smoking or buying drinks. When I see a kid wearing a tie I have the same reaction as when I see a chimp wearing pants. I know that whoever's in charge of the creature thinks that it's cute and gets a kick out of it, but that the animal itself must feel like a complete dick. So it was on the night of the Ball.

I stood there in the living room in front of my assembled family looking absolutely *ludicrous*. The shirt and tie were bad enough, but it was all of Mum's 'grooming' that had really done the damage. My face had been scrubbed, my nails had been clipped and everything stunk of Sard Wonder Soap. Worst of all was my hair. Mum had blow-waved it for hours and then combed it over my ears (as was the fashion back then) so that it curved around my head like a soft, fluffy motorcycle helmet. It's fair to say that on this, my night of nights, the most important date in my childhood calendar, I looked worse than I ever had before or was ever likely to again.

Of course, my family didn't agree.

'Doesn't he look grand,' Mum gushed.

'Sure scrubs up well,' Dad enthused.

'*Naaaaah*, I think he looks terrific!' countered Pop.

'That's what we just said.'

'Ey?'

'THAT'S WHAT WE JUST SAID. HE LOOKS GREAT!'

'Yeah, that's right. Marvellous! Still reckon he'd look better in a hat, though.'

I giggled at this comment and thanked God for small mercies.

The Ball was being held at a nearby town hall (the multi-purpose room's many purposes not extending that far). As I sat in the back seat fiddling with my collar, the tension inside me slowly increased. From my point of view, there was a lot to be afraid of. I had to dance for a start, and this was not one of the Daffey family's traditional fortes. I also had to hang out with, and *touch*, Virginia; which had been bad enough during dancing classes, but would be an absolute nightmare in front of our parents. Then, of course, there was Jenny and the diary.

Somehow or another during the course of the night I had to achieve *all* of the following objectives:

(1) find the courage to ask Jenny for the last two dances before anyone else did;
(2) convince her to accept this request;
(3) make some sort of 'move' on her as we shuffled around the dance floor;
(4) and do all of this while under the constant threat of being exposed as a liar and a suck.

Naturally, it was the last of these scenarios that really freaked me. Sure, McEvoy hadn't read the diary *yet*, but what if he flicked through it on the way to the Ball? What if, at the very moment I was worrying about it, the entire McEvoy family was pissing themselves and pointing at my Ace Freeley picture? It didn't bear thinking about.

If McEvoy did find out the truth, the night would be catastrophic. He'd arrive, he'd tell his friends, they'd tell their friends, and before I knew it, the entire dance floor would be a hotbed of rumour and ridicule. I couldn't survive that. No-one could. And so, as we pulled up next to the hall and my parents drove off to find a park, I entered the building determined but afraid. My grade six year had come down to just one night, and this time, there'd be no tomorrows.

*****

My confidence received an unexpected boost almost as soon as I walked through the door. Much to my relief, all of the other guys looked as stupid as me. The hall was awash with clean, tie-wearing, spherically headed children, all of whom had spent too much time under the blow dryer. When I caught up with my friends there was a moment or two of awkwardness as we each surveyed the others' carefully coiffed hairstyles.

'You boys look lovely tonight,' I said smiling.

'Same to you, Daff,' quipped Simon.

'Shove it up your arse,' replied Mart.

Compliments and well wishes out of the way, the three of us huddled together like a 1950s rock 'n' roll band (the type that wore suits and looked like computer technicians). What we saw around us astonished us. The boys may have looked silly, but the girls looked sensational! It wasn't just the dresses either. It was everything. Nails had been painted, hair had been curled, and there was even, unless my eyes deceived me, a smattering of make-up! For the first time in my life, I made the connection between the girls I'd grown up with and the women I saw on TV. Amazingly enough, they were one and the same species.

I couldn't find Jenny's face in the crowd, but I did spot a much prettier version of Virginia, who walked right up to me and demanded to take my hand.

'You look, um, you look really *nice*, Virginia,' I said, sounding a little more surprised that I'd meant to.

'Thanks,' she said, blushing. 'You look . . . . Thanks, thanks a lot.'

Then she tilted her face towards the dance floor and we wandered off to find our spots.

The structure of the Ball was simple. Our parents sat on one side of the hall, watching and gently applauding, while us kids occupied the other. Each couple had been given a specific position by Mrs Quong, who strode around the perimeter making sure we kept formation.

Our first number was a waltz of sorts. It wasn't a 'flowing' type of waltz, at least not the way we did it. It was more like the kind of waltz you'd do if you were performing in front of the Gestapo – nervous, mechanical and hoping like hell to avoid mistakes. I wasn't too bad at it, really. Under Mrs Quong's watchful eye, I managed to guide Virginia around the hall with a minimum of energy and fuss. It helped that Virginia was such a good partner, being smallish and light and not complaining too much when I stepped on her feet.

The hardest part about the whole thing was not getting too close to her. Although us boys had finally reached an age where we found the opposite sex appealing, the idea of compulsory physical contact was still pretty spooky. To combat this (and to eliminate the possibility of embarrassing 'chest touches') we developed a style of dancing designed to limit physical contact:

1. Place your left hand in the girl's right (compulsory).
2. Put your arm around her waist (compulsory).
3. Take as many steps away from her as you could, while still technically satisfying 1 and 2.

Girls seemed to follow similar guidelines and the result was two people who looked like they were linking arms around an imaginary fridge. The dance floor was full of couples like this. In fact, I'd have to say it was the predominant dancing style – move your partner to the left, move your partner to the right, and do it all from the comfort of three feet away.

There were, of course, exceptions to this rule. One of them was poor old Martin. There was less space between Martin's chin and Donna Gobbo's nose then there is between your average pair of hydrogen atoms. She clung to him like a drowning swimmer and it was all Martin could do to keep his feet.

Bobbing somewhere in between these two extremes were Simon and Nadine, who began the night only a few pairs away from me. One minute they were close together (as a result of a Jackson advance) and the next they were far apart (as Nadine beat a hasty retreat). This to-and-fro motion meant that they tended to move in the direction Simon was facing instead of round and round like everyone else. It made for an interesting sight. There were fifty pairs of twirling children and one making a beeline right through the middle.

It wasn't until the third number that I caught side of Jenny. She was dancing on the opposite side of the hall with a klutz called Robert Dan (famous at school for being the only kid ever to strike out in T-ball). Rob was a godsend in terms of non-threatening partners and it gladdened my heart to see him with her.

Like all of the other girls at the Ball, Jenny looked much

older than when I'd last seen her. Not to mention more attractive; and more intimidating; and more likely to laugh in my face when I asked her to dance. Looking over at her, I suddenly felt terribly inadequate. There was no way she was going to say yes. She'd probably already been asked by someone else before the Ball even started. Why on earth I hadn't done this myself, I didn't know. Maybe it had something to do with being a massive chicken? Or maybe it was my tendency to leave everything until the last minute? Either way, it was sloppy work. I now ran the risk of being rejected for timeliness, as well as merit, and so had doubled my risk of failure. Oh well – no point worrying about it now, I thought to myself. And then proceeded to worry like hell.

We performed eight dances in all before the first intermission. My favourite was a barn-dance type of thing involving the clapping of hands, the yeeing of haws, and the chance to swap partners frequently. (Note: My personal award for Clammiest Hands of the Evening went to Sarah Davidson, who must have stuck her fists under her arms before coming out to dance.)

Most of my energy during this time was spent looking out for Jenny and/or McEvoy. My enemy proved elusive. On the two or three occasions he scooted past, it was impossible to gauge his intentions. He could have handed me the diary before we started dancing but had chosen not to. Why? Was it because he'd forgotten to bring it? Was it because he couldn't find it? I certainly hoped so.

The intermission was a chance for the dancers to catch their breath. It was also an opportunity for Mrs Newport to say a few words to our parents. She gave the sort of speech teachers always give on these occasions: how it had been one of the best years she could remember; how we were all a bunch of colourful funsters; and how she was confident that within our ranks were the future leaders of Australian society (which, scanning down the list of people who did grade six with me, turned out to be patently untrue).

While our teacher prattled on, we helped ourselves to cups of lemon-lime cordial and went about the business of socialising. For most of us, this meant ditching our partners and re-forming into single-sex groups. There were a number of smaller rooms adjacent to our side of the hall and these proved perfect for semi-private conversations. Martin, Simon and I ducked into the cloakroom, which was crammed to the rafters with our parents' stuff.

'Liked your moves out there, Mart,' Simon began. 'Could try getting a bit closer to Donna though.' Martin flushed and gave Simon the finger.

'So what about you, Sime?' I asked. 'How's it going with Nadine?'

'You saw it for yourself, Daff. It's embarrassing! I mean, I try to keep my distance, but the girl keeps pulling me closer!'

Martin and I snorted and bit down on our fingernails. Sensing, perhaps, that his version of events was about to be challenged, Simon seized the opportunity to make a quick exit.

'You guys want some more cordial? I'm *so* thirsty.'

We shook our heads and waved him away.

When I was sure he'd gone, I leaned closer to Martin and began whispering surreptitiously. 'So you remember what you have to do?'

'Yes, Daff,' he replied.

'You're going to be closer to Jenny than I am – so when they get to the free choice bit, you've got to make sure no-one gets to her first.'

'Um, yeah, I've been thinking about this part, Daff. No offence or anything, but what am I supposed to do? Hide her? Stand in front of her? Punch out anyone who comes close?'

'Do anything you have to, Mart,' I said with the utmost seriousness. 'Anything you have to.'

'Okay, Captain Blood. Whatever you say.'

*****

The last few dances rushed by in a blur. There was a jive, another waltz, a rumba, a cha-cha, a foxtrot, and a step we called 'the tango', which seemed remarkably similar to all of the others. The only highlight from a spectator's point of view was watching a slightly tipsy Mrs Newport drag Mr Weathershaw onto the floor. The crowd loved it, but the man himself looked furious. This indignation only increased when Mrs Newport called him an 'old fusspot' and ordered him to 'get down and shake his booty'. Having witnessed what followed, let me say this: some booties were never meant to be disturbed.

As I waited impatiently for the last two dances, a cold, squarish object in my pocket began to irritate me. It was one of those miniature boxes of chocolates you can buy, containing four or five pieces, and its purpose was to win over Jenny. I'd stuffed it in there just before I left the house, having stored it in the freezer for an hour to make sure they wouldn't melt. The idea was to ask Jenny to dance and then whip out the chockies before she had a chance to say no. I would have bought her a bigger box, but there are limits to what you can carry around in your pants.

When our final tango came to end and Mrs Newport began explaining the new format, I pulled out my bribe and straightened its bow. *Come on little fella*, I said to it encouragingly. *Work your magic!* Then I glanced around the hall in search of Jenny. I spotted her on the far side of the dance floor, near the storerooms. She was chatting to a female friend and Martin was only a few feet away. *Perfect*! The chocolates were cold; my man was in place. Now all I had to do was pull it off!

Mrs Newport's introductory address went on forever. She took care to point out that the last two dances were just 'a bit of fun' and that no-one had to participate if they didn't want to. This was to spare the feelings of those unable or unwilling to find partners (a merciful consideration that no-one bothered with once you got to high school). When she was finally done, a full third of all the kids headed immediately for the sidelines, including Nadine Fawkner, who fled a pleading Simon Jackson at Mach 5. The rest of us battled it out for a date.

I moved purposefully towards Jenny, secure in the knowledge that Martin would delay things until I got there. I saw him walk up to her and smiled at the genius of my plan. But then something terrible happened! His partner, Donna Gobbo, grabbed him by the arm, yanked him into one of the storerooms, and then slammed the door shut behind them. *What the . . . ?*

I almost broke into a run. Martin was out of the picture and now there was no-one left to help. Damn it! If only I'd told Simon!

I shoved my way through the throng and rapidly closed the gap on Jenny. I would have made it too had I not slammed smack bang into Andrew McEvoy.

'What's your hurry, Ducky?' he smirked, deliberately blocking my path.

'Yeah, where you off to, bird-boy?' his mate Trimble parroted.

'Look, girls, it's been great knowing you and everything, but I've got to . . .'

'I brought your stupid diary,' McEvoy interrupted.

My diary? Shit. I'd almost forgotten!

'I would have thrown it out, but Mum said I had to bring it. It's in her handbag with all the other stuff,' he said, waving his hand in the direction of the cloakroom.

I didn't know how to respond. His manner suggested he

hadn't read the diary and that he simply wanted to give it back. This was great news, but why *now*? Why did it have to happen ten seconds before I asked Jenny to dance? I didn't have time for this, and I couldn't afford any last minute 'discoveries'.

'Don't worry. Keep it! I don't want it anymore.'

'Don't be silly, Ducky. It's just over *there*,' he repeated, stepping towards the cloakroom.

'I DON'T CARE! I don't want it! It's yours. Merry Christmas!'

McEvoy took a step back, and his eyes narrowed warily.

'What's the matter with you, Ducky? You come up to me at school acting all weird and asking for your diary back. And now that I've got it, you won't let me give it to you! What's the big deal?'

'Nothing. Nothing it all. Definitely no big deal. It's just, look...'

'Come on, Mark. Let's get this diary. There's something funny going on here.'

Then they stomped off towards the cloakroom.

Damn it! I started to follow them, and then stopped. I turned back and moved towards Jenny, and then I stopped that too. *Damn it, damn it, DAMN IT!* What was I supposed to do?

I tried to tell myself that the diary wasn't important anymore. What did it matter if they read it? It was too late to stop me from dancing with Jenny, and after that, they'd never see me again. The worst they could do was giggle at us from the sidelines. And maybe point at us. And show the book to their friends. And whistle. And laugh. And try to get our attention. And make duck and horse noises. And... and... Well you can see my dilemma.

I cast one final look at Jenny before making up my mind. She was still chatting with a female friend. There was still time! Right – get the diary first and *THEN* deal with Jenny.

When I entered the cloakroom, McEvoy had just pulled the diary out of his mum's bag and was about to open it.

'Great, thanks, Andrew,' I said, walking towards him with my hand out. 'It was nice of you to bring it. Really. Thanks a lot.'

'Not so fast, Ducky. Think I might have a bit of a squiz first.'

'Hey! Give it here! It's mine!' I snarled, charging forward and tripping neatly over Trimble's outstretched foot.

My body arced gracelessly through the air and I came crashing down on my chest, the chocolates in my left hand breaking open and spilling all over the floor.

'Oh no! My present!' I exclaimed, throwing an arm out and sweeping the chocolates back towards me.

I managed to scoop up four of them this way, but the fifth was just beyond my reach. *It's still okay*, I said to myself, lunging forward. *I can just wipe it clean!* THUMP! Trimble's heel came plunging out of the sky and squished it, spurting soft centre all over my forehead.

'Ah, HA HA!' he boomed, his burly face jiggling with mirth. 'Guess you won't be eating that one, hey, Ducky?'

I didn't respond. Instead, I wiped a finger across my forehead and then pressed it to my tongue (in the manner of a policeman checking for cocaine). It was even worse than I thought. Not only had Trimble destroyed one fifth of my total present, he'd also managed to knock out the best and most 'girly' chocolate of them all – the Strawberry Cream! All thoughts of dancing disappeared and were replaced with white-hot fury. This fucker was going to pay!

Springing to my feet, I tackled him around the waist and sent him flying into the shelves. What followed was a brief, undignified struggle, in which the aggressor was quickly overcome by superior size and strength. I don't know how many Weetbix this kid ate for breakfast, but I'm guessing it was quite a few.

'I'm going to rip your head off and then shove it up your arse!' I screamed, as he bent my arm behind my back. 'Do you hear me? You're gone, Trimble. Gone!'

Trimble chuckled to himself and McEvoy walked up and bopped me on the nose with my own diary.

It was at about this point that my arm really started to hurt and I realised I was in a lot of trouble. Just as my shoulder threatened to pop out of its socket, a voice drifted in from outside. It was Simon.

'Daff? Where are you? They're about to start the . . .'

The voice fell silent as Simon stepped inside and laid his eyes upon the scene.

'Simon! Help! They've got my diary – and they've wrecked my chocolates – and they won't let me go!'

Simon didn't move.

'*Sime*! What are you doing? Help me!'

My friend remained still. He looked at me, he looked at my opponents, he looked back at the dance floor, and then he fled.

'Hey, come back here!' I screamed after him. 'You *chickenshit*!'

'Nice mates you've got there, Ducky,' McEvoy sneered. 'Now how about we take a look at this diary?'

There was nothing more I could do. I stood there, thrashing around in Trimble's arms and watching the Golden Boy leaf through my book. Music drifted in from the hall, and with it, the realisation that all was lost. Jenny would have chosen a partner by now – or someone would have chosen her – and thus my hopes of a romantic dance were dashed. I couldn't believe it had all come to this. All my plans, all my schemes, all that effort. After a year's worth of work, I found myself imprisoned in a cloakroom watching my enemies stamp on my chocolates and page through my private thoughts. I had hoped for better.

'You know, Ducky,' McEvoy began, as he picked through January, 'I've always thought you had something to do with that video. Remember that? Just a few days before the election I was going to win, some porn movie ends up in my schoolbag and I almost get expelled. Know anything about that, do you?'

I maintained a scowling silence.

'I was pretty annoyed about it, you know. I lost the election, I got into trouble with the Principal, and this girl I liked stopped talking to me. Probably for the best, though. She was a bit of a mole anyway.'

'*Yaaaaaaaaargh!*' I bellowed, plunging my elbow into Trimble's stomach and launching myself across the room.

'Settle down, Ducky,' McEvoy oozed, as Trimble's hand caught the back of my shirt. 'No need to get yourself in a flap.' The two of them laughed heartily at this gag, and I hung my head in defeat.

'Well, Ducky, if you did have something to do with that tape, maybe there's something about it in here. The funny thing is, though, it looks empty! There's this crap at the start about Christmas and then nothing, nothing, nothing, noth . . . *Hang on a second!*'

'G'day, fellas!' interrupted a familiar voice from the doorway.

Thank God! I exclaimed to myself, turning around. *Simon had come back to rescue me*! But the voice didn't belong to Simon. It was, of all people, *the Gibbon*! He was standing in the entrance, hands on hips, wearing his trademark cocky grin. Directly behind him loomed Julian, who towered over him with crossed arms, as still and silent as a totem pole.

'Hello, T-Bird,' said the Gibbon, turning towards me and executing some sort of bizarre 'gangland' salute. 'What's the problem here?'

'Oh, um, hello, *Jubbin*,' I stammered back, attempting an awkward imitation of the same. 'That guy's got my book and he won't give it back.'

McEvoy sighed impatiently and turned to our guest.

'Listen, Gibbon, it's none of your business. This here is between Ducky and me. Now get lost, and take lard-arse there with you!'

I raised an eyebrow and glanced nervously across at Julian. He didn't respond as such, but there was an almost imperceptible tightening of his face. *Hmmmmm*, I thought to myself. *This could get interesting.*

'Lard-arse, huh?' the Gibbon replied. 'You'd better watch your mouth, McEvoy, or you might just regret it. Now gimme that book.'

'Piss off, *weed*,' McEvoy shot back, shoving the advancing Gibbon in the chest and sending him sprawling onto the ground.

This, it has to be said, was a very dumb thing to do. Sensing he'd made a mistake, McEvoy raised his left hand as if to calm things and backed away instinctively.

'Um, sorry, Gibbon, I didn't mean to . . .'

But it was too late. A pair of arms the size of small hams were uncrossing themselves, and Julian Crowler was on the march.

Stepping over his fallen comrade, Julian took two massive strides towards his victim and balled his fists, ready to pounce. He looked furious. I must have seen Julian beat up a dozen kids that year, but I'd never seen him angry. When he fought in the sandpit, he did so in a professional, detached manner; like a lumberjack chopping wood. Not so today. There was a dark, desolate rage burning in those deep-set eyes – the rage of a kid who'd been picked on by people like this all his life, and who saw a rare chance to get even. For a second or two, I almost felt sorry for Andrew McEvoy.

Julian lumbered up to his target and then stopped about two inches short. Turning his meaty skull sideways, he cast a menacing look at Trimble, who was cowering in a corner. It was a look of hate, and of fury, and of impending violence, and it said, better than any words ever could:

'Get the fuck out of this room before I smash in your face!'

Trimble nodded his head politely, and disappeared.

Left on his own and facing a veritable boy–mountain, McEvoy suddenly became a lot more conciliatory.

'Listen, Jules, I've always been a big fan of yours, you know that. And look, if you want this diary here, it's yours. There we go, I've dropped it. And if you want anything else I've got, you're welcome to that too, and . . . *blurgh!*'

Julian seized hold of his tie and tugged on it savagely. Adjusting the knot until McEvoy turned a bright shade of purple, Julian leaned close and opened his mouth for the first time in living memory.

'I don't like you, McEvoy,' he said. 'You shit me.'

Then he lifted him up off the ground and tossed him into a coat stand.

This was to be the last I would ever see of Andrew McEvoy. Pulling his shirt-collar loose and gasping for breath, he scrambled back into the hall and out of my life. As soon as he was gone, Julian stooped down to retrieve my diary and handed it to me smiling.

'Thanks,' I said, not knowing quite what to say.

'No problem,' said Julian.

With the confrontation over and no common foe left to bind us, we quickly discovered there was little left to chat about. After some embarrassingly awkward small talk, I prepared to take my leave, but not before one final, heartfelt thank you.

'Have a good life, guys,' I began sincerely, 'and by the way, this is the second time you've saved my arse. I don't know why you did it or how it happened, but thanks a lot for putting that porno in McEvoy's bag. It saved me a lot of trouble.'

The Jubbins started at me blankly.

'You know – the tape? The one you stole from the Log Fort and then dumped in McEvoy's schoolbag?'

Still nothing.

'Oh well. Thanks anyway.'

The Jubbins saluted and I waved them goodbye.

I emerged from the cloakroom relieved but unhappy. The forces of evil had finally been defeated, but the main battle of the night had been lost. The last two dances of the Ball were now over, and they were about to start the first encore. Scanning the assembled onlookers, I allowed myself one last shred of optimism. Maybe Jenny hadn't been picked out after all? Maybe she was standing patiently on the sidelines waiting for her champion to arrive? But alas, she wasn't there. With considerable reluctance, I tossed my diary into the nearest bin and then turned my attention to the dance floor.

I made up my mind to hate the guy even before I saw him. I didn't care that it wasn't his fault. It didn't matter to me that he couldn't possibly have known. Whoever this person was, he had waltzed off with my one chance at happiness. And for that, he deserved to *die*.

The couples were milling around the centre of the hall, waiting for the music to restart, and it took some time before I made out Jenny. She was standing with her back to me chatting with her partner, and her head was obscuring his face. This left me hopping from one foot to the other, waiting to get a good view. He was slightly taller than she was and I could see the top of his head. He had sandy hair, a pale complexion, and what looked like a smattering of freckles. *Wait a minute* . . . Jenny shifted slightly to the left and the face that I saw floored me.

SIMON! You stupid, blundering *tool*! Not only do you abandon me in my hour of need, but then you go off and pinch my girlfriend! Anger welled up inside me until my fingernails sliced into my palms. How could he do this to me? Why, why, WHY did he have to pick Jenny? After all we'd been through! After all that I'd done for him! I caught myself halfway through this final thought, when it occurred to me that I probably hadn't done that much. Other than keep things from him; and leave him out of stuff; and continually favour Martin. But this was precisely why! Because he was hopeless.

Because he was a coward. Because he was a screw-up who couldn't be trusted! Simon deserved to be treated like a second-class friend, because that's exactly what he was!

I had half a mind to storm over to my parents and demand they take me home, but thoughts about what I might do to Simon kept me standing there. I stared at my friend with such venom and focused ferocity that he ended up looking over at me. When our eyes met, he proceeded to do something strange. He started to wave! I tried to pretend I hadn't seen him, but then Jenny started waving too. They were mouthing things at me and beckoning me towards them and generally making it difficult to stay away. Grinding my teeth together, I stomped over to see what was wrong.

'Shouldn't you two be getting ready to dance?' I said, in the calmest tone I could muster.

'Don't worry, Daff, they're waiting for Weathershaw.'

I looked over to where Simon was pointing and saw my teacher desperately clinging to a chair.

'Newport won't leave him alone,' Simon chuckled, 'the poor old bugger. Anyway, Daff, glad to see you made it and you're okay!'

'Yeah, nice one, Sime,' I hissed. '*No thanks to you!*'

'Hello, Chris,' said Jenny (whose gaze I'd been steadfastly ignoring).

'Um, hello, Jen. Nice to see you.'

'Nice to see you, too,' she smiled. 'So, shall we dance?'

'What?'

'Simon said you wanted to dance with me, but were too afraid to ask.'

'He said *what*?' I looked to Simon for an explanation, but he just grinned at me.

'Well, if you *would* like to dance, you'll have to wait a minute. I have to go and do something.' Then she smiled again and was off.

'Okay, Simon, what the hell is going on?'

'Nothing, Daff. You weren't going to get back in time, so I grabbed her before anyone else could.'

'But . . . but . . . how did you know I wanted to dance with her? How did you even know I *liked* her???'

'What do you mean – *how did I know*? Jenny Hartnett – JART. Just how dumb do you think I am?'

I stared at my friend in disbelief.

'I saw her standing on her own and I went off to find you. But when I saw you with McEvoy, I knew you weren't going to make it. So I asked her myself and sent the Jubbins in to help.'

'*You* sent the Jubbins in? How did you manage that?'

'Easy. I told them there was a rumble.'

'A *rumble*?'

'Yeah, like in *Happy Days*. What did you expect me to do? Fight them myself? They would have killed me!'

At this point, the tension broke, and I started giggling like a madman.

'Anyway, Daff, what happened in there?'

'Oh, um, Julian half-strangled McEvoy, and then threw

him into some coats.' Now it was Simon's turn to laugh. 'Weird thing is, though, when I tried to thank them for putting that video in McEvoy's bag, they didn't seem to know anything about it. I was *sure* it was them!'

My friend coughed and looked exceedingly uncomfortable.

'Oh, come on! Don't tell me you know something about this too?'

'Actually, Daff, I've been meaning to tell you something. Promise you won't kill me?'

'No – no, I don't promise.'

'Okay – well, anyway. I knew it wasn't the Jubbins that did it.'

'How?'

'Because it was *me*.'

'*You?*'

'Yep. Remember that argument we had about tactics for your election?'

'Yeah,' I said, scratching my head and casting my mind back.

'And I wanted to fight dirty but you and Martin wouldn't listen to me? Well, I thought of the perfect way to get him! Plant our porno in his bag and then have him kicked out! I knew you wouldn't go for it, so I did it myself and pretended it had been stolen.'

'But, hang on, how did you know the teachers would search our bags?'

'Oh, that was easy. I told the Principal someone had stolen

my Oil Panic and then demanded they look for it. I even cried and everything! I was going to tell you afterwards, but then I remembered I'd left our names on the tape.'

'Bloody hell, Sime! You almost got us expelled!'

'I know, I know,' he said, putting up his hands defensively. 'But if I hadn't done it, McEvoy would have won the election, and then you would have been stuffed!'

'Hmmm,' I replied begrudgingly. He had a point.

'Shit, better go, here comes your girl! Wooooooooo, Daffa's in *luuuuuuv*,' he taunted as he left, providing a timely reminder of why I hadn't told him in the first place.

As Jenny approached, I fought hard to stay composed. Too much had happened too quickly and I was feeling a little dazed. *C'mon, Daff, this is it – this is the big one!* I said to myself, slapping my legs and trying to gee myself up.

'Sorry I took so long,' she said, smiling. 'What are *they*?'

I looked down at the crumpled box of chocolates in my hand and tried to explain.

'Oh, um, they were for you. But they got spilt, and then stepped on, and I tried to pick them up, but . . .'

'Don't worry. I know. Simon told me.'

'Really?' I said suspiciously. 'What else did he tell you?'

'Oh, you know, this 'n' that,' she said coyly, placing her right hand into my left. It was cool and soft, and the feel of it made me jump.

'He told me you don't have a horse.'

'*Glurgh!*' I replied, choking.

'It's okay. I didn't think you had one anyway. Every time you mentioned him, he kept changing colour!'

I blushed furiously and was unable to speak for some time.

Mr Weathershaw was eventually prized from his stronghold, and with him came the return of the music. The last dance of the night was to be yet another waltz, and this meant putting my arm around Jenny. I tried to do it in a casual, offhand manner, but my wide-eyed look of terror may have given things away.

I danced better than I thought I would. When I'd been with Virginia, my focus had been entirely on my feet (and the damage they were doing to hers). Now, it was on Jenny, and this seemed to help.

'Were any of the other things you told me true?' Jenny asked, as we swept past Mrs Quong.

'Um, well . . .'

'Do your parents own a farm?'

'No.'

'Ever been on *Family Feud*?'

'Nup.'

'Pop sick?'

'Naah, not really. Nan's a bit dodgy though.'

'I thought so,' she said, laughing and twirling around. 'Boys are such bad liars!'

Jenny's knowledge and acceptance of my lies was both humiliating and endearing. I felt exposed; outmanoeuvred and outplayed by a vastly superior opponent. All this time I'd thought it was the strength of my lies that had kept me in it – but it turned out that it was their transparency that might have done the trick. For the first time in my grade six year, I felt happy. Not contented, mind you, but happy. Everything I'd done had been worth it. The smock, the breezeway, the act, the election, my disastrous foray into the world of elite sport: they'd all played their part in bringing me to this moment. And what a moment it was. Swirling around the room with my dream girl in my arms, I felt like the king of Templestowe Heights (or at least a very high-ranking prince). And this, surely, was only the beginning.

Given my euphoric, trance-like state, it came as quite a shock when the music suddenly wound down and Mrs Newport told us it was time to go home. Naturally, I'd never planned past this moment. I'd never imagined what would happen *after* we danced; it had always been the getting there that was important. It was a strange oversight, really. What I'd always regarded as the 'beginning' of our relationship also happened to fall on the very last day of school. Tomorrow, this whole world wouldn't even exist.

'Thanks for being my partner,' Jenny said warmly, as our parents stood and applauded. 'I guess I'll be seeing you around.'

'Oh yeah, for sure,' I replied, performing a quick calculation of the distance between our high schools. 'For sure,' I repeated confidently.

Not knowing what to do next, I made a feeble attempt at shaking hands, before Jenny brushed my arm aside and kissed me gently on the cheek. Blushing, embarrassed, and hoping she'd do it again, I put my hand to my face and watched her walk away.

Hey, come back! the Hollywood version of me cried out. *Now it's my turn to kiss YOU!* But the real me was afraid to push his luck.

'Way to go, Romeo!' came Simon's voice from behind me, as dancers streamed past on their way to their parents.

'Hey, Sime. Where've you been?'

'On the sidelines, watching with everyone else,' he said. 'You were good, Daff. I thought you danced really well.'

'Yeah, thanks.'

'No, seriously. I mean it.'

'Fuck off.'

'Anyway, I don't know why you're asking where *I've* been. It's where Martin's been that I'd like to know. I haven't seen him for *ages.*'

That's right – *Martin*! I turned my attention to a doorway on the other side of the dance floor – a doorway that had remained securely shut for almost half an hour. Right on cue, it burst open, and Donna Gobbo waltzed out grinning from ear to ear.

'He's in there,' I said pointing.

Martin took some time to emerge from the storeroom, and when he did, he was a mess. His hair was all ruffled, his tie was skew-whiff, and the bottom half of his face was drenched in lip-gloss.

'Crikey!' exclaimed Simon, as Martin walked gingerly towards us. 'It's a bird, it's a plane, no, it's *pash*-man!'

Martin didn't say anything and wiped his mouth with the back of his hand.

'Geez, Mart. Attacked by the Gobbo-monster! A fate worse than death! How'd you get through it?'

'Settle down, Sime,' said our friend, smiling oddly. 'She's actually quite nice when you get to know her.'

After ridiculing Martin as much as we could, the three of us walked off to find our parents and started planning what we'd do over the holidays. We never discussed what we'd do after the holidays – when we were all at different schools. We just assumed that would take care of itself.

There was a moment or two of awkwardness when Martin greeted his mother and Simon wanted to know where his dad was – but it passed, and I bid goodbye to my two best friends: one of whom I'd always assumed was incompetent, and the other who I'd always assumed had a perfect life.

As I approached Mum and Dad, I caught one final glimpse of Jenny leaving the building. It was hard watching her go. Hard because she wasn't just walking out of a dance hall, she was walking out of my reach. Although I couldn't possibly have known it then, I think I had an inkling that our paths were about to diverge, and that by the time they next crossed, nothing would be the same.

I wasn't going to see Jenny tomorrow. I wasn't going to see her next week. Or next month. Or next term. It would be eighteen long years before I laid eyes upon her again, and when I did, I was going to have a lot of explaining to do. I was going to have to tell her that not only did I remember who she was, but that I'd just spent three years and eighty-five thousand words writing a book about her.

I wonder if she'll be impressed?